Frommer's

PORTABLE

Puerto Vallarta, Manzanillo & Guadalajara

5th Edition

by David Baird & Lynne Bairstow

Here's what critics say about Frommer's:

"Amazingly easy to use. Very portable, very complete."

—*Booklist*

"Detailed, accurate, and easy-to-read information for all price ranges."

—*Glamour Magazine*

WILEY

Wiley Publishing, Inc.

Published by:

WILEY PUBLISHING, INC.

111 River St.
Hoboken, NJ 07030-5774

ISBN-13: 978-0-7645-8897-6
ISBN-10: 0-7645-8897-4

Editor: Maureen Clarke
Production Editor: Melissa S. Bennett
Photo Editor: Richard Fox
Cartographer: Tim Lohnes
Production by Wiley Indianapolis Composition Services

For information on our other products and services or to obtain technical
support, please contact our Customer Care Department within the U.S. at
800/762-2974, outside the U.S. at 317/572-3993 or fax 317/572-4002.

Wiley also publishes its books in a variety of electronic formats. Some content that appears in print may not be available in electronic formats.

Manufactured in the United States of America

5 4 3 2 1

Contents

List of Maps

About the Authors

David Baird is a writer, editor, and translator who doesn't like writing about himself in the third person (too close to being an obituary). Texan by birth, Mexican by disposition, he has lived several years in different parts of Mexico. Now based in Austin, Texas, he spends as much time in Mexico as possible.

For **Lynne Bairstow**, Mexico has become more like home than her native United States. She has lived in Puerto Vallarta for most of the past 13 years, where she has deepened her appreciation and respect for Mexico's customs, culture, and natural treasures. Her articles on Mexico have appeared in the *New York Times, Los Angeles Times,* Mexicana's and Alaska Airlines' in-flight magazines, and other publications. In 2000, Lynne received the Pluma de Plata, a top honor awarded by the Mexican government to foreign writers, for her work on Frommer's guidebook to Puerto Vallarta. She wishes to thank her research assistant, **Alejandra Macedo,** for her invaluable contribution to this book.

An Invitation to the Reader

In researching this book, we discovered many wonderful places—hotels, restaurants, shops, and more. We're sure you'll find others. Please tell us about them, so we can share the information with your fellow travelers in upcoming editions. If you were disappointed with a recommendation, we'd love to know that, too. Please write to:

Frommer's Portable Puerto Vallarta, Manzanillo
& Guadalajara, 5th Edition
Wiley Publishing, Inc. • 111 River St. • Hoboken, NJ 07030-5774

An Additional Note

Please be advised that travel information is subject to change at any time—and this is especially true of prices. We therefore suggest that you write or call ahead for confirmation when making your travel plans. The authors, editors, and publisher cannot be held responsible for the experiences of readers while traveling. Your safety is important to us, however, so we encourage you to stay alert and be aware of your surroundings. Keep a close eye on cameras, purses, and wallets, all favorite targets of thieves and pickpockets.

FROMMER'S STAR RATINGS, ICONS & ABBREVIATIONS

Every hotel, restaurant, and attraction listing in this guide has been ranked for quality, value, service, amenities, and special features using a **star-rating system.** In country, state, and regional guides, we also rate towns and regions to help you narrow down your choices and budget your time accordingly. Hotels and restaurants are rated on a scale of zero (recommended) to three stars (exceptional). Attractions, shopping, nightlife, towns, and regions are rated according to the following scale: zero stars (recommended), one star (highly recommended), two stars (very highly recommended), and three stars (must-see).

In addition to the star-rating system, we also use **seven feature icons** that point you to the great deals, in-the-know advice, and unique experiences that separate travelers from tourists. Throughout the book, look for:

Finds	Special finds—those places only insiders know about
Fun Fact	Fun facts—details that make travelers more informed and their trips more fun
Kids	Best bets for kids—advice for the whole family
Moments	Special moments—those experiences that memories are made of
Overrated	Places or experiences not worth your time or money
Tips	Insider tips—great ways to save time and money
Value	Great values—where to get the best deals

The following **abbreviations** are used for credit cards:

| AE | American Express | DISC | Discover | V | Visa |
| DC | Diners Club | MC | MasterCard | | |

FROMMERS.COM

Now that you have the guidebook to a great trip, visit our website at **www.frommers.com** for travel information on more than 3,000 destinations. With features updated regularly, we give you instant access to the most current trip-planning information available. At Frommers.com, you'll also find the best prices on airfares, accommodations, and car rentals—and you can even book travel online through our travel booking partners. At Frommers.com, you'll also find the following:

- Online updates to our most popular guidebooks
- Vacation sweepstakes and contest giveaways
- Newsletter highlighting the hottest travel trends
- Online travel message boards with featured travel discussions

Planning Your Trip to Mid-Pacific Mexico

Along the Pacific coast of Mexico, palm-studded jungles sweep down to meet the deep blue of the Pacific Ocean, providing spectacular backdrops for three modern resort cities, as well as smaller coastal villages. This lovely stretch of coastline, which extends from Puerto Vallarta down to Manzanillo, is known as the Mexican Riviera. Modern hotels, easy air access, and a growing array of activities and adventure tourism attractions have transformed this region into one of Mexico's premier resort areas.

A little advance planning can make the difference between a good trip and a great trip to this popular destination. When should you go? What's the best way to get there? How much should you plan on spending? What festivals or special events will be taking place during your visit? What safety or health precautions are advised? We'll answer these and other questions for you in this chapter.

In addition to these basics, I highly recommend taking the time to learn a little about the culture and traditions of Mexico. It can make the difference between simply "getting away" and coming back with an enriched understanding.

1 The Region in Brief

Puerto Vallarta, with its traditional Mexican architecture and gold-sand beaches bordered by jungle-covered mountains, is currently the second most visited resort in Mexico (trailing only Cancún). Vallarta (as the locals refer to it) maintains a small-town charm despite sophisticated hotels, great restaurants, a thriving arts community, an active nightlife, and a growing variety of ecotourism attractions. **Manzanillo** is surprisingly relaxed, even though it's one of Mexico's most active commercial ports; it also offers great fishing and golf. And along the **Costa Alegre,** between Puerto Vallarta and Manzanillo, pristine coves are home to unique luxury and value-priced resorts that cater to travelers seeking seclusion and privacy. Just north of Puerto Vallarta is **Punta Mita,** home of the first Four Seasons resort in Latin America and a Jack Nicklaus golf course. With three more luxury resorts— including ones by Rosewood and Starwood—and two more golf courses on tap, it is emerging as Mexico's most exclusive address.

If you're looking for a more essentially Mexican experience, head inland over the mountains to **Guadalajara,** Mexico's second-largest city and the birthplace of many of the country's traditions.

International airports at all three cities make getting to each easier; Guadalajara and Puerto Vallarta have the most frequent connections. Distances in the region are easily managed by car; most drives between major points take from 45 minutes to 6 hours on roads that are in generally good condition.

If you decide to visit this region, you have several choices about how to allot your time. Most people pick one coastal resort and stay there for the duration of their vacations, but, if you wish, you can easily enjoy more than one resort during your time in Mexico.

Barra de Navidad, for example, is so close to Manzanillo that it's easy to combine several days there with a stay in Manzanillo. From Puerto Vallarta, **Bucerías, Yelapa, San Sebastian,** and **San Blas** all offer a change of pace and scenery. Hotelito Desconocido and Las Alamandas are both closer to Puerto Vallarta, with the remainder of the luxury coastal resorts between Manzanillo and Puerto Vallarta, nearer to Manzanillo. There are more frequent flights, however, to and from Puerto Vallarta, and many people find that Puerto Vallarta provides the best access to the coastal area.

2 Visitor Information

The **Mexico Hot Line** (© 800/44-MEXICO) is an excellent source for general information; you can request brochures and get answers to the most common questions from the exceptionally well-trained, knowledgeable staff.

More information (15,000 pages' worth) about Mexico is available on the official site of Mexico's Tourism Promotion Board, **www.visitmexico.com.** The **U.S. State Department** (© 202/647-5225; www.travel.state.gov) offers **Travel Warnings** and a **Consular Information Sheet** on Mexico with consistently updated safety, medical, driving, and general travel information gleaned from reports by its offices in Mexico. You can also request the Consular Information Sheet by fax (© 202/647-3000).

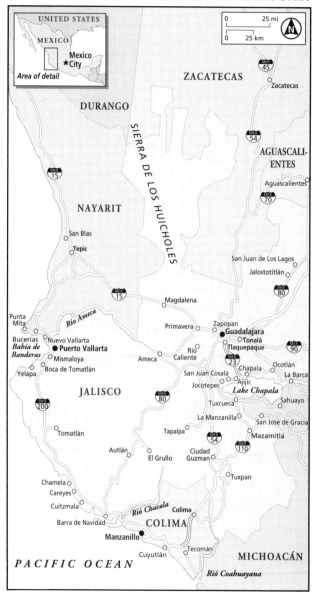

The **Centers for Disease Control and Prevention Hot Line** (℃ **800/311-3435** or 404/639-3534; www.cdc.gov) is a source of medical information for travelers to Mexico and elsewhere. For travelers to Mexico and Central America, the number with recorded messages is ℃ **877/FYI-TRIP.** The toll-free fax number for requesting information is ℃ 888/232-3299. Information available by fax is also available at **www.cdc.gov/travel**. The U.S. State Department website (see above) also offers medical information for Americans traveling abroad and a list of air ambulance services.

The **Mexican Government Tourist Board** has offices in major North American cities, in addition to the main office in Mexico City (℃ **555/203-1103**). In the **United States:** Chicago (℃ **312/606-9252**), Houston (℃ **713/772-2581**, ext. 105, or 713/772-3819), Los Angeles (℃ **310/282-9112**), and New York (℃ **212/308-2110**).

The **Mexican Embassy** in the United States is at 1911 Pennsylvania Ave. NW, Washington, DC 20005 (℃ **202/728-1750**). In Canada: 1 Place Ville-Marie, Suite 1931, Montreal, QUE, H3B 2C3 (℃ **514/871-1052**); 2 Bloor St. W., Suite 1502, Toronto, ON, M4W 3E2 (℃ **416/925-0704**); 999 W. Hastings, Suite 1110, Vancouver, BC, V6C 2W2 (℃ **604/669-2845**). Embassy office: 1500-45 O'Connor St., Ottawa, ON, K1P 1A4 (℃ **613/233-8988;** fax 613/235-9123).

3 Entry Requirements & Customs

ENTRY REQUIREMENTS

All travelers to Mexico are required to present **proof of citizenship,** such as an original birth certificate with a raised seal, a valid passport, or naturalization papers. Those using a birth certificate should also have current photo identification, such as a driver's license or official ID. If the last name on the birth certificate is different from your current name, bring a photo identification card *and* legal proof of the name change, such as the original marriage license or certificate. *Note:* Photocopies are *not* acceptable.

The best ID is a passport. Safeguard your passport in an inconspicuous, inaccessible place like a money belt, and keep a copy of the critical pages with your passport number in a separate place. If you lose your passport, visit the nearest consulate of your native country as soon as possible for a replacement.

For information on how to get a passport, go to "Passports" in the "Fast Facts: Mexico" section, later in this chapter—the websites

> **⟨Tips⟩ Passport Savvy**
>
> Allow plenty of time before your trip to apply for a passport; processing normally takes **3 weeks** but can take longer during busy periods (especially spring). And keep in mind that if you need a passport in a hurry, you'll pay a higher processing fee. When traveling, safeguard your passport in an inconspicuous, inaccessible place like a money belt and keep a copy of the critical pages with your passport number in a separate place. If you lose your passport, visit the nearest consulate or embassy of your native country as soon as possible for a replacement.

listed provide downloadable passport applications as well as the current fees for processing passport applications. For an up-to-date country-by-country listing of passport requirements around the world, go to the "Foreign Entry Requirement" Web page of the U.S. State Department at **http://travel.state.gov/foreignentryreqs.html**.

You must carry a **Mexican Tourist Permit (FMT),** the equivalent of a tourist visa, which Mexican border officials issue, free of charge, after proof of citizenship is accepted. Airlines generally provide the necessary forms aboard your flight to Mexico. The FMT is more important than a passport, so guard it carefully. If you lose it, you may not be permitted to leave until you can replace it—a bureaucratic hassle that can take anywhere from a few hours to a week.

The FMT can be issued for up to 180 days. Sometimes officials don't ask but just stamp a time limit, so be sure to say "6 months," or at least twice as long as you intend to stay. If you decide to extend your stay, you may request that additional time be added to your FMT from an official immigration office in Mexico.

Note that children under age 18 traveling without parents or with only one parent must have a notarized letter from the absent parent or parents authorizing the travel.

CUSTOMS
WHAT YOU CAN BRING INTO MEXICO
When you enter Mexico, Customs officials will be tolerant as long as you have no illegal drugs or firearms. You're allowed to bring in two cartons of cigarettes or 50 cigars, plus 1 kilogram (2.2 lb.) of smoking tobacco; two 1-liter bottles of wine or hard liquor, and 12 rolls of film. A laptop computer, camera equipment, and sports equipment that could feasibly be used during your stay are also

allowed. The underlying guideline is: Don't bring anything that looks as if it's meant to be resold in Mexico.

WHAT YOU CAN TAKE HOME FROM MEXICO

Returning **U.S. citizens** who have been away for at least 48 hours are allowed to bring back, once every 30 days, $800 worth of merchandise duty-free. You'll be charged a flat rate of 4% duty on the next $1,000 worth of purchases. Any dollar amount beyond that is dutiable at whatever rates apply. On mailed gifts, the duty-free limit is $200. Be sure to have your receipts or purchases handy to expedite the declaration process. *Note:* If you owe duty, you are required to pay on your arrival in the United States, by either cash, personal check, government or traveler's check, or money order (and in some locations, a Visa or MasterCard).

To avoid having to pay duty on foreign-made personal items you owned before you left on your trip, bring along a bill of sale, insurance policy, jeweler's appraisal, or receipts of purchase. Or you can register items that can be readily identified by a permanently affixed serial number or marking—think laptop computers, cameras, and CD players—with Customs before you leave. Take the items to the nearest Customs office or register them with Customs at the airport from which you're departing. You'll receive, at no cost, a Certificate of Registration, which allows duty-free entry for the life of the item.

With some exceptions, you cannot bring fresh fruits and vegetables into the United States. For specifics on what you can bring back, download the invaluable free pamphlet *Know Before You Go* online at **www.cbp.gov**. (Click on "Travel," and then click on "Know Before You Go."). Or contact the **U.S. Customs & Border Protection (CBP),** 1300 Pennsylvania Ave., NW, Washington, DC 20229 (© **877/287-8667**), and request the pamphlet.

For a clear summary of **Canadian** rules, write for the booklet *I Declare,* issued by the **Canada Customs and Revenue Agency** (© **800/461-9999** in Canada, or 204/983-3500; www.cra-arc.gc.ca). Canada allows its citizens a C$750 exemption, and you're allowed to bring back duty-free one carton of cigarettes, 1 can of tobacco, 40 imperial ounces of liquor, and 50 cigars. In addition, you're allowed to mail gifts to Canada valued at less than C$60 a day, provided they're unsolicited and don't contain alcohol or tobacco (write on the package "Unsolicited gift, under C$60 value"). All valuables should be declared on the Y-38 form before departure from Canada, including serial numbers of valuables you already own, such as expensive foreign cameras. *Note:* The C$750 exemption can only be used once a year and only after an absence of 7 days.

U.K. citizens returning from **a non-E.U. country** have a customs allowance of: 200 cigarettes; 50 cigars; 250 grams of smoking tobacco; 2 liters of still table wine; 1 liter of spirits or strong liqueurs (over 22% volume); 2 liters of fortified wine, sparkling wine, or other liqueurs; 60 cubic centimeters (ml) perfume; 250 cubic centimeters (ml) of toilet water; and £145 worth of all other goods, including gifts and souvenirs. People under 17 cannot have the tobacco or alcohol allowance. For more information, contact **HM Customs & Excise** at ☏ **0845/010-9000** (020/8929-0152 from outside the U.K.), or consult the website at www.hmce.gov.uk.

The duty-free allowance in **Australia** is A$400 or, for those under 18, A$200. Citizens can bring in 250 cigarettes or 250 grams of loose tobacco, and 1,125 milliliters of alcohol. If you're returning with valuables you already own, such as foreign-made cameras, you should file form B263. A helpful brochure available from Australian consulates or Customs offices is *Know Before You Go.* For more information, call the **Australian Customs Service** at ☏ **1300/363-263,** or log on to www.customs.gov.au.

The duty-free allowance for **New Zealand** is NZ$700. Citizens over 17 can bring in 200 cigarettes, 50 cigars, or 250 grams of tobacco (or a mixture of all three if their combined weight doesn't exceed 250g); plus 4.5 liters of wine and beer, or 1.125 liters of liquor. New Zealand currency does not carry import or export restrictions. Fill out a certificate of export, listing the valuables you are taking out of the country; that way, you can bring them back without paying duty. Most questions are answered in a free pamphlet available at New Zealand consulates and Customs offices: *New Zealand Customs Guide for Travellers, Notice no. 4.* For more information, contact **New Zealand Customs,** The Customhouse, 17–21 Whitmore St., Box 2218, Wellington (☏ **04/473-6099** or 0800/428-786; www.customs.govt.nz).

GOING THROUGH CUSTOMS

Mexican Customs inspection has been streamlined. At most points of entry, tourists must press a button in front of what looks like a traffic signal, which alternates between red and green. A green light lets you pass without inspection; if the light flashes red, your luggage or car may be inspected. If you have an unusual amount of luggage or an oversized piece, you may be subject to inspection in any case.

4 Money

CASH/CURRENCY

The currency in Mexico is the **peso.** Paper currency comes in denominations of 20, 50, 100, 200, and 500 pesos. Coins come in denominations of 1, 2, 5, 10, and 20 pesos, and 20 and 50 **centavos** (100 centavos = 1 peso). The current exchange rate for the U.S. dollar, and the one used in this book, is around 11 pesos; at that rate, an item that costs 11 pesos would be equivalent to US$1.

Getting **change** is a problem. Small-denomination bills and coins are hard to come by, so start collecting them early in your trip. Shopkeepers everywhere always seem to be out of change and small bills; that's doubly true in markets.

Many establishments that deal with tourists, especially in coastal resort areas, quote prices in dollars. To avoid confusion, they use the abbreviations "Dlls." for dollars and "M.N." (*moneda nacional,* or national currency) for pesos.

The rate of exchange fluctuates daily, so you probably are better off not exchanging too much currency at once. Don't forget to have

---

Tips A Few Words About Prices

The peso's value continues to fluctuate—at press time, it was roughly 11 pesos to the dollar. Prices in this book (which are always given in U.S. dollars) have been converted to U.S. dollars at 11 pesos to the dollar. Most hotels in Mexico—with the exception of places that receive little foreign tourism—quote prices in U.S. dollars. Thus, currency fluctuations are unlikely to affect the prices most hotels charge.

Mexico has a **value-added tax** of 15% (*Impuesto de Valor Agregado,* or IVA; pronounced "ee-vah") on most everything, including restaurant meals, bus tickets, and souvenirs. (Exceptions are Cancún, Cozumel, and Los Cabos, where the IVA is 10%; as ports of entry, they receive a break on taxes.) Hotels charge the usual 15% IVA, plus a locally administered bed tax of 2% (in most areas), for a total of 17%. The prices quoted by hotels and restaurants do not necessarily include IVA. You may find that upper-end properties (three or more stars) quote prices without IVA included, while lower-priced hotels include IVA. Always ask to see a printed price sheet and always ask if the tax is included.

---

enough pesos to carry you over a weekend or Mexican holiday, when banks are closed. In general, avoid carrying the U.S. $100 bill, the bill most commonly counterfeited in Mexico and therefore the most difficult to exchange, especially in smaller towns. Because small bills and coins in pesos are hard to come by in Mexico, the $1 bill is very useful for tipping. **Note:** A tip of U.S. coins, which cannot be exchanged into Mexican currency, is of no value to the service provider.

The bottom line on exchanging money: Ask first, and shop around. Banks generally pay the top rates.

Casas de cambio (exchange houses) generally have more locations and longer hours than banks; the exchange rate may be the same as a bank's or slightly lower. Before leaving a bank or exchange-house window, count your change in front of the teller before the next client steps up.

Large airports have currency-exchange counters that often stay open whenever flights are operating. Though convenient, they generally do not offer the most favorable rates.

A hotel's exchange desk commonly pays less favorable rates than banks; however, when the currency is in a state of flux, higher-priced hotels are known to pay higher rates than banks, in an effort to attract dollars. *Note:* In almost all cases, you receive a better rate by changing money first, then paying.

It's a good idea to exchange at least some money—just enough to cover airport incidentals and transportation to your hotel—before you leave home (though don't expect the exchange rate to be ideal), so you can avoid lines at airport ATMs (automated teller machines). You can exchange money at your local American Express or Thomas Cook office or your bank. If you're far away from a bank with currency-exchange services, **American Express** offers traveler's checks and foreign currency, though with a $15 order fee and additional shipping costs, at © **800/807-6233** or www.americanexpress.com.

BANKS & ATMs

Banks in Mexico are rapidly expanding and improving services. They tend to be open weekdays from 9am until 5pm, and often for at least a half-day on Saturday. In larger resorts and cities, they can generally accommodate the exchange of dollars (which used to stop at noon) anytime during business hours. During times when the currency is in flux, a particular bank may not exchange dollars, so check before standing in line. Some, but not all, banks charge a service fee of about 1% to exchange traveler's checks. However, you can

Money Matters

Note: The universal currency sign **($)** is used to indicate pesos in Mexico. The use of this symbol in this book, however, denotes U.S. currency. Many establishments dealing with tourists, especially in coastal resort areas, quote prices in dollars. To avoid confusion, they use the abbreviations "Dlls." for dollars and "M.N." (*moneda nacional,* or national currency) for pesos. All dollar equivalencies in this book were based on an exchange rate of 11 pesos per dollar.

pay for most purchases directly with traveler's checks at the establishment's stated exchange rate. Don't even bother with personal checks drawn on a U.S. bank—the bank will wait for your check to clear, which can take weeks, before giving you your money.

ATMs (automated teller machines) are available in most major cities and resort areas. The U.S. State Department has an advisory against using ATMs in Mexico for safety reasons, stating that they should only be used during business hours, but this pertains primarily to Mexico City, where crime remains a significant problem. In most resorts in Mexico, the use of ATMs is perfectly safe—just use the same precautions you would at any ATM. Universal bank cards (such as the Cirrus and PLUS systems) can be used. This is a convenient way to withdraw money and avoid carrying too much with you at any time. The exchange rate is generally more favorable than that at a *casas de cambio.* Most machines offer Spanish/English menus and dispense pesos, but some offer the option of withdrawing dollars. The **Cirrus** (© **800/424-7787;** www.mastercard.com) and **PLUS** (© **800/843-7587;** www.visa.com) networks span the globe; look at the back of your bank card to see which network you're on, then call or check online for ATM locations at your destination. Be sure you know your personal identification number (PIN) before you leave home and be sure to find out your daily withdrawal limit before you depart. Also keep in mind that many banks impose a fee every time a card is used at a different bank's ATM, and that fee can be higher for international transactions (up to $5 or more) than for domestic ones (where they're rarely more than $1.50). On top of this, the bank from which you withdraw cash may charge its own fee. To compare banks' ATM fees within the U.S., use www.bankrate.com. For international withdrawal fees, ask your bank.

You can also get cash advances on your credit card at an ATM. Keep in mind that credit card companies try to protect themselves from theft by limiting the funds someone can withdraw outside their home country, so call your credit card company before you leave home. And keep in mind that you'll pay interest from the moment of your withdrawal, even if you pay your monthly bills on time.

TRAVELER'S CHECKS

Traveler's checks are less popular now that most cities have 24-hour ATMs. If a bank is not your own, however, you will be charged an ATM fee, so if you're withdrawing money every day, you might be better off with traveler's checks. You'll have to show identification, however, every time you cash one. You should also keep a record of their serial numbers separate from your checks in the event that they are stolen or lost. You'll get a refund faster if you know the numbers.

You can get traveler's checks at almost any bank. You can also get **American Express** traveler's checks over the phone at © **800/221-7282** (Amex gold and platinum cardholders who use this number are exempt from the 1% fee). **Visa** offers traveler's checks at Citibanks nationwide, as well as at several other banks. Call © **800/732-1322** for information. AAA members can obtain Visa checks without a fee at most AAA offices or by calling © **866/339-3378.** **MasterCard** also offers traveler's checks. Call © **800/223-9920** for a location near you.

CREDIT CARDS

Credit cards are a safe way to carry money: They also provide a convenient record of all your expenses, and they generally offer relatively good exchange rates. You can also withdraw cash advances from your credit cards at banks or ATMs, provided you know your PIN. If you've forgotten yours, or didn't even know you had one,

---

Tips **Small Change**

When you change money, ask for some small bills or loose change. Petty cash will come in handy for tipping and public transportation. Consider keeping the change separate from your larger bills, so that it's readily accessible and you'll be less of a target for theft.

Tips **Dear Visa: I'm Off to Mexico!**

Some credit card companies recommend that you notify them of any impending trip abroad so that they don't become suspicious and block your charges when the card is used numerous times in a foreign destination. Even if you don't call your credit card company in advance, you can always call the toll-free emergency number (see "Fast Facts: Mexico," later in this chapter) if a charge is refused—a good reason to carry the phone number with you. But perhaps the most important lesson is to carry more than one card on your trip; if one card doesn't work for any number of reasons, you'll have a backup.

---

call the number on the back of your credit card and ask the bank to send it to you. It usually takes 5 to 7 business days, though some banks will provide the number over the phone if you tell them your mother's maiden name or some other personal information.

Keep in mind that when you use your credit card abroad, most banks assess a 2% fee above the 1% fee charged by Visa, Master-Card, or American Express for currency conversion on credit charges. But credit cards still may be the smart way to go when you factor in things like exorbitant ATM fees and higher traveler's check exchange rates (and service fees).

In Mexico, Visa, MasterCard, and American Express are the most accepted cards. You'll be able to charge most hotel, restaurant, and store purchases, as well as almost all airline tickets, on your credit card. You generally can't charge gasoline purchases in Mexico. You can get cash advances of several hundred dollars on your card, but there may be a wait of 20 minutes to 2 hours.

Charges will be made in pesos, then converted into dollars by the bank issuing the credit card. Generally you receive the favorable bank rate when paying by credit card. However, be aware that some establishments in Mexico add a 5% to 7% surcharge when you pay with a credit card. This is especially true when using American Express. Many times, advertised discounts will not apply if you pay with a credit card.

For tips and telephone numbers to call if your wallet is stolen or lost, go to "Lost & Found" in the "Fast Facts: Mexico" section, later in this chapter.

5 When to Go

SEASONS

Mexico has two principal travel seasons: high and low. High season begins around December 20 and continues through Easter, although in some places high season can begin as early as mid-November. Low season begins the day after Easter and continues through mid-December; during low season, prices may drop 20% to 50%. In beach destinations, the prices may also increase during the months of July and August, the traditional national summer vacation period. Prices in inland cities, such as Guadalajara, seldom fluctuate from high to low season, but may rise dramatically during Easter and Christmas weeks.

CLIMATE

From Puerto Vallarta south to Huatulco, Mexico offers one of the world's most perfect winter climates—dry and balmy with temperatures ranging from the 80s during the day to the 60s at night. From Puerto Vallarta south, you can swim year-round. High mountains shield Pacific beaches from *nortes* (northers—freezing blasts out of Canada via the Texas Panhandle).

HOLIDAYS & SPECIAL EVENTS

During national holidays, Mexican banks and governmental offices—including immigration—are closed.

January

New Year's Day (Año Nuevo). National holiday. Parades, religious observances, parties, and fireworks welcome in the New Year everywhere. In traditional indigenous communities, new tribal leaders are inaugurated with colorful ceremonies rooted in the pre-Hispanic past. January 1.

Three Kings Day (Día de los Reyes). Commemorates the Three Kings' bringing of gifts to the Christ Child. Children receive gifts, and friends and families gather to share the *Rosca de Reyes,* a special cake. Inside the cake is a small doll representing the Christ Child; whoever receives the doll in his or her piece must host a tamales-and-atole party the next month. January 6.

February

Candlemas. Music, dances, processions, food, and other festivities lead up to a blessing of seed and candles, a ritual that mixes pre-Hispanic and European traditions marking the end of winter. All those who attended the Three Kings' Celebration reunite to share atole and tamales at a party hosted by the recipient of the doll found in the Rosca. February 2.

Carnaval. Carnaval takes place the 3 days preceding Ash Wednesday and the start of Lent. It is celebrated with special gusto in Mazatlán. Here, the celebration resembles New Orleans's Mardi Gras, with festivities and parades. Transportation and hotels are packed, so it's best to make reservations 6 months in advance and arrive a couple of days ahead of the beginning of celebrations.

Ash Wednesday. The start of Lent and time of abstinence. It's a day of reverence nationwide, but some towns honor it with folk dancing and fairs. Lent begins on March 1 in 2006, and February 21 in 2007.

March

Benito Juárez's Birthday. National holiday. March 21.

April

Holy Week. Celebrates the last week in the life of Christ, from Palm Sunday to Easter Sunday, with somber religious processions almost nightly, spoofings of Judas, and reenactments of specific biblical events, plus food and craft fairs. Businesses close during this week of Mexican national vacations.

If you plan on traveling to or around Mexico during Holy Week, make your reservations early. Airline seats on flights into and out of the country are often reserved months in advance. Buses to almost anywhere in Mexico will be full, so try arriving on the Wednesday or Thursday before Good Friday. Easter Sunday is quiet. In 2006, Easter Sunday is April 16, and the week following is a traditional vacation period.

May

Labor Day. Nationwide parades; everything closes. May 1.

Holy Cross Day (Día de la Santa Cruz). Workers place a cross on top of unfinished buildings and celebrate with food, bands, folk dancing, and fireworks around the work site. May 3.

Cinco de Mayo. A national holiday that celebrates the defeat of the French at the Battle of Puebla. May 5.

June

National Ceramics Fair and Fiesta, Tlaquepaque, Jalisco. This pottery center outside Guadalajara hosts crafts demonstrations and contests, mariachis, dancers, and parades. June 14.

Día de San Pedro (St. Peter and St. Paul's Day). Celebrated wherever St. Peter is the patron saint, and honors anyone named

Pedro or Peter. It's especially festive at San Pedro Tlaquepaque, near Guadalajara, with numerous mariachi bands, folk dancers, and parades with floats. In Mexcatitlan, Nayarit, shrimpers hold a regatta to celebrate the season opening. June 29.

September

Mariachi Festival, Guadalajara, Jalisco. Public mariachi concerts, with groups from around the world (even Japan!). Workshops and lectures are given on the history, culture, and music of the mariachi. Plans for an extension of this festival in Puerto Vallarta are being worked out—call ☏ **800-44-MEXICO** to confirm dates and performance schedules. September 1 to 15.

Independence Day. Celebrates Mexico's independence from Spain. A day of parades, picnics, and family reunions throughout the country. At 11pm on September 15, the president of Mexico gives the famous independence *grito* (shout) from the National Palace in Mexico City, which is duplicated by every *presidente municipal* (mayor) in every town plaza in Mexico. Both Guadalajara and Puerto Vallarta have great parties in the town plaza on the nights of September 15 and 16.

October

Fiestas de Octubre (October Festivals), Guadalajara. This "most Mexican of cities" celebrates for a whole month with its mariachi music trademark. A bountiful display of popular culture and fine arts, and a spectacular spread of traditional foods, Mexican beers, and wines all add to the celebration. All month.

November

Day of the Dead. The Day of the Dead is actually 2 days, All Saints' Day (honoring saints and deceased children) and All Souls' Day (honoring deceased adults). Relatives gather at cemeteries carrying candles and food, and often spend the night beside the graves of loved ones. Weeks before, bakers begin producing bread shaped like mummies or round loaves decorated with bread "bones." Decorated sugar skulls emblazoned with glittery names are sold everywhere. Many days ahead, homes and churches erect special altars laden with Day of the Dead bread, fruit, flowers, candles, and favorite foods and photographs of saints and of the deceased. Children, dressed in costumes and masks, carry mock coffins and pumpkin lanterns through the streets at night, expecting people to drop money in them. November 1 and 2.

The 2006 Puerto Vallarta Film Festival, Puerto Vallarta, Jalisco. Featuring a wide range of North American independent and Latin American productions, this elaborate showcase of full-length films and documentaries includes galas, art expos, and concerts, with celebrity attendees. www.puertovallartafilm.com. Check local calendars or call © **800/44-MEXICO** for details. Mid-November.

Gourmet Festival. Puerto Vallarta, Jalisco. In this culinary capital of Mexico, chefs from around the world join with local restaurateurs to create special menus, as well as host wine tastings, tequila tastings, cooking classes, gourmet food expos, and other special events. For a detailed schedule and more information visit www.festivalgourmet.com. November 10 to 19.

Revolution Day. Commemorates the start of the Mexican Revolution in 1910 with parades, speeches, rodeos, and patriotic events. November 20.

December

Feast of the Virgin of Guadalupe. Throughout the country, the patroness of Mexico is honored with religious processions, street fairs, dancing, fireworks, and Masses. It is one of Mexico's most moving and beautiful displays of traditional culture. The Virgin of Guadalupe appeared to a young man, Juan Diego, in December 1531, on a hill near Mexico City. He convinced the bishop that he had seen the apparition by revealing his cloak, upon which the Virgin was emblazoned. Children dress up as Juan Diego, wearing mustaches and red bandannas. December 12.

In Puerto Vallarta, the celebration begins on December 1 and extends through December 12, with traditional processions to the church for a brief *misa* (mass) and blessing. In the final days, the processions and festivities take place around the clock, with many of the processions featuring floats, mariachis, Aztec dancers, and fireworks. The central plaza is filled with street vendors and a festive atmosphere, and a major fireworks exhibition takes place on December 12 at 11pm.

Christmas Posadas. On each of the 9 nights before Christmas, it's customary to reenact the Holy Family's search for an inn, with door-to-door candlelit processions in cities and villages nationwide. Most business and community organizations host them in place of the northern tradition of a Christmas party. December 15 to 24.

Christmas. Mexicans extend this celebration, often starting 2 weeks before Christmas, through New Year's. Many businesses close, and resorts and hotels fill up. December 24 and 25.

New Year's Eve. As in the rest of the world, New Year's Eve is celebrated with parties and fireworks.

6 Travel Insurance

Check your existing insurance policies and credit card coverage before you buy travel insurance. You may already be covered for lost luggage, canceled tickets, or medical expenses. The cost of travel insurance varies widely, depending on the cost and length of your trip, your age and health, and the type of trip you're taking, but expect to pay between 5% and 8% of the vacation itself.

If you'll be driving in Mexico, see "Getting There: By Car" and "Getting Around: By Car," later in this chapter, for information on **collision**, **damage**, and **accident insurance.**

TRIP-CANCELLATION INSURANCE   Trip-cancellation insurance helps you get your money back if you have to back out of a trip, if you have to go home early, or if your travel supplier goes bankrupt. Allowed reasons for cancellation can range from sickness to natural disasters to the State Department declaring your destination unsafe for travel. (Insurers usually won't cover vague fears, though, as many travelers discovered who tried to cancel their trips after the Sept. 11, 2001, terrorist attacks because they were wary of flying.) In this unstable world, trip-cancellation insurance is a good buy if you're getting tickets well in advance—who knows what the state of the world, or of your airline, will be in 9 months? Insurance policy details vary, so read the fine print—and make sure that your airline or cruise line is on the list of carriers covered in case of bankruptcy. A good resource is **"Travel Guard Alerts,"** a list of companies considered high-risk by Travel Guard International (see website below). Protect yourself further by paying for the insurance with a credit card—by law, consumers can get their money back on goods and services not received if they report the loss within 60 days after the charge is listed on their credit card statement.

Note: Many tour operators, particularly those offering trips to remote or high-risk areas, include insurance in the cost of the trip or can arrange insurance policies through a partnering provider, a convenient and often cost-effective way for the traveler to obtain insurance. Make sure the tour company is a reputable one, however: Some experts suggest you avoid buying insurance from the tour or cruise company you're traveling with, saying it's better to buy from a "third party" insurer than to put all your money in one place.

For more information, contact one of the following recommended insurers: **Access America** (✆ 866/807-3982; www.access america.com); **Travel Guard International** (✆ 800/826-4919;

www.travelguard.com); **Travel Insured International** (© 800/243-3174; www.travelinsured.com); and **Travelex Insurance Services** (© 888/457-4602; www.travelex-insurance.com).

MEDICAL INSURANCE   For travel overseas, most health plans (including Medicare and Medicaid) do not provide coverage, and the ones that do often require you to pay for services upfront and reimburse you only after you return home. Even if your plan does cover overseas treatment, most out-of-country hospitals make you pay your bills upfront, and send you a refund only after you've returned home and filed the necessary paperwork with your insurance company. As a safety net, you may want to buy travel medical insurance, particularly if you're traveling to a remote or high-risk area where emergency evacuation is a possible scenario. If you require additional medical insurance, try **MEDEX Assistance** (© 410/453-6300; www.medexassist.com) or **Travel Assistance International** (© 800/821-2828; www.travelassistance.com; for general information on services, call the company's Worldwide Assistance Services, Inc., at © **800/777-8710**).

LOST-LUGGAGE INSURANCE   On domestic flights, checked baggage is covered up to $2,500 per ticketed passenger. On international flights (including U.S. portions of international trips), baggage coverage is limited to approximately $9.07 per pound, up to approximately $635 per checked bag. If you plan to check items more valuable than the standard liability, see if your valuables are covered by your homeowner's policy or get baggage insurance as part of your comprehensive travel-insurance package. Don't buy insurance at the airport, as it's usually overpriced. Be sure to take any valuables or irreplaceable items with you in your carry-on luggage, as many valuables (including books, money, and electronics) aren't covered by airline policies.

If your luggage is lost, immediately file a lost-luggage claim at the airport, detailing the luggage contents. For most airlines, you must report delayed, damaged, or lost baggage within 4 hours of arrival. The airlines are required to deliver luggage, once found, directly to your house or destination free of charge.

Keep in mind that in these uncertain times, insurers no longer cover some airlines, cruise lines, and tour operators. *The bottom line:* Always, always check the fine print before you sign; more and more policies have built-in exclusions and restrictions that may leave you out in the cold if something goes awry.

7 Health & Safety

In most of Mexico's resort destinations, health care meeting U.S. standards is now available. Mexico's major cities are also known for their excellent health care, although the facilities available may be fewer, and equipment older than what is available at home. Prescription

Tips **What to Do If You Get Sick**

"Montezuma's revenge"—persistent diarrhea, often with fever, nausea, and vomiting—used to attack many travelers to Mexico. Widespread improvements in infrastructure, sanitation, and education have practically eliminated this ailment, especially in well-developed resort areas. Most travelers drink only bottled water, which also helps to protect against unfamiliar bacteria. In resort areas, and generally throughout Mexico, only purified ice is used. If you do get sick, nothing beats Pepto Bismol, readily available in Mexico. Imodium is also available in Mexico and is used by many travelers for a quick fix. A good high-potency (or "therapeutic") vitamin supplement and even extra vitamin C can help; yogurt is good for healthy digestion.

Since dehydration can quickly become life-threatening, the Public Health Service advises that you be careful to replace fluids and electrolytes (potassium, sodium, and the like) during a bout of diarrhea. Drink Pedialyte, a rehydration solution available at most Mexican pharmacies, or natural fruit juice, such as guava or apple (stay away from orange juice, which has laxative properties), with a pinch of salt added.

How to Prevent It: The U.S. Public Health Service recommends the following measures for preventing travelers' diarrhea: **Drink only purified water** (boiled water, canned or bottled beverages, beer, or wine). **Choose food carefully.** In general, avoid salads (except in first-class restaurants), uncooked vegetables, undercooked protein, and unpasteurized milk or milk products, including cheese. Choose food that is freshly cooked and still hot. In addition, something as simple as **clean hands** can go a long way toward preventing *turista*.

Over-the-Counter Drugs

Antibiotics and other drugs that you'd need a prescription to buy in the States are available over the counter in Mexican pharmacies. Mexican pharmacies also carry a limited selection of common over-the-counter cold, sinus, and allergy remedies.

medicine is broadly available at Mexico pharmacies; however, be aware that you may need a copy of your prescription, or obtain a prescription from a local doctor. This is especially true in the border towns, such as in Tijuana, where many Americans have been crossing into Mexico specifically for the purpose of purchasing lower priced prescription medicines.

Contact the **International Association for Medical Assistance to Travelers (IAMAT; ℂ 716/754-4883** or, in Canada, 416/652-0137; www.iamat.org) for tips on travel and health concerns in the countries you're visiting, and lists of local, English-speaking doctors. The U.S. **Centers for Disease Control and Prevention (ℂ 800/311-3435;** www.cdc.gov) provides up-to-date information on health hazards by region or country and offers tips on food safety.

STAYING HEALTHY

BUG OFF   Mosquitoes and gnats are prevalent along the coast. Insect repellent *(repelente contra insectos)* is a must, and it's not always available in Mexico. If you'll be in these areas and are prone to bites, bring a repellent along that contains the active ingredient DEET. Avon's "Skin So Soft" also works well. If you're sensitive to bites, pick up some antihistamine cream from a drugstore at home. Another good remedy to keep the mosquitoes away is to mix citronella essential oil with basil, clove, and lavender essential oils.

Most visitors won't ever see an *alacrán* (scorpion). But if one stings you, go immediately to a doctor. In Mexico you can buy scorpion toxin antidote at any drugstore. It is an injection and it costs around $25. This is a good idea if you plan to camp in a remote area where medical assistance can be several hours away.

MORE SERIOUS DISEASES   You shouldn't be overly concerned about tropical diseases if you stay on the normal tourist routes and don't eat street food. However, both dengue fever and cholera have appeared in Mexico in recent years. Talk to your doctor or to a medical specialist in tropical diseases about precautions you should take. You can also get medical bulletins from the U.S. State Department and the Centers for Disease Control and Prevention (see "Visitor Information," earlier in this chapter). Watch what you eat and drink; don't swim in stagnant water (ponds, slow-moving rivers, or wells); and avoid mosquito bites by covering up, using repellent, and sleeping under netting. The most dangerous areas seem to be on Mexico's west coast, away from the big resorts.

WHAT TO DO IF YOU GET SICK AWAY FROM HOME

Any foreign consulate can provide a list of area doctors who speak English. If you get sick, consider asking your hotel concierge to recommend a local doctor—even his or her own. You can also try the emergency room at a local hospital. Many hospitals also have walk-in clinics for emergency cases that are not life-threatening; you may not get immediate attention, but you won't pay the high price of an emergency room visit. We list hospitals and emergency numbers under "Fast Facts," in each destination's chapter.

If you suffer from a chronic illness, consult your doctor before your departure. For conditions like epilepsy, diabetes, or heart problems, wear a **MedicAlert identification tag** (© 888/633-4298; www.medic alert.org), which will immediately alert doctors to your condition and give them access to your records through MedicAlert's 24-hour hot line.

Avoiding "Economy Class Syndrome"

Deep vein thrombosis or, as it's known in the world of flying, "economy-class syndrome," is a blood clot that develops in a deep vein. It's a potentially deadly condition that can be caused by sitting in cramped conditions—such as an airplane cabin—for too long. During a flight (especially a long one), get up, walk around, and stretch your legs every 60 to 90 minutes to keep your blood flowing. Also frequently flex your legs while sitting, drink lots of water, and avoid alcohol and sleeping pills. If you have a history of deep vein thrombosis, heart disease, or another condition that puts you at high risk, some experts recommend wearing compression stockings or taking anticoagulants when you fly; always ask your physician about the best course for you. Symptoms of deep vein thrombosis include leg pain or swelling, or even shortness of breath.

Pack **prescription medications** in your carry-on luggage, and carry them in their original containers, with pharmacy labels—otherwise they won't make it through airport security. Also bring along copies of your prescriptions in case you lose your pills or run out. Don't forget an extra pair of contact lenses or prescription glasses. Carry the generic name of prescription medicines, in case a local pharmacist is unfamiliar with the brand name.

Contact the **International Association for Medical Assistance to Travelers** (see above under "Staying Healthy") for tips on travel and health concerns in Mexico and lists of local English-speaking doctors. The U.S. **Centers for Disease Control and Prevention** (see above) provides up-to-date information on necessary vaccines and health hazards by region or country.

EMERGENCY CARE   Puerto Vallarta has a modern, U.S.-standards health care facility that offers insured care. **Ameri-Med,** Plaza Neptuno, in Marina Vallarta (© **322/221-0023;** fax 322/221-0026; www.amerimed-hospitals.com), provides complete, 24-hour, emergency health care adhering to U.S. medical standards. Facilities include CAT scan, radiology, ultrasound, and emergency air-evacuation services. Prices are in line with the standard of care, meaning that it's more costly than other medical facilities in Mexico.

For extreme medical emergencies, a service from the United States will fly people to American hospitals: **Global Lifeline** (© **888/554-9729,** or 01-800/305-9400 in Mexico) is a 24-hour air ambulance. Several other companies offer air evac service; for a list refer to the U.S. State Department website at http://travel.state.gov/medical.html.

EMERGENCY EVACUATION   **Global Lifeline** (© **888/554-9729,** or 01-800/305-9400 in Mexico), a 24-hour air ambulance, will fly sick or injured U.S. citizens to American hospitals.

STAYING SAFE

I have lived and traveled in Mexico for a decade, have never had any serious trouble, and rarely feel suspicious of anyone or any situation. You will probably feel physically safer in most Mexican cities and villages than in any comparable place at home. However, crime in Mexico has received attention in the North American press over the past several years. Many feel this unfairly exaggerates the real dangers, but note that crime rates, including taxi robberies, kidnappings, and highway carjackings, have risen. The most severe crime problems were concentrated in Mexico City, far away from the Mexican Riviera; however, Guadalajara has experienced an increase in street crime. See "Crime, Bribes & Scams," below, for more information and how to access the latest U.S. State Department advisories.

CRIME, BRIBES & SCAMS
CRIME

The crime rate is, on the whole, much lower in Mexico than in most parts of the United States, and the nature of crimes in general is less violent. Random, violent, or serial crime is essentially unheard of in Mexico. You are much more likely to meet kind and helpful Mexicans than you are to encounter those set on thievery and deceit. A good rule of thumb is that you can generally trust people whom you approach for help, assistance, or directions—but be wary of anyone who approaches you offering the same. The more insistent they are, the more cautious you should be.

BRIBES & SCAMS

As is the case around the world, there are the occasional bribes and scams in Mexico, targeted at people believed to be naive—such as the telltale tourist. For years Mexico was known as a place where bribes—called *mordidas* (bites)—were expected; however, the country is rapidly changing. Frequently, offering a bribe today, especially to a police officer, is considered an insult, and it can land you in deeper trouble.

If you believe a **bribe** is being requested, here are a few tips on dealing with the situation. Even if you speak Spanish, don't utter a word of it to Mexican officials. That way you'll appear innocent, all the while understanding every word.

When you are crossing the border, should the person who inspects your car ask for a tip, you can ignore the request—but understand that the official may decide to thoroughly search your belongings. If faced with a situation where you feel you're being asked for a *propina* (literally, "tip"; colloquially, "bribe"), how much should you offer? Usually $3 to $5 or the equivalent in pesos will do the trick. Many tourists have the impression that everything works better in Mexico if you "tip"; however, in reality, this only perpetuates the *mordida* attitude. If you are pleased with a service, feel free to tip, but you shouldn't tip simply to attempt to get away with something illegal or inappropriate, whether it is crossing the border without having your car inspected or not getting a ticket that's deserved.

Whatever you do, **avoid impoliteness;** under no circumstances should you insult a Latin American official. Extreme politeness, even in the face of adversity, rules Mexico. In Mexico, *gringos* have a reputation for being loud and demanding. By adopting the local custom of excessive courtesy, you'll have greater success in negotiations of any kind. Stand your ground, but do it politely.

In Mexico, you may encounter several types of **scams,** which are typical throughout the world. One involves some kind of a **distraction** or feigned commotion. While your attention is diverted, a pickpocket makes a grab for your wallet. In another common scam, an **unaccompanied child** pretends to be lost and frightened and takes your hand for safety. Meanwhile the child or an accomplice plunders your pockets. A third involves **confusing currency.** A shoeshine boy, street musician, guide, or other individual might offer you a service for a price that seems reasonable—in pesos. When it comes time to pay, he or she tells you the price is in dollars, not pesos. Be very clear on the price and currency when services are involved.

8 Specialized Travel Resources

FAMILY TRAVEL

Children are considered the national treasure of Mexico, and Mexicans will welcome and cater to them. Many parents were reluctant to bring young children into Mexico in the past, primarily due to health concerns, but I can't think of a better place to introduce children to the adventure of exploring a different culture. Puerto Vallarta is among the best destinations for traveling with little ones.

Hotels can often arrange for a babysitter. Some hotels in the moderate-to-luxury range even have small playgrounds and pools for children, and hire caretakers with special activity programs during the day. Few budget hotels offer these amenities.

Before leaving, ask your doctor which medications to take along. Disposable diapers cost about the same in Mexico but are of poorer quality. You can get high-quality brands, but at a higher price. Many stores sell Gerber's baby foods. Dry cereals, powdered formulas, baby bottles, and purified water are easily available in midsize and large cities or resorts.

Only the largest, most luxurious hotels provide cribs, but rollaway beds are often available. Child seats or high chairs at restaurants are common, but bring your own car seat; they are not readily available for rent in Mexico.

Every country's regulations differ, but in general children traveling abroad should have plenty of documentation on hand, particularly if they're traveling with someone other than their own parents (in which case a notarized form letter from a parent is often required). For details on entry requirements for children traveling abroad, go to the U.S. State Department website (www.travel.state.gov); click on "International Travel," "Travel Brochures," and "Foreign Entry Requirements."

Throughout this book, the "Kids" icon distinguishes attractions, hotels, restaurants, and other destinations that are particularly attractive and accommodating to children and families.

Familyhostel (© 800/733-9753; www.learn.unh.edu/family hostel) takes the whole family, including kids ages 8 to 15, on moderately priced domestic and international learning vacations. Lectures, field trips, and sightseeing are guided by a team of academics.

Recommended family travel Internet sites include **Family Travel Forum** (www.familytravelforum.com), a comprehensive site that offers customized trip planning; **Family Travel Network** (www.familytravelnetwork.com), an award-winning site that offers travel features, deals, and tips; **Traveling Internationally with Your Kids** (www.travelwithyourkids.com), a comprehensive site offering sound advice for long-distance and international travel with children; and **Family Travel Files** (www.thefamilytravelfiles.com), which offers an online magazine and a directory of off-the-beaten-path tours and tour operators for families.

GAY & LESBIAN TRAVELERS

Mexico is a conservative country, with deeply rooted Catholic religious traditions. As such, public displays of same-sex affection are rare and still considered shocking for men, especially outside of urban or resort areas. Women in Mexico frequently walk hand in hand, but anything more would cross the boundary of acceptability. However, gay and lesbian travelers are generally treated with respect and should not experience any harassment, assuming the appropriate regard is given to local culture and customs.

Puerto Vallarta is perhaps the most welcoming and accepting destination in Mexico. Susan Weisman's travel service **Bayside Properties** (© 322/223-4424; www.baysidepuertovallarta.com) rents gay-friendly condos, villas, and hotels for individuals and large groups. Her services are customized to individual needs, and she can offer airport pickups and in-villa cooks.

The **International Gay and Lesbian Travel Association (IGLTA)** (*©* 800/448-8550 135 or 954/776-2626; www.iglta.org) is the trade association for the gay and lesbian travel industry, and offers an online directory of gay- and lesbian-friendly travel businesses; go to their website and click on "Members."

Many agencies offer tours and travel itineraries specifically for gay and lesbian travelers. **Above and Beyond Tours** (*©* 800/397-2681; www.abovebeyondtours.com) is the exclusive gay and lesbian tour operator for United Airlines. **Now, Voyager** (*©* 800/255-6951; www.nowvoyager.com) is a well-known San Francisco–based gay-owned and operated travel service. **Olivia Cruises & Resorts** (*©* 800/631-6277; www.olivia.com) charters entire resorts and ships for exclusive lesbian vacations and offers smaller group experiences for both gay and lesbian travelers.

The following travel guides are available at most travel bookstores and gay and lesbian bookstores, or you can order them from **Giovanni's Room** bookstore, 1145 Pine St., Philadelphia, PA 19107 (*©* 215/923-2960; www.giovannisroom.com): *Out and About* (*©* 800/929-2268; www.outandabout.com), which offers guidebooks and a newsletter ($20/year; 10 issues) packed with solid information on the global gay and lesbian scene; *Spartacus International Gay Guide* (Bruno Gmünder Verlag; www.spartacus world.com/gayguide) and *Odysseus: The International Gay Travel Planner* (Odysseus Enterprises Ltd.), both good, annual English-language guidebooks focused on gay men; the *Damron* guides (www.damron.com), with separate, annual books for gay men and lesbians; and *Gay Travel A to Z: The World of Gay & Lesbian Travel Options at Your Fingertips* by Marianne Ferrari (Ferrari International; Box 35575, Phoenix, AZ 85069), a very good gay and lesbian guidebook series.

TRAVELERS WITH DISABILITIES

Mexico may seem like one giant obstacle course to travelers in wheelchairs or on crutches. At airports, you may encounter steep stairs before finding a well-hidden elevator or escalator—if one exists. Airlines will often arrange wheelchair assistance to the baggage area. Porters are generally available to help with luggage at airports and large bus stations, once you've cleared baggage claim.

Mexican airports are upgrading their services, but it is not uncommon to board from a remote position, meaning you either descend stairs to a bus that ferries you to the plane, which you board by climbing stairs, or you walk across the tarmac to your plane and ascend the stairs. Deplaning presents the same problem in reverse.

Escalators (and there aren't many in the country) are often out of order. Stairs without handrails abound. Few restrooms are equipped for travelers with disabilities; when one is available, access to it may be through a narrow passage that won't accommodate a wheelchair or a person on crutches. Many deluxe hotels (the most expensive) now have rooms with bathrooms for people with disabilities. Those traveling on a budget should stick with one-story hotels or hotels with elevators. Even so, there will probably still be obstacles somewhere. Generally speaking, no matter where you are, someone will lend a hand, although you may have to ask for it.

One exception is Puerto Vallarta, which has recently renovated the majority of its downtown sidewalks and plazas with ramps to accommodate wheelchairs (and baby strollers). Even the airport has ramps adjacent to stairways, and special wheelchair lifts. A local citizen with disabilities deserves the credit for this impressive task—setting the stage for greater accessibility in other towns and resorts.

Most disabilities shouldn't stop anyone from traveling. There are more options and resources out there than ever before.

Many travel agencies offer customized tours and itineraries for travelers with disabilities. **Flying Wheels Travel** (© 507/451-5005; www.flyingwheelstravel.com) offers escorted tours and cruises that emphasize sports and private tours in minivans with lifts. **Access-Able Travel Source** (© 303/232-2979; www.access-able.com) offers extensive access information and advice for traveling around the world with disabilities. **Accessible Journeys** (© 800/846-4537 or 610/521-0339; www.disabilitytravel.com) caters specifically to slow walkers and wheelchair travelers and their families and friends.

Organizations that offer assistance to travelers with disabilities include **MossRehab** (www.mossresourcenet.org), which provides a library of accessible-travel resources online; **Society for Accessible Travel & Hospitality** (SATH; © 212/447-7284; www.sath.org; annual membership fees: $45 adults, $30 seniors and students), which offers a wealth of travel resources for all types of disabilities and informed recommendations on destinations, access guides, travel agents, tour operators, vehicle rentals, and companion services; and the **American Foundation for the Blind** (AFB; ⓒ **800/232-5463;** www.afb.org), a referral resource for the blind or visually impaired that includes information on traveling with Seeing Eye dogs.

The website **iCan** (www.icanonline.net/channels/travel) has destination guides and regular columns on accessible travel. Also check out the magazines *Emerging Horizons* ($15 per year, $20 outside the U.S.; www.emerginghorizons.com); and *Open World,* published by SATH (see above; subscription: $13 per year, $21 outside the U.S.).

SENIOR TRAVEL

Mexico is popular with retirees, and some of the most popular places for long-term stays are Puerto Vallarta and Guadalajara. For decades, North Americans have been living indefinitely in Mexico by returning to the border and recrossing with a new tourist permit every 6 months. Mexican immigration officials have caught on, and now limit the maximum time in the country to 6 months per year. This is to encourage even partial residents to acquire proper documentation.

AIM, Apdo Postal 31–70, 45050 Guadalajara, Jal., is a well-written, informative newsletter for prospective retirees. Issues have evaluated retirement in Aguascalientes, Puebla, San Cristóbal de las Casas, Puerto Angel, Puerto Escondido and Huatulco, Oaxaca, Taxco, Tepic, Manzanillo, Melaque, and Barra de Navidad. Subscriptions are $18 to the United States and $21 to Canada. Back issues are three for $5.

Sanborn Tours, 2015 S. 10th St., Post Office Drawer 519, McAllen, TX 78505-0519 (ⓒ **800/395-8482**), offers a "Retire in Mexico" orientation tour.

Mention that you're a senior when you make reservations. Most major U.S. airlines have canceled their senior discounts and coupon books, but many hotels still offer senior discounts.

Members of **AARP** (formerly known as the American Association of Retired Persons), 601 E St. NW, Washington, DC 20049 (ⓒ **888/687-2277;** www.aarp.org), get discounts on hotels, airfares, and car rentals. AARP offers members a wide range of benefits, including *AARP: The Magazine* and a monthly newsletter. Anyone over 50 can join.

Many reliable agencies and organizations target the 50-plus market. **Elderhostel** (ⓒ **877/426-8056;** www.elderhostel.org) arranges study programs for those ages 55 and over (and a spouse or companion of any age) in the U.S. and in more than 80 countries around the world. Most courses abroad last 2 to 4 weeks, and many include air-fare, accommodations in university dormitories or modest inns, meals, and tuition. **ElderTreks** (© **800/741-7956;** www.eldertreks.com) offers small-group tours to off-the-beaten-path or adventure-travel locations, restricted to travelers 50 and older. **INTRAV** (© **800/456-8100;** www.intrav.com) is a high-end tour operator that caters to the mature, discerning traveler (not specifically seniors), with trips around the world that include guided safaris, polar expeditions, private-jet adventures, and small-boat cruises down jungle rivers.

Recommended publications offering travel resources and discounts for seniors include: the quarterly magazine *Travel 50 & Beyond* (www.travel50andbeyond.com); *Travel Unlimited: Uncommon Adventures for the Mature Traveler* (Avalon); *101 Tips for Mature Travelers,* available from Grand Circle Travel (© **800/221-2610** or 617/350-7500; www.gct.com); and *Unbelievably Good Deals and Great Adventures That You Absolutely Can't Get Unless You're Over 50* (McGraw-Hill), by Joann Rattner Heilman.

SINGLE TRAVELERS

Mexico may be an old favorite for romantic honeymoons, but it's also a great place to travel on your own without really being or feeling alone. Although many Mexican hotels are starting to offer the same rates for single or double occupancies, many of the establishments in this book still offer singles at lower rates.

Mexicans are very friendly, and it's easy to meet other foreigners. But if you don't like the idea of traveling alone, then try **Travel Companion Exchange (TCE)** (© **631/454-0880;** www.travelcompanions.com), one of the nation's oldest roommate finders for single travelers. Register with them and find a travel mate who will split the cost of the room with you and be around as little, or as often, as you like during the day.

For more information, check out Eleanor Berman's *Traveling Solo: Advice and Ideas for More Than 250 Great Vacations* (Globe Pequot), for individuals traveling alone at large, or on a group tour. (It was last updated in 2003.) The **Travel Alone and Love It** website (www.travelaloneandloveit.com) was designed by former flight attendant Sharon Wingler, the author of the book of the same name. Her site is full of tips for single travelers.

WOMEN TRAVELERS

As a female traveling alone, I can tell you firsthand that I feel safer traveling in Mexico than in the United States. But I use the same common-sense precautions I use anywhere else in the world and am alert to what's going on around me.

Mexicans in general, and men in particular, are nosy about single travelers, especially women. If a taxi driver or anyone else with whom you don't want to become friendly asks about your marital status, family, and so forth, my advice is to make up a set of answers (regardless of the truth): "I'm married, traveling with friends, and I have three children." Saying you are single and traveling alone may send the wrong message. U.S. television—widely viewed now in Mexico—has given many Mexican men the image of American single women as being sexually promiscuous. Check out the award-winning website **Journeywoman** (www.journeywoman.com), a "real life" women's travel information network where you can sign up for a free e-mail newsletter and get advice on everything from etiquette and dress to safety; or the travel guide *Safety and Security for Women Who Travel* by Sheila Swan and Peter Laufer (Travelers' Tales, Inc.), offering common-sense tips on safe travel.

9 Planning Your Trip Online

SURFING FOR AIRFARES

The "big three" online travel agencies, **Expedia.com, Travelocity. com,** and **Orbitz.com,** sell most of the air tickets bought on the Internet. (Canadian travelers should try expedia.ca and Travelocity. ca; U.K. residents can go for expedia.co.uk and opodo.co.uk.) Each has different business deals with the airlines and may offer different fares on the same flights, so it's wise to shop around. Expedia and Travelocity will also send you **e-mail notification** when a cheap fare becomes available to your favorite destination. Of the smaller travel agency websites, **SideStep** (www.sidestep.com) has gotten the best reviews from Frommer's authors. It's a browser add-on that purports to "search 140 sites at once," but in reality only beats competitors' fares as often as other sites do.

Also remember to check **airline websites,** especially those for low-fare carriers such as Southwest, whose fares are often misreported or simply missing from travel agency websites. Even with major airlines, you can often shave a few bucks from a fare by booking directly through the airline and avoiding a travel agency's transaction fee. But

Tips Frommers.com: The Complete Travel Resource

For an excellent travel-planning resource, we highly recommend **Frommers.com** (www.frommers.com), voted Best Travel Site by *PC Magazine*. We're a little biased, of course, but we guarantee that you'll find the travel tips, reviews, monthly vacation giveaways, bookstore, and online-booking capabilities thoroughly indispensable. Among the special features are our popular **Destinations** section, where you'll get expert travel tips, hotel and dining recommendations, and advice on the sights to see for more than 3,500 destinations around the globe; the **Frommers.com Newsletter**, with the latest deals, travel trends, and money-saving secrets; our **Community** area featuring **Message Boards**, where Frommer's readers post queries and share advice (sometimes even our authors show up to answer questions); and our **Photo Center**, where you can post and share vacation tips. When your research is done, the **Online Reservations System** (www.frommers.com/book_a_trip) takes you to Frommer's preferred online partners for booking your vacation at affordable prices.

you'll get these discounts only by **booking online:** Most airlines now offer online-only fares that even their phone agents know nothing about. For the websites of airlines that fly to and from your destination, go to "Getting There," later in this chapter.

Great **last-minute deals** are available through free weekly e-mail services provided directly by the airlines. Most of these are announced on Tuesday or Wednesday and must be purchased online. Most are only valid for travel that weekend, but some (such as Southwest's) can be booked weeks or months in advance. Sign up for weekly e-mail alerts at airline websites or check megasites that compile comprehensive lists of last-minute specials, such as **SmarterTravel.com**. For last-minute trips, **site59.com** and **lastminutetravel.com** in the U.S. and **lastminute.com** in Europe often have better air-and-hotel package deals than the major-label sites. A website listing numerous bargain sites and airlines around the world is **www.itravelnet.com**.

If you're willing to give up some control over your flight details, use what is called an **"opaque" fare service** like **Priceline** (www.priceline.com, or www.priceline.co.uk for Europeans) or its smaller competitor **Hotwire** (www.hotwire.com). Both offer rock-bottom prices in exchange for travel on a "mystery airline" at a mysterious time of day, often with a mysterious change of planes en route. The mystery airlines are all major, well-known carriers—and the possibility of being sent from Philadelphia to Chicago via Tampa is remote; the airlines' routing computers have gotten a lot better than they used to be. But your chances of getting a 6am or 11pm flight are pretty high. Hotwire tells you flight prices before you buy; Priceline usually has better deals than Hotwire, but you have to play their "name your price" game. If you're new at this, the helpful folks at **BiddingForTravel** (www.biddingfortravel.com) do a good job of demystifying Priceline's prices and strategies. Priceline and Hotwire are great for flights within North America and between the U.S. and Europe. But for flights to other parts of the world, consolidators will almost always beat their fares. ***Note:*** In 2004 Priceline added nonopaque service to its roster. You now have the option to pick exact flights, times, and airlines from a list of offers—or opt to bid on opaque fares as before.

For much more about airfares and savvy air-travel tips and advice, pick up a copy of ***Frommer's Fly Safe, Fly Smart*** (Wiley Publishing, Inc.). See also "Flying for Less: Tips for Getting the Best Airfare," later in this chapter.

SURFING FOR HOTELS

Generally, you can shop online for hotels in one of two ways: by booking through the hotel's own website or through an independent booking agency (or a fare-service agency like Priceline; see above). These Internet hotel agencies have multiplied in mind-boggling numbers of late, competing for the business of millions of consumers surfing for accommodations around the world. This competitiveness can be a boon to consumers who have the patience and time to shop and compare the online sites for good deals—but shop they must, for prices can vary considerably from site to site. And keep in mind that hotels at the top of a site's listing may be there for no other reason than that they paid money to get the placement.

Of the "big three" sites, **Expedia** offers a long list of special deals and "virtual tours" or photos of available rooms so you can see what you're paying for (a feature that helps counter the claims that the best rooms are often held back from bargain-booking websites). **Travelocity** posts unvarnished customer reviews and ranks its properties according to the AAA rating system. Also reliable are **Hotels.com** and **Quikbook.com**. An excellent free program, **TravelAxe** (www.travelaxe.net), can help you search multiple hotel sites at once, even ones you may never have heard of—and conveniently lists the total price of the room, including the taxes and service charges. Another booking site, **Travelweb** (www.travelweb), is partly owned by the hotels it represents (including the Hilton, Hyatt, and Starwood chains) and is therefore plugged directly into the hotels' reservations systems—unlike independent online agencies, which have to fax or e-mail reservation requests to the hotel, a good portion of which get misplaced in the shuffle. More than once, travelers have arrived at the hotel, only to be told that they have no reservation. To be fair, many of the major sites are undergoing improvements in service and ease of use, and Expedia will soon be able to plug directly into the reservations systems of many hotel chains—none of which can be bad news for consumers. In the meantime, it's a good idea to **get a confirmation number** and **make a printout** of any online booking transaction.

SURFING FOR RENTAL CARS

For booking rental cars online, the best deals are usually at rental-car company websites, although all the major online travel agencies also offer rental-car reservations services. Priceline and Hotwire work well for rental cars, too; the only "mystery" is which major rental company you get, and for most travelers the difference between Hertz, Avis, and Budget is negligible.

10 The 21st-Century Traveler

INTERNET ACCESS AWAY FROM HOME

Travelers have any number of ways to check their e-mail and access the Internet on the road. Of course, using your own laptop—or even a PDA (personal digital assistant) or electronic organizer with a modem—gives you the most flexibility. But even if you don't have a computer, you can still access your e-mail and even your office computer from cybercafes.

WITHOUT YOUR OWN COMPUTER

It's hard nowadays to find a city or town in Mexico that *doesn't* have a few cybercafes. The "Fast Facts" sections in this book list cybercafes in major destinations. Although there's no definitive directory for cybercafes—these are independent businesses, after all—two places to start looking are at **www.cybercaptive.com** and **www.cybercafe.com**.

Hotels that cater to business travelers often have **in-room dataports** and **business centers,** but the charges can be hefty—and downright frightful if you're trying to connect to a U.S.-based access number.

Most major airports now have **Internet kiosks** scattered throughout their gates. These kiosks, which you'll also see in shopping malls, hotel lobbies, and tourist information offices around the world, give you basic Web access for a per-minute fee that's usually higher than cybercafe prices. The kiosks' clunkiness and high price mean they should be avoided whenever possible.

To retrieve your e-mail, ask your **Internet service provider (ISP)** if it has a Web-based interface tied to your existing e-mail account. If your ISP doesn't have such an interface, you can use the free **mail2web** service (www.mail2web.com) to view and reply to your home e-mail. For more flexibility, you may want to open a free, Web-based e-mail account with **Yahoo! Mail** (mail.yahoo.com). Microsoft's **Hotmail** is another popular option, but Hotmail has severe spam problems. Your home ISP may be able to forward your e-mail to the Web-based account automatically.

If you need to access files on your office computer, look into a service called **GoToMyPC** (www.gotomypc.com). The service provides a Web-based interface for you to access and manipulate a distant PC from anywhere—even a cybercafe—provided your "target" PC is on and has an always-on connection to the Internet (such as with Road Runner cable). The service offers top-quality security, but if you're worried about hackers, use your own laptop rather than a cybercafe computer to access the GoToMyPC system.

WITH YOUR OWN COMPUTER

Wi-Fi (wireless fidelity) is the buzzword in computer access, and more and more hotels, cafes, and retailers are signing on as wireless "hotspots" from where you can get high-speed connection without cable wires, networking hardware, or a phone line (see below). You can get Wi-Fi connection one of several ways. Many laptops sold in the last year have built-in Wi-Fi capability (an 802.11b wireless Ethernet connection). Mac owners have their own networking technology, Apple AirPort. For those with older computers, an 802.11b/**Wi-Fi card** (around $50) can be plugged into your laptop. You sign up for wireless access service much as you do cellphone service, through a plan offered by one of several commercial companies that have made wireless service available in airports, hotel lobbies, and coffee shops, primarily in the U.S. (followed by the U.K. and Japan). **T-Mobile Hotspot** (www.t-mobile.com/hotspot) serves up wireless connections at more than 1,000 Starbucks coffee shops nationwide. **Boingo** (www.boingo.com) and **Wayport** (www.wayport.com) have set up networks in airports and high-class hotel lobbies. iPass providers (see below) also give you access to a few hundred wireless hotel lobby setups. Best of all, you don't need to cough up the cash to stay at a place like the Four Seasons to use the hotel's network; just set yourself up on a nice couch in the lobby. The companies' pricing policies can be byzantine, with a variety of monthly, per-connection, and per-minute plans, but in general you pay around $30 a month for limited access—and, as more and more companies jump on the wireless bandwagon, prices are likely to get even more competitive.

There are also places that provide **free wireless networks** in cities around the world. To locate these free hotspots, go to www.personaltelco.net/index.cgi/wirelesscommunities.

If Wi-Fi is not available at your destination, most business-class hotels throughout the world offer dataports for laptop modems, and many hotels are now offering free high-speed Internet access using an Ethernet network cable. You can bring your own cables, but most hotels rent them for around $10. **Call your hotel in advance** to see what your options are.

In addition, major Internet service providers (ISPs) have **local access numbers** around the world, allowing you to go online by simply placing a local call. Check your ISP's website or call its toll-free number and ask how you can use your current account away from home, and how much it will cost.

If you're traveling outside the reach of your ISP, try the **iPass** network, which has dial-up numbers in most countries around the world. You'll have to sign up with an iPass provider, who will then tell you how to set up your computer for your destination(s). For a list of iPass providers, go to www.ipass.com and click on "Individual

Purchase." One solid provider is **i2roam** (© **866/811-6209** or 920/235-0475; www.i2roam.com).

Wherever you go, bring a **connection kit** of the right power and phone adapters, a spare phone cord, and a spare Ethernet network cable—or find out whether your hotel supplies them to guests.

USING A CELLPHONE

The three letters that define much of the world's **wireless capabilities** are GSM (Global System for Mobiles), a big, seamless network that makes for easy cross-border cellphone use throughout Europe and dozens of other countries worldwide, including Mexico. In the U.S., T-Mobile, AT&T Wireless, and Cingular use this quasi-universal system; in Canada, Microcell and some Rogers customers are GSM, and all Europeans and most Australians use GSM.

If your cellphone is on a GSM system, and you have a world-capable multiband phone such as many Sony Ericsson, Motorola, or Samsung models, you can make and receive calls across civilized areas on much of the globe, from Andorra to Uganda. Just call your

---

Digital Photography on the Road

Many travelers are going digital these days with their vacation photographs. Not only are digital cameras left relatively unscathed by airport X-rays, but with digital equipment you don't need to lug armloads of film with you as you travel. In fact, nowadays you don't even need to carry your laptop to download the day's images to make room for more. With a **media storage card,** sold by all major camera dealers, you can store hundreds of images in your camera. These "memory" cards come in different configurations—from memory sticks to flash cards to secure digital cards—with varying storage capacities (the more megabytes of memory, the more images a card can hold). They range in price from $30 to over $200. (**Note:** Each camera model works with a specific type of card, so you'll need to determine which storage card is compatible with your camera.) When you get home, you can print the images out on your own color printer or take the storage card to a camera store, drugstore, or chain retailer. Or have the images developed online with a service like **Snapfish** (www.snapfish.com) for something like 25¢ a shot. See "Flying with Film & Video," p. 43.

Online Traveler's Toolbox

Veteran travelers usually carry some essential items to make their trips easier. Following is a selection of handy online tools to bookmark and use.

- **Airplane Seating and Food**. Find out which seats to reserve and which to avoid (and more) on all major domestic airlines at www.seatguru.com. And check out the type of meal (with photos) you'll likely be served on airlines around the world at www.airlinemeals.com.
- **Visa ATM Locator** (www.visa.com) and **MasterCard ATM Locator** (www.mastercard.com), for locations of PLUS (Visa) and Cirrus (MasterCard) ATMs worldwide.
- **Foreign Languages for Travelers** (www.travlang.com). Learn basic terms in more than 70 languages and click on any underlined phrase to hear what it sounds like.
- **Intellicast** (www.intellicast.com) and **Weather.com** (www.weather.com). Weather forecasts for all 50 states and cities around the world.
- **Universal Currency Converter** (www.xe.net/currency). See what your dollar or pound is worth in more than 100 other countries.
- **Travel Warnings** (http://travel.state.gov/travel_warnings. html, www.fco.gov.uk/travel, www.voyage.gc.ca, www. dfat.gov.au/consular/advice). These sites report on places where health concerns or unrest might threaten American, British, Canadian, and Australian travelers. Generally, U.S. warnings are the most paranoid; Australian warnings are the most relaxed.

wireless operator and ask for "international roaming" to be activated on your account. Unfortunately, per-minute charges can be high— usually $1 to $1.50 in western Europe and up to $5 in places like Russia and Indonesia.

That's why it's important to buy an "unlocked" world phone from the get-go. Many cellphone operators sell "locked" phones that restrict you from using any removable computer memory phone chip card (called an SIM card) other than the ones they supply. Having an unlocked phone allows you to install a cheap, prepaid

SIM card (found at a local retailer) in your destination country. Show your phone to the salesperson; not all phones work on all networks. You'll get a local phone number—and much, much lower calling rates. Getting an already locked phone unlocked can be a complicated process, but it can be done; just call your cellular operator and say you'll be going abroad for several months and want to use the phone with a local provider.

For many, **renting** a phone is a good idea. (Even world phone owners will have to rent new phones if they're traveling to non-GSM regions, such as Japan or Korea.) While you can rent a phone from any number of overseas sites, including kiosks at airports and at car-rental agencies, we suggest renting the phone before you leave home. That way you can give loved ones and business associates your new number, make sure the phone works, and take the phone wherever you go—especially helpful for overseas trips through several countries, where local phone-rental agencies often bill in local currency and may not let you take the phone to another country.

Phone rental isn't cheap. You'll usually pay $40 to $50 per week, plus airtime fees of at least a dollar a minute. The bottom line: Shop around.

Two good wireless rental companies are **InTouch USA** (© **800/872-7626;** www.intouchglobal.com) and **RoadPost** (© **888/290-1606** or 905/272-5665; www.roadpost.com). Give them your itinerary, and they'll tell you what wireless products you need. InTouch will also, for free, advise you on whether your existing phone will work overseas; simply call © **703/222-7161** between 9am and 4pm EST, or go to www.intouchglobal.com/travel.htm.

For trips of more than a few weeks spent in one country, **buying a phone** becomes economically attractive, as many nations have cheap, no-questions-asked prepaid phone systems. In Mexico, both of the two major cell service providers, **TelCel** and **USACell,** sell inexpensive phones that use prepaid cards.

Once you arrive at your destination, stop by a local cellphone shop and get the cheapest package; you'll probably pay less than $100 for a phone and a starter calling card. Local calls may be as low as 10¢ per minute, and in many countries incoming calls are free.

True wilderness adventurers, or those heading to less-developed countries, should consider renting a **satellite phone ("satphone"),** which is different from cellphones in that they connect to satellites rather than ground-based towers. A satphone is more costly than a cellphone but works where there's no cellular signal and no towers. You can rent satellite phones from **RoadPost** (✆ **888/290-1606** or 905/272-5665; www.roadpost.com). InTouch USA (see above) offers a wider range of satphones but at higher rates. Per-minute call charges can be even cheaper than roaming charges with a regular cellphone, but the phone itself is more expensive (up to $150 a week), and depending on the service you choose, people calling you may incur high long-distance charges. As of this writing, satphones were outrageously expensive to buy.

11 Getting There

BY PLANE

The airline situation in Mexico is rapidly improving, with many new regional carriers offering scheduled service to areas previously not served. In addition to regularly scheduled service, charter service direct from U.S. cities to resorts is making Mexico more accessible. For information about saving money on airfares using the Internet, see "Planning Your Trip Online," earlier in this chapter.

THE MAJOR INTERNATIONAL AIRLINES   The main airlines operating direct or nonstop flights from the United States to Mexico include **Aero California** (✆ 800/237-6225), **Aeromexico** (✆ 800/237-6639; www.aeromexico.com), **Air France** (✆ 800/237-2747; www.airfrance.com), **Alaska Airlines** (✆ 800/426-0333; www.alaskaair.com), **America West** (✆ 800/235-9292; www.americawest.com), **American Airlines** (✆ 800/433-7300; www.aa.com), **Continental** (✆ 800/525-0280; www.continental.com), **Frontier Airlines** (✆ 800/432-1359; www.frontierairlines.com), **Mexicana** (✆ 800/531-7921; www.mexicana.com), **Northwest/KLM** (✆ 800/225-2525; www.nwa.com), **Taca** (✆ 800/225-2272; www.taca.com), **United** (✆ 800/241-6522; www.united.com), and **US Airways** (✆ 800/428-4322; www.usairways.com). **Southwest Airlines** (✆ 800/435-9792; www.southwest.com) serves the U.S. border.

The main departure points in North America for international airlines are Atlanta, Chicago, Dallas/Fort Worth, Denver, Houston, Las Vegas, Los Angeles, Miami, New York, Orlando, Philadelphia, Phoenix, Raleigh/Durham, San Antonio, San Francisco, Seattle, Toronto, and Washington, D.C.

GETTING THROUGH THE AIRPORT

With the federalization of security, procedures at U.S. airports are more stable and consistent than ever. Generally, you'll be fine if you arrive at the airport **1 hour** before a domestic flight and **2 hours** before an international flight; if you show up late, tell an airline employee and she'll probably whisk you to the front of the line.

Bring a **current, government-issued photo ID** such as a driver's license or passport. Keep your ID at the ready to show at check-in, the security checkpoint, and sometimes even the gate. (Children under 18 do not need government-issued photo IDs for domestic flights, but they do for international flights to most countries.)

In 2003, the TSA phased out **gate check-in** at all U.S. airports. And **e-tickets** have made paper tickets nearly obsolete. Passengers with e-tickets can beat the ticket-counter lines by using airport **electronic kiosks** or even **online check-in** from their home computers. Online check-in involves logging on to your airline's website, accessing your reservation, and printing out your boarding pass—and the airline may even offer you bonus miles to do so! If you're using a kiosk at the airport, bring the credit card you used to book the ticket or your frequent-flier card. Print out your boarding pass from the kiosk and simply proceed to the security checkpoint with your pass and a photo ID. If you're checking bags or looking to snag an exit-row seat, you will be able to do so using most airline kiosks. Even the smaller airlines are employing the kiosk system, but always call your airline to make sure these alternatives are available. Note that at press time, these check-in services were not available at Mexico's airports, so plan on checking in the old-fashioned way—by standing in line. **Curbside check-in** is also a good way to avoid lines, although a few airlines still ban curbside check-in; call before you go.

Security checkpoint lines are getting shorter than they were during 2001 and 2002, but some doozies remain. If you have trouble standing for long periods of time, tell an airline employee; the airline will provide a wheelchair. Speed up security by **not wearing metal objects** such as big belt buckles. If you've got metallic body parts, a note from your doctor can prevent a long chat with the security screeners. Keep in mind that only **ticketed passengers** are allowed past security, except for folks escorting passengers with disabilities or children.

Federalization has stabilized **what you can carry on** and **what you can't.** The general rule is that sharp things are out, nail clippers are okay, and food and beverages must be passed through the X-ray machine—but that security screeners can't make you drink from your coffee cup. Bring food in your carry-on rather than checking it, as explosive-detection machines used on checked luggage have been known to mistake food (especially chocolate, for some reason) for bombs. Travelers in the U.S. are allowed one carry-on bag, plus a "personal item" such as a purse, briefcase, or laptop bag. Carry-on hoarders can stuff all sorts of things into a laptop bag; as long as it has a laptop in it, it's still considered a personal item. The Transportation Security Administration (TSA) has issued a list of restricted items; check its website (www.tsa.gov/public/index.jsp) for details.

Airport screeners may decide that your checked luggage needs to be searched by hand. You can now purchase luggage locks that allow screeners to open and relock a checked bag if hand-searching is necessary. Look for Travel Sentry certified locks at luggage or travel shops and Brookstone stores (you can buy them online at www.brookstone.com). These locks, approved by the TSA, can be opened by luggage inspectors with a special code or key. For more information on the locks, visit www.travelsentry.org. If you use something other than TSA-approved locks, your lock will be cut off your suitcase if a TSA agent needs to hand-search your luggage.

FLYING FOR LESS: TIPS FOR GETTING THE BEST AIRFARE

Passengers sharing the same airplane cabin rarely pay the same fare. Travelers who need to purchase tickets at the last minute, change their itinerary at a moment's notice, or fly one-way often get stuck paying the premium rate. Here are some ways to keep your airfare costs down.

- Passengers who can book their tickets **far in advance,** who can **stay over Saturday night,** or who **fly midweek** or **at less-trafficked hours** may pay a fraction of the full fare. If your schedule is flexible, say so, and ask if you can secure a cheaper fare by changing your flight plans.
- You can also save on airfares by keeping an eye out in local newspapers for **promotional specials** or **fare wars,** when airlines lower prices on their most popular routes. You rarely see

fare wars offered for peak travel times, but if you can travel in the off-months, you may snag a bargain.

- Search the **Internet** for cheap fares (see "Planning Your Trip Online," earlier in this chapter).
- **Consolidators,** also known as bucket shops, are great sources for international tickets, although they usually can't beat the Internet on fares within North America. Start by looking in Sunday newspaper travel sections; U.S. travelers should focus on the *New York Times,* the *Los Angeles Times,* and the *Miami Herald.* For less-developed destinations, small travel agents who cater to immigrant communities in large cities often have the best deals. ***Beware:*** Bucket shop tickets are usually nonrefundable or rigged with stiff cancellation penalties, often as high as 50% to 75% of the ticket price, and some put you on charter airlines, which may leave at inconvenient times and experience delays. Several reliable consolidators are worldwide and available on the Net. **STA Travel** (© **800/781-4040** in North America; www.statravel.com) is now the world's leader in student travel, thanks to their purchase of Council Travel. It also offers good fares for travelers of all ages. **ELTExpress** (© **800/TRAV-800;** www.eltexpress.com) started in Europe and has excellent fares worldwide, but particularly to that continent. It also has "local" websites in 12 countries. **FlyCheap** (© **800/FLY-CHEAP;** www.1800flycheap.com) is owned by package-holiday megalith MyTravel and so has especially good access to fares for sunny destinations. **Air Tickets Direct**

Travel in the Age of Bankruptcy

Airlines go bankrupt, so protect yourself by **buying your tickets with a credit card**, as the Fair Credit Billing Act guarantees that you can get your money back from the credit card company if a travel supplier goes under (and if you request the refund within 60 days of the bankruptcy). **Travel insurance** can also help, but make sure it covers against "carrier default" for your specific travel provider. And be aware that if a U.S. airline goes bust mid-trip, a 2001 federal law requires other carriers to take you to your destination (albeit on a space-available basis) for a fee of no more than $25, provided you rebook within 60 days of the cancellation.

Flying with Film & Video

Never pack film—exposed or unexposed—in checked bags, as the new, more powerful scanners in U.S. airports can fog film. The film you carry with you can be damaged by scanners as well. X-ray damage is cumulative; the faster the film, and the more times you put it through a scanner, the more likely the damage. Film under 800 ASA is usually safe for up to five scans. If you're taking your film through additional scans, U.S. regulations permit you to demand hand inspections. In international airports, you're at the mercy of airport officials. On international flights, store your film in transparent baggies, so you can remove it easily before you go through scanners. Keep in mind that airports are not the only places where your camera may be scanned: Highly trafficked attractions are X-raying visitors' bags with increasing frequency.

Most photo supply stores sell protective pouches designed to block damaging X-rays. The pouches fit both film and loaded cameras. They should protect your film in checked baggage, but they also may raise alarms and result in a hand inspection.

You'll have little to worry about if you are traveling with **digital cameras.** Unlike film, which is sensitive to light, the digital camera and storage cards are not affected by airport X-rays, according to Nikon. Still, if you plan to travel extensively, you may want to play it safe and hand-carry your digital equipment or ask that it be inspected by hand. See "Digital Photography on the Road," p. 36.

Carry-on scanners will not damage **videotape** in video cameras, but the magnetic fields emitted by the walk-through security gateways and handheld inspection wands will. Always place your loaded camcorder on the screening conveyor belt or have it hand-inspected. Be sure your batteries are charged, as you may be required to turn the device on to ensure that it's what it appears to be.

(© **800/778-3447;** www.airticketsdirect.com) is based in Montreal and leverages the currently weak Canadian dollar for low fares; it'll also book trips to places that U.S. travel agents won't touch, such as Cuba.

• Join **frequent-flier clubs.** Accrue enough miles, and you'll be rewarded with free flights and elite status. It's free, and you'll get the best choice of seats, faster response to phone inquiries, and prompter service if your luggage is stolen, your flight is canceled or delayed, or if you want to change your seat. You don't need to fly to build frequent-flier miles—**frequent-flier credit cards** can provide thousands of miles for doing your everyday shopping.

• For many more tips about air travel, including a rundown of the major frequent-flier credit cards, pick up a copy of *Frommer's Fly Safe, Fly Smart* (Wiley Publishing, Inc.).

BY CAR

Driving is not the cheapest way to get to Mexico, but it is the best way to see the country. Even so, you may think twice about taking your own car south of the border once you've pondered the bureaucracy involved. One option is to rent a car once you arrive and tour around a specific region. Rental cars in Mexico are generally new, clean, and well maintained. Although they're pricier than in the United States, discounts are often available for rentals of a week or longer, especially when you make arrangements in advance from the United States. (See "Car Rentals," later in this chapter, for more details.)

If, after reading the section that follows, you have additional questions or you want to confirm the current rules, call your nearest Mexican consulate or the Mexican Government Tourist Office. Although travel insurance companies are generally helpful, they may not have the most accurate information. To check on road conditions or to get help with any travel emergency while in Mexico, call © **01-800/903-9200,** or 555/250-0151 in Mexico City. English-speaking operators staff both numbers.

In addition, check with the **U.S. State Department** (see "Visitor Information," earlier in this chapter) for warnings about dangerous driving areas.

CAR DOCUMENTS

To drive your car into Mexico, you'll need a **temporary car-importation permit,** which is granted after you provide a required list of documents (see below). The permit can be obtained through Banco del Ejército (Banjercito) officials, who have a desk, booth, or office at the *aduana* (Mexican Customs) building after you cross the border into Mexico.

The following strict requirements for border crossing were accurate at press time:

- **A valid driver's license,** issued outside of Mexico.
- **Current, original car registration and a copy of the original car title.** If the registration or title is in more than one name and not all the named people are traveling with you, a notarized letter from the absent person(s) authorizing use of the vehicle for the trip is required; have it ready. The registration and your credit card (see below) must be in the same name.
- **A valid international major credit card.** With a credit card, you are required to pay only a $23 car-importation fee. The credit card must be in the same name as the car registration. If you do not have a major credit card (American Express, Diners Club, MasterCard, or Visa), you must post a bond or make a deposit equal to the value of the vehicle. Check cards are not accepted.
- **Original immigration documentation.** This is either your tourist permit (FMT) or the original immigration booklet, FM2 or FM3, if you hold more permanent status.
- **A signed declaration promising to return to your country of origin with the vehicle.** Obtain this form *(Carta Promesa de Retorno)* from AAA or Sanborn's before you go, or from Banjercito officials at the border. There's no charge. The form does not stipulate that you must return by the same border entry through which you entered.
- **Temporary Importation Application.** By signing this form, you state that you are only temporarily importing the car for your personal use and will not be selling it. This is to help regulate the entry and restrict the resale of unauthorized cars and trucks. Make sure the permit is canceled when you return to the U.S.

If you receive your documentation at the border, Mexican officials will make two copies of everything and charge you for copies. For up-to-the-minute information, a great source is ´ toms office in Nuevo Laredo, or *Módulo de Importació´ Automóviles, Aduana Nuevo Laredo* (**©** **867/712-**˘

Important reminder: Someone else may drive, but the person (or relative of the person) whose name appears on the car-importation permit must *always* be in the car. (If stopped by police, a non-registered family member driving without the registered driver must be prepared to prove familial relationship to the registered driver—no joke.) Violation of this rule subjects the car to impoundment and the driver to imprisonment, a fine, or both. You can drive a car with foreign license plates only if you have a foreign (non-Mexican) driver's license.

MEXICAN AUTO INSURANCE

Liability auto insurance is legally required in Mexico. U.S. insurance is invalid; to be insured in Mexico, you must purchase Mexican insurance. Any party involved in an accident who has no insurance may be sent to jail and have his or her car impounded until all claims are settled. This is true even if you just drive across the border to spend the day. U.S. companies that broker Mexican insurance are commonly found at the border crossing, and several quote daily rates.

You can also buy car insurance through **Sanborn's Mexico Insurance,** P.O. Box 52840, 2009 S. 10th, McAllen, TX (*©* **956/686-3601;** fax 800/222-0158 or 956/686-0732; www.sanbornsinsurance.com). The company has offices at all U.S. border crossings. Its policies cost the same as the competition's do, but you get legal coverage (attorney and bail bonds if needed) and a detailed mile-by-mile guide for your proposed route. Most of the Sanborn's border offices are open Monday through Friday, and a few are staffed on Saturday and Sunday. **AAA** auto club (www.aaa.com) also sells insurance.

RETURNING TO THE U.S. WITH YOUR CAR

You *must* return the car documents you obtained when you entered Mexico when you cross back with your car, or at some point within 180 days. (You can cross as many times as you wish within the 180 days.) If the documents aren't returned, heavy fines are imposed ($250 for each 15 days late), your car may be impounded and confiscated, or you may be jailed if you return to Mexico. You can only return the car documents to a Banjercito official on duty at the Mexican *aduana* (Customs) building *before* you cross back into the United States. Some border cities have Banjercito officials on duty 24 hours a day, but others do not; me do not have Sunday hours.

BY SHIP

Numerous cruise lines serve Mexico. Some (including whale-watching trips) cruise from California to the Baja Peninsula and ports of call on the Pacific coast, or from Houston or Miami to the Caribbean (which often includes stops in Cancún, Playa del Carmen, and Cozumel). Several cruise-tour specialists offer substantial discounts on unsold cabins if you're willing to take off at the last minute. One such company is **The Cruise Line,** 150 NW 168 St., North Miami Beach, FL 33169 (ⓒ **800/777-0707** or 305/521-2200).

BY BUS

Greyhound-Trailways (or its affiliates) offers service from around the United States to the Mexican border, where passengers disembark, cross the border, and buy a ticket for travel into Mexico. Many border crossings have scheduled buses from the U.S. bus station to the Mexican bus station.

12 Packages for the Independent Traveler

Before you start your search for the lowest airfare, you may want to consider booking your flight as part of a travel package. Package tours are not the same thing as escorted tours. Package tours are simply a way to buy the airfare, accommodations, and other elements of your trip (such as car rentals, airport transfers, and sometimes even activities) at the same time and often at discounted prices—kind of like one-stop shopping. Packages are sold in bulk to tour operators—who resell them to the public at a cost that usually undercuts standard

---

Tips **Before You Book a Package**

- **Read the fine print.** Make sure you know *exactly* what's included in the price you're being quoted, and what's not.
- **Know what you're getting yourself into—and if you can get yourself out of it.** Before you commit, make sure you know how much flexibility you have. Often, packagers will offer trip cancellation insurance (for around $25–$30), which will return your payment if you need to change your plans.

rates. Frommers.com regularly covers the latest package deals for destinations all around the world; new stories are posted every Monday, Wednesday, and Friday.

You can buy a package at any time of the year, but the best deals usually coincide with high season—from mid-December to April—when demand is at its peak, and companies are more confident about filling planes. You might think that package rates would be better during low season, when room rates and airfares plunge. But the key is air access, which is much easier during the winter. Packages vary widely, with some companies offering a better class of hotels than others. Some offer the same hotels for lower prices. Some offer flights on scheduled airlines, while others book charters. In some packages, your choices of accommodations and travel days may be limited. Each destination usually has some packagers that are better than the rest because they buy in even bigger bulk. Not only can that mean better prices, it can also mean more choices.

You are often required to make a large payment upfront. On the plus side, packages can save you money, offering group prices but allowing for independent travel. Some even let you add on a few guided excursions or escorted day trips (also at prices lower than if you booked them yourself) without booking an entirely escorted tour.

Before you invest in a package tour, get some answers. Ask about the **accommodations choices** and prices for each. Then look up the hotels' reviews in a Frommer's guide and check their rates online for your specific dates of travel. You'll also want to find out what **type of room** you get. If you need a certain type of room, ask for it; don't take whatever is thrown your way. Request a nonsmoking room, a quiet room, a room with a view, or whatever you fancy.

Finally, look for **hidden expenses.** Ask whether airport departure fees and taxes, for example, are included in the total cost.

Beyond those described below, travel packages are also listed in the travel section of your local Sunday newspaper. Or check ads in the national travel magazines such as *Arthur Frommer's Budget Travel Magazine, Travel & Leisure, National Geographic Traveler,* and *Condé Nast Traveler.*

WHERE TO BROWSE

- One specialist in Mexico vacation packages is **www.mexico travelnet.com**, an agency that offers most of the well-known

> ⎛Finds **Out-of-the-Ordinary Places to Stay**
>
> Mexico lends itself beautifully to the concept of small, private hotels in idyllic settings. They vary in style from grandiose estate to palm-thatched bungalow. **Mexico Boutique Hotels** (www.MexicoBoutiqueHotels.com) specializes in smaller places to stay with a high level of personal attention and service. Most options have less than 50 rooms, and the accommodations consist of entire villas, *casitas,* bungalows, or a combination.

travel packages to Mexico beach resorts, plus offers last-minute specials.

- Check out **www.2travel.com** and find the page with links to a number of the big-name Mexico packagers, including several of those listed here.

- For last-minute air-only or package bargains, check out **Vacation Hot Line** (www.vacationhotline.net). Once you find your deal, you'll need to call to make booking arrangements. This service offers packages from the popular Apple and Funjet vacation wholesalers.

- Several big **online travel agencies**—Expedia.com, Travelocity. com, Orbitz.com, Site59.com, and Lastminute.com—also do a brisk business in packages. If you're unsure about the pedigree of a smaller packager, check with the Better Business Bureau in the city where the company is based, or go online at www.bbb.org. If a packager won't tell you where they're based, don't fly with them.

RECOMMENDED PACKAGERS

- **Aeromexico Vacations** (✆ **800/245-8585;** www.aeromexico. com) offers year-round packages to almost every destination it serves, including Puerto Vallarta. Aeromexico has a large (more than 100) selection of resorts in these destinations and more, in a variety of price ranges. The best deals are from Houston, Dallas, San Diego, Los Angeles, Miami, and New York, in that order.

- **Alaska Airlines Vacations** (✆ **800/468-2248;** www.alaskaair. com) sells packages to Manzanillo/Costa Alegre and Puerto Vallarta. Alaska flies direct from Los Angeles, San Diego, San

Jose, San Francisco, Seattle, Vancouver, Anchorage, and Fairbanks. The website offers unpublished discounts that are not available through the phone operators.

- **American Airlines Vacations** (© 800/321-2121; www.aavacations.com) has year-round deals to Guadalajara and Puerto Vallarta. You don't have to fly with American if you can get a better deal on another airline; land-only packages include hotel, hotel tax, and airport transfers. American's hubs to Mexico are Dallas/Fort Worth, Chicago, and Miami. The website offers unpublished discounts that are not available through the operators.

- **America West Vacations** (© 800/356-6611; www.americawestvacations.com) has deals to Guadalajara, Manzanillo, and Puerto Vallarta, mostly from its Phoenix gateway. Many packages to Los Cabos include car rentals. The website offers discounted featured specials that are not available through the operators. You can also book hotels without air by calling the toll-free number.

- **Apple Vacations** (© 800/365-2775; www.applevacations.com) offers inclusive packages to all the beach resorts, and has the largest choice of hotels in Manzanillo and Puerto Vallarta. Scheduled carriers for the air portion include American, United, Mexicana, Delta, US Airways, Reno Air, Alaska Airlines, Aero California, and Aeromexico. Apple perks include baggage handling and the services of a company representative at major hotels.

- **Classic Custom Vacations** (© 800/635-1333; www.classiccustomvacations.com) specializes in package vacations to Mexico's finest luxury resorts. It combines discounted first-class and economy airfare on American, Continental, Mexicana, Alaska, America West, and Delta with stays at the most exclusive hotels in Guadalajara, Puerto Vallarta, and Manzanillo. In many cases, packages also include meals, airport transfers, and upgrades. The prices are not for bargain hunters but for those who seek luxury, nicely packaged.

- **Continental Vacations** (© 800/301-3800; www.covacations.com) has year-round packages to Puerto Vallarta and Guadalajara. The best deals are from Houston; Newark, N.J.; and Cleveland. You must fly Continental. The Internet deals offer savings not available elsewhere.

- **Funjet Vacations** (book through any travel agent; www. funjet.com for general information) is one of the largest vacation packagers in the United States. Funjet has packages to Puerto Vallarta. You can choose a charter or fly on American, Continental, Delta, Aeromexico, US Airways, Alaska Air, or United.
- **GOGO Worldwide Vacations** (✆ **888/636-3942;** www.gogo wwv.com) has trips to all the major beach destinations, including Puerto Vallarta. It offers several exclusive deals from higher-end hotels. Book through any travel agent.
- **Mexicana Vacations,** or MexSeaSun Vacations (✆ **800/531-9321;** www.mexicana.com) offers getaways to all the resorts. Mexicana operates daily direct flights from Los Angeles to Puerto Vallarta and Manzanillo.
- **Online Vacation Mall** (✆ **800/839-9851;** www.onlinevacation mall.com) allows you to search for and book packages offered by a number of tour operators and airlines to Puerto Vallarta.
- **Pleasant Mexico Holidays** (✆ **800/448-3333;** www.pleasant holidays.com) is one of the largest vacation packagers in the United States, with hotels in Puerto Vallarta and other destinations.

REGIONAL PACKAGERS

From the East Coast: Liberty Travel (✆ **888/271-1584;** www. libertytravel.com), one of the biggest packagers in the Northeast, often runs a full-page ad in the Sunday papers, with frequent Mexico specials. You won't get much in the way of service, but you will get a good deal.

From the West: Suntrips (✆ **800/SUNTRIPS,** or 800/786-8747 for departures within 14 days; www.suntrips.com) is one of the largest West Coast packagers for Mexico, with departures from San Francisco and Denver; regular charters to Puerto Vallarta and other destinations; and a large selection of hotels.

From the Southwest: Town and Country (book through travel agents) packages regular deals to Puerto Vallarta, Manzanillo, and other destinations with America West from the airline's Phoenix and Las Vegas gateways.

Resort Packages: The biggest hotel chains and resorts also sell packages. To take advantage of these offers, contact your travel agent or call the hotels directly.

13 Special-Interest Trips

The diverse geography of the Mexican Riviera and its wealth of eco- and adventure-tour options have made it a natural favorite of travelers looking for more active vacations.

Excellent golf courses are located in Guadalajara, Puerto Vallarta, Punta Mita, and along the coastline down to Manzanillo. Tennis, water-skiing, surfing, biking, and horseback riding are all sports visitors can enjoy in this region. Scuba diving is excellent along the Pacific Coast at Puerto Vallarta and Manzanillo, where a wide array of sea life can be observed, including dolphins, sea turtles, and giant mantas.

ORGANIZATIONS & TOUR OPERATORS

AMTAVE (Asociación Mexicana de Turismo de Aventura y Ecoturismo, A.C.) is an active association in Mexico of eco- and adventure-tour operators. They publish an annual catalog of participating firms and their offerings, all of which must meet certain criteria for security, and for quality and training of the guides, as well as for sustainability of natural and cultural environments. For more information, contact AMTAVE (© **800/509-7678;** www.amtave.com.mx).

Culinary Adventures, 6023 Reid Dr. NW, Gig Harbor, WA 98335 (© **253/851-7676;** fax 253/851-9532), offers a short but special list of cooking tours of particular regions in Mexico known for excellent cuisine, and featuring well-known cooks. The owner, Marilyn Tausend, is the co-author of *Mexico the Beautiful Cookbook,* and *Cocinas de la Familia (Family Kitchens).*

One World Workforce, P.O. Box 3188, La Mesa, CA 91944 (© **800/451-9564**), has weeklong "hands-on conservation trips" that offer working volunteers a chance to help with sea-turtle conservation along the Majahuas beach 60 miles south of Puerto Vallarta during the summer and fall.

Open Air Expeditions, Calle Guerrero 339, Col. Centro, Apdo. Postal 105-B, Puerto Vallarta, Jal. C.P. 48300 (© **322/222-3310;** fax 322/223-2407; www.vallartawhales.com), offers true eco-adventures guided by experts trained as marine biologists, oceanographers, or geologists. Their specialty is whale-watching tours (Dec–May); they have documented the returning whale population in an annual photo-ID study for the past 5 years. Other offerings include tours to sea turtle preservation camps, hiking, sea kayaking, and bird-watching. All are in small groups, with minimal environmental impact and great sensitivity to the natural surroundings.

Trek America, P.O. Box 189, Rockaway, NJ 07866 (© **800/221-0596** or 973/983-1144; fax 973/983-8551), organizes lengthy, active trips that combine trekking, hiking, van transportation, and camping in Mexico's Pacific coast, Guadalajara, and other destinations.

Vallarta Adventures, Edif. Marina Golf Local 13c, Marina Vallarta, Puerto Vallarta, Jal., C.P. 48354 (© **322/297-1212,** or 322/221-0657; www.vallarta-adventures.com), Puerto Vallarta's premier adventure-tour company, offers expeditions by boat to the Marietas Islands nature preserve, by land to the foothills of the Sierra Madre, and by air to the remote mining village of San Sebastian and the town of Tequila. They also have two adjacent dolphin-swim facilities, with an emphasis on education and interactive communication, a canopy tour which takes you swinging from treetop to treetop, and a day spa at the private cove of Caletas, the former home of film great John Huston. All adventures are top quality, led by enthusiastic guides who mix adventure with spirited fun.

14 Tips on Accommodations

MEXICO'S HOTEL RATING SYSTEM

The hotel rating system in Mexico is called "Stars and Diamonds." Hotels may qualify to earn one to five stars, or five diamonds. Many hotels that have excellent standards are not certified, but all rated hotels adhere to strict standards. The guidelines relate to service, facilities, and hygiene more than to prices.

Five-diamond hotels meet the highest requirements for rating: The beds are comfortable, bathrooms are in excellent working order, all facilities are renovated regularly, infrastructure is top-tier, and services and hygiene meet the highest international standards.

Five-star hotels usually offer similar quality, but with lower levels of service and detail in the rooms. For example, a five-star hotel may have less-luxurious linens, or perhaps room service during limited hours rather than 24 hours.

Four-star hotels are less expensive and more basic, but they still guarantee cleanliness and basic services such as hot water and purified drinking water. Three-, two-, and one-star hotels are at least working to adhere to certain standards: Bathrooms are cleaned and linens are washed daily, and you can expect a minimum standard of service. Two- and one-star hotels generally provide bottled water rather than purified water.

The nonprofit organization Calidad Mexicana Certificada, A.C., known as **Calmecac** (www.calmecac.com.mx), is responsible for hotel ratings. For additional details about the rating system, visit Calmecac's website or www.starsanddiamonds.com.mx.

HOTEL CHAINS

In addition to the major international chains, you'll run across a number of less-familiar brands as you plan your trip to Mexico. They include:

- **Brisas Hotels & Resorts** (www.brisas.com.mx). These were the hotels that originally attracted jet-set travelers to Mexico. Spectacular in a retro way, these properties offer the laid-back luxury that makes a Mexican vacation so unique.

- **Fiesta Americana** and **Fiesta Inn** (www.posadas.com). Part of the Mexican-owned Grupo Posadas company, these hotels set the country's midrange standard for facilities and services. They generally offer comfortable, spacious rooms and traditional Mexican hospitality. Fiesta Americana hotels offer excellent beach-resort packages. Fiesta Inn hotels are usually more business oriented. Grupo Posadas also owns the more luxurious Caesar Park hotels and the eco-oriented Explorean hotels.

- **Hoteles Camino Real** (www.caminoreal.com). The premier Mexican hotel chain, Camino Real maintains a high standard of service at its properties, all of which carry five stars (see "Mexico's Hotel Rating System," above). Its beach hotels are traditionally located on the best beaches in the area. This chain also focuses on the business market. The hotels are famous for their vivid and contrasting colors.

- **Hoteles Krystal NH** (www.nh-krystal.mexico-hoteles.com). Grupo Chartwell recently acquired this family-owned chain. The hotels are noted for their family-friendly facilities and five-star standards. The beach properties' signature feature is a pool, framed by columns, overlooking the sea.

- **Plaza Las Glorias** (www.sidek.com.mx/hotel/ing/glorias. asp). Sidek Situr group, the company responsible for building the first mega-developments in Mexico's resort areas,

---

Tips **Dial "E" for "Easy"**

For quick directions on how to call Mexico, see "Telephone & Fax" in "Fast Facts: Mexico," later in this chapter, or check out the "Telephone Tips" on the inside front cover of the book.

---

built these hotels. The chain usually represents a more affordable option than its competitors but maintains international standards.

- **Quinta Real Grand Class Hotels and Resorts** (www.quinta real.com). These hotels, owned by Summit Hotels and Resorts, are noted for architectural and cultural details that reflect their individual regions. At these luxury properties, attention to detail and excellent service are the rule.

HOUSE RENTALS & SWAPS

House and villa rentals and swaps are becoming more common in Mexico, but no single recognized agency or business provides this service exclusively for Mexico. In the chapters that follow, we have provided information on independent services that we have found to be reputable.

With regard to general online services, the most extensive inventory of homes is found at **VRBO** (Vacation Rentals by Owner; www.vrbo.com). They have over 33,000 homes and condominiums worldwide, including a large selection in Mexico. Another good option is **VacationSpot** (www.vacationspot.com), owned by Expedia, and a part of its sister company, Hotels.com. It has fewer choices, but the company's criteria for adding inventory is much more selective, and often includes onsite inspections. They also offer toll-free phone support.

SAVING ON YOUR HOTEL ROOM

The **rack rate** is the maximum rate that a hotel charges for a room. Hardly anybody pays this price, however, except in high season or on holidays. To lower the cost of your room:

- **Ask about special rates or other discounts.** Always ask whether a room less expensive than the first one quoted is available, or whether any special rates apply to you. You may qualify for corporate, student, military, senior, or other discounts. Mention membership in AAA, AARP, frequent-flier programs, or trade unions, which may entitle you to special deals as well. Find out the hotel policy on children—do kids stay free in the room or is there a special rate?

- **Dial direct.** When booking a room in a chain hotel, you'll often get a better deal by calling the individual hotel's reservation desk rather than the chain's main number.

- **Book online.** Many hotels offer Internet-only discounts, or supply rooms to Priceline, Hotwire, or Expedia at rates much lower than the ones you can get through the hotel itself. Shop around. And if you have special needs—a quiet room, a room with a view—call the hotel directly and make your needs known after you've booked online.

- **Remember the law of supply and demand.** Resort hotels are most crowded and therefore most expensive on weekends, so discounts are usually available for midweek stays. Business hotels in downtown locations are busiest during the week, so you can expect big discounts over the weekend. Many hotels have high-season and low-season prices, and booking the day after "high season" ends can mean big discounts.

- **Look into group or long-stay discounts.** If you come as part of a large group, you should be able to negotiate a bargain rate, since the hotel can then guarantee occupancy in a number of rooms. Likewise, if you're planning a long stay (at least 5 days), you might qualify for a discount. As a general rule, expect 1 night free after a 7-night stay.

- **Avoid excess charges and hidden costs.** When you book a room, ask whether the hotel charges for parking. Use your own cellphone, pay phones, or prepaid phone cards instead of dialing direct from hotel phones, which usually have exorbitant rates. And don't be tempted by the room's minibar offerings: Most hotels charge through the nose for water, soda, and snacks. Finally, ask about local taxes and service charges, which can increase the cost of a room by 15% or more. If a hotel insists upon tacking on a surprise "resort fee" for amenities you didn't use, you can often make a case for getting it removed.

- **Consider the pros and cons of all-inclusive resorts and hotels.** The term "all-inclusive" means different things at different hotels. Many all-inclusive hotels will include three meals daily, sports equipment, spa entry, and other amenities; others may include all or most drinks. In general, you'll save money going the "all-inclusive" way—as long as you use the facilities provided. The downside is that your choices are limited and you're stuck eating and playing in one place for the duration of your vacation.

- **Carefully consider your hotel's meal plan.** If you enjoy eating out and sampling the local cuisine, it makes sense to choose a **Continental Plan (CP),** which includes breakfast only, or a **European Plan (EP),** which doesn't include any meals and allows you maximum flexibility. If you're more interested in saving money, opt for a **Modified American Plan (MAP),** which includes breakfast and one other meal, or the **American Plan (AP),** which includes three meals. If you must choose a MAP, see if you can get a free lunch at your hotel if you decide to go out for dinner.
- **Book an efficiency.** A room with a kitchenette allows you to shop for groceries and cook your own meals. This is a big money saver, especially for families on long stays.
- **Consider enrolling in hotel "frequent-stay" programs,** which reward repeat customers who accumulate enough points or credits to earn free hotel nights, airline miles, complimentary in-room amenities, or even merchandise. These are offered not only by many chain hotels and motels (Hilton HHonors, Marriott Rewards, Wyndham ByRequest, to name a few), but also individual inns and B&Bs. Many chain hotels partner with other hotel chains, car-rental firms, airlines, and credit card companies to give consumers additional ways to accumulate points in the program.

LANDING THE BEST ROOM

Somebody has to get the best room in the house. It might as well be you. You can start by joining the hotel's frequent-guest program, which may make you eligible for upgrades. A hotel-branded credit card usually gives its owner "silver" or "gold" status in frequent-guest programs for free. Always ask about a corner room. They're often larger and quieter, with more windows and light, and they often cost the same as standard rooms. When you make your reservation, ask if the hotel is renovating; if it is, request a room away from the construction. Ask about nonsmoking rooms, rooms with views, rooms with twin, queen- or king-size beds. If you're a light sleeper, request a quiet room away from vending machines, elevators, restaurants, bars, and dance clubs. Ask for a room that has been renovated or redecorated most recently.

If you aren't happy with your room when you arrive, ask for another one. Most lodgings will be willing to accommodate you.

In resort areas, ask the following questions before you book a room:

- What's the view like? Cost-conscious travelers may be willing to pay less for a back room facing the parking lot, especially if they don't plan to spend much time in their room.
- Does the room have air-conditioning or ceiling fans? Do the windows open? If they do, and the nighttime entertainment takes place alfresco, you may want to find out when show time is over.
- What's included in the price? If you're charged for beach chairs, towels, sports equipment, and other amenities, you could end up spending more than you bargained for.
- How far is the room from the beach and other amenities? If it's far, is there transportation to and from the beach, and is it free?

15 Getting Around

An important note: If your travel schedule depends on a vital connection—say, a plane trip or a ferry or bus connection—use the telephone numbers in this book or other resources to find out if the connection is still available. Don't assume that it is, even if you used it two years ago.

BY PLANE

To fly from point to point within Mexico, you'll rely on Mexican airlines. Mexico has two large, privately owned national carriers: **Mexicana** (© 800/366-5400) and **Aeromexico** (© 800/021-4000), in addition to several up-and-coming regional carriers. Mexicana and Aeromexico both offer extensive connections to the United States as well as within Mexico.

Several of the new regional carriers are operated by or can be booked through Mexicana or Aeromexico. Regional carriers are **Aerocaribe** (see Mexicana); **Aerolitoral** (see Aeromexico); and **Aero Mar** (see Mexicana). The regional carriers are expensive, but they go to places that are difficult to reach. In each applicable section of this book, we mention regional carriers, with all pertinent telephone numbers.

Because major airlines can book some regional carriers, read your ticket carefully to see if your connecting flight is on one of these smaller carriers. They may leave from a different airport or check in at a different counter; this may be especially true in the Guadalajara airport.

AIRPORT TAXES Mexico charges an airport tax on all departures. Passengers leaving the country on international flights pay $18—in dollars or the peso equivalent. It has become a common practice to include this departure tax in your ticket price, but double-check to make sure so you're not caught by surprise at the airport. Taxes on each domestic departure within Mexico are around $13, unless you're on a connecting flight and have already paid at the start of the flight.

Mexico charges an $18 "tourism tax," the proceeds of which go into a tourism promotional fund. Your ticket price may not include it, so be sure to have enough money to pay it at the airport upon departure.

RECONFIRMING FLIGHTS Although Mexican airlines say it's not necessary to reconfirm a flight, it's still a good idea. To avoid getting bumped on popular, possibly overbooked flights, check in for an international flight 1½ hours in advance of travel.

BY CAR

Most Mexican roads are not up to U.S. standards of smoothness, hardness, width of curve, grade of hill, or safety markings. Driving at night is dangerous—the roads are rarely lit; trucks, carts, pedestrians, and bicycles usually have no lights; and you can hit potholes, animals, rocks, dead ends, or uncrossable bridges without warning.

The spirited style of Mexican driving sometimes requires super vision and reflexes. Be prepared for new customs, as when a truck driver flips on his left turn signal when there's not a crossroad for miles. He's probably telling you the road's clear ahead for you to pass. Another custom that's very important to respect is turning left. Never turn left by stopping in the middle of a highway with your left signal on. Instead, pull onto the right shoulder, wait for traffic to clear, then proceed across the road.

GASOLINE There's one government-owned brand of gas and one gasoline station name throughout the country—**Pemex** (Petroleras Mexicanas). There are two types of gas in Mexico: *magna*, 87-octane unleaded gas, and premium 93 octane. In Mexico, fuel and oil are sold by the liter, which is slightly more than a quart (40 liters equals about 11 gal.). Many franchise Pemex stations have bathroom facilities and convenience stores—a great improvement over the old ones. *Important note:* No credit cards are currently accepted for gas purchases.

TOLL ROADS   Mexico charges some of the highest tolls in the world for its network of new toll roads; as a result, they are rarely used. Generally speaking, though, using toll roads cuts travel time. Older toll-free roads are generally in good condition, but travel times tend to be longer.

BREAKDOWNS   If your car breaks down on the road, help might already be on the way. Radio-equipped green repair trucks operated by uniformed English-speaking officers patrol major highways during daylight hours. These **"Green Angels"** perform minor repairs and adjustments free, but you pay for parts and materials.

Your best guide to repair shops is the Yellow Pages. For repairs, look under *Automóviles y Camiones: Talleres de Reparación y Servicio;* auto-parts stores are under *Refacciones y Accesorios para Automóviles.* To find a mechanic on the road, look for a sign that says TALLER MECANICO.

Places called *vulcanizadora* or *llantera* repair flat tires, and it is common to find them open 24 hours a day on the most traveled highways.

MINOR ACCIDENTS   When possible, many Mexicans drive away from minor accidents, or try to make an immediate settlement, to avoid involving the police. If the police arrive while the involved persons are still at the scene, everyone may be locked in jail until blame is assessed. In any case, you have to settle up immediately, which may take days. Foreigners who don't speak fluent Spanish are at a distinct disadvantage when trying to explain their version of the event. Three steps may help the foreigner who doesn't wish to do as the Mexicans do: If you were in your own car, notify your Mexican insurance company, whose job it is to intervene on your behalf. If you were in a rental car, notify the rental company immediately and ask how to contact the nearest adjuster. (You did buy insurance with the rental, right?) Finally, if all else fails, ask to contact the nearest Green Angel, who may be able to explain to officials that you are covered by insurance. See also "Mexican Auto Insurance" in "Getting There," earlier in this chapter.

CAR RENTALS You'll get the best price if you reserve a car at least a week in advance in the United States. U.S. car-rental firms include **Advantage** (© 800/777-5500 in the U.S. and Canada; www.arac.com), **Avis** (© 800/331-1212 in the U.S., or 800/TRY-AVIS in Canada; www.avis.com), **Budget** (© 800/527-0700 in the U.S. and Canada; www.budget.com), **Hertz** (© 800/654-3131 in the U.S. and Canada; www.hertz.com), **National** (© 800/CAR-RENT in the U.S. and Canada; www.nationalcar.com), and **Thrifty** (© 800/367-2277 in the U.S. and Canada; www.thrifty.com), which often offers discounts for rentals in Mexico. For European travelers, **Kemwel Holiday Auto** (© 800/678-0678; www.kemwel.com) and **Auto Europe** (© 800/223-5555; www.autoeurope.com) can arrange Mexican rentals, sometimes through other agencies. These and some local firms have offices in Mexico City and most other large Mexican cities. You'll find rental desks at airports, all major hotels, and many travel agencies.

Cars are easy to rent if you are 25 or over and have a major credit card, valid driver's license, and passport with you. Without a credit card you must leave a cash deposit, usually a big one. One-way rentals are usually simple to arrange but more costly.

Car-rental costs are high in Mexico because cars are more expensive. The condition of rental cars has improved greatly over the years, and clean new cars are the norm. The basic cost of the 1-day rental of a Volkswagen Beetle at press time, with unlimited mileage (but before 15% tax and $15 daily insurance), was $48 in Cancún, $52 in Mexico City, $44 in Puerto Vallarta, $48 in Oaxaca, and $38 in Mérida. Renting by the week gives you a lower daily rate. Avis was offering a basic 7-day rate for a VW Beetle (before tax or insurance) of $220 in Cancún and Puerto Vallarta, $180 in Mérida, and $250 in Mexico City. Prices may be considerably higher if you rent around a major holiday. Also double-check charges for insurance—some companies will increase the insurance rate after several days. Always ask for detailed information about all charges you will be responsible for. Car-rental companies usually write credit card charges in U.S. dollars.

Deductibles Be careful—these vary greatly; some are as high as $2,500, which comes out of your pocket immediately in case of damage. On a VW Beetle, Hertz's deductible is $1,000 and Avis's is $500.

Insurance   Insurance is offered in two parts: **Collision and damage** insurance covers your car and others if the accident is your fault, and **personal accident** insurance covers you and anyone in your car. Read the fine print on the back of your rental agreement and note that insurance may be invalid if you have an accident while driving on an unpaved road.

Damage   Always inspect your car carefully and note every damaged or missing item, no matter how minute, on your rental agreement, or you may be charged.

Trouble Number   It's advisable to note the rental company's trouble number, as well as the direct number of the agency where you rented the car.

BY TAXI

Taxis are the preferred way to get around almost all of the resort areas of Mexico, and also within Guadalajara. Short trips within towns are generally charged by preset zones, and are quite reasonable compared with U.S. rates. For longer trips or excursions to nearby cities, taxis can generally be hired for around $10 to $15 per hour, or for a negotiated daily rate. Even drops to different destinations, say between Puerto Vallarta and Barra de Navidad, can be arranged. A negotiated one-way price is usually much less than the cost of a rental car for a day, and service is much faster than traveling by bus. For anyone who is uncomfortable driving in Mexico, this is a convenient, comfortable route. An added bonus is that you have a Spanish-speaking person with you in case you run into any car or road trouble. Many taxi drivers speak at least some English. Your hotel can assist you with the arrangements.

BY BUS

Mexican buses run frequently, are readily accessible, and can get you to almost anywhere you want to go. They're often the only way to get from large cities to other nearby cities and small villages. Don't hesitate to ask questions if you're confused about anything, but note that little English is spoken in bus stations.

Dozens of Mexican companies operate large, air-conditioned, Greyhound-type buses between most cities. Classes are *segunda*

Tips Know Spanish for the Bus Ride

There's little English spoken at bus stations, so come prepared with your destination written down, then double-check the departure.

(second), *primera* (first), and *ejecutiva* (deluxe), which goes by a variety of names. Deluxe buses often have fewer seats than regular buses, show video movies, are air-conditioned, and make few stops. Many run express from point to point. They are well worth the few dollars more. In rural areas, buses are often of the school-bus variety, with lots of local color.

Whenever possible, it's best to buy your reserved-seat ticket, often using a computerized system, a day in advance on long-distance routes and especially before holidays. See the appendix for a list of helpful bus terms in Spanish.

16 Recommended Books & Film

Studying up on Mexico can be one of the most fun bits of "research" you'll ever do. If you'd like to learn more about this fascinating country before you go—which I encourage—these books and movies are an enjoyable way to do it.

BOOKS

HISTORY & CULTURE   For an overview of pre-Hispanic cultures, pick up a copy of Michael D. Coe's *Mexico: From the Olmecs to the Aztecs* or Nigel Davies's *Ancient Kingdoms of Mexico.* Richard Townsend's *The Aztecs* is a thorough, well-researched examination of the Aztec and the Spanish conquest. For the Maya, Michael Coe's *The Maya* is probably the best general account. For a survey of Mexican history through modern times, *A Short History of Mexico* by J. Patrick McHenry (Doubleday) provides a complete, yet concise account.

John L. Stephens' *Incidents of Travel in the Yucatan, Vol. I and II* (Dover Publications) are travel classics, among the great books about archeological discovery. The two volumes chart the course of Stephens' discoveries of the Yucatan, beginning in 1841. Before his expeditions, little was known of the region, and the Maya culture had not been discovered. During his travels, Stephens found and described 44 Maya sites, and his account of these remains the most authoritative in existence.

For a more modern exploration of the archaeology of the region, Peter Tompkins' *Mysteries of the Mexican Pyramids* is a visually rich book, which explores not only the ruins of the Maya in the Yucatan, but also the whole of Mexico's archaeological treasures.

For contemporary culture, start with Octavio Paz's classic, *The Labyrinth of Solitude,* which still generates controversy among Mexicans. For a recent collection of writings by Subcomandante Marcos, leader of the Zapatista movement, try *Our Word is Our Weapon.* Another source is *Basta! Land and the Zapatista Rebellion* by George Collier and others. For those already familiar with Mexico and its culture, Guillermo Bonfil's *Mexico Profundo: Reclaiming a Civilization* is a rare bottom-up view of Mexico today.

Lesley Byrd Simpson's *Many Mexicos* (University of California Press) provides a comprehensive account of Mexican history with a cultural context. A classic on understanding the culture of this country is *Distant Neighbors*, by Alan Riding (Vintage).

ART & ARCHITECTURE   *Art and Time in Mexico: From the Conquest to the Revolution,* by Elizabeth Wilder Weismann, covers religious, public, and private architecture. *Casa Mexicana,* by Tim Street-Porter, takes readers through the interiors of some of Mexico's finest homes-turned-museums, public buildings, and private homes.

Folk Treasures of Mexico, by Marion Oettinger, is the fascinating story behind the 3,000-piece Mexican folk-art collection amassed by Nelson Rockefeller over a 50-year period.

Maya Art and Architecture, by Mary Ellen Miller (Thames and Hudson), showcases the best of the artistic expression of this culture, with interpretations of its meanings.

For a wonderful read on the food of the Yucatan and Mexico, pick up *Mexico, One Plate at a Time,* by celebrity chef and Mexico aficionado Rick Bayless (Scribner).

NATURE   *A Naturalist's Mexico,* by Roland H. Wauer, is a fabulous guide to birding. *A Hiker's Guide to Mexico's Natural History,* by Jim Conrad, covers flora and fauna and tells how to find the easy-to-reach as well as out-of-the-way spots he describes. *Peterson Field Guides: Mexican Birds,* by Roger Tory Peterson and Edward L. Chalif, is an excellent guide.

MOVIES

Mexico has served as a backdrop for countless movies. Here are just a few of my favorites, all available on DVD.

The 2003 blockbuster *Frida* starring Selma Hayak and Alfred Molina is not only an entertaining way to learn about two of Mexico's most famous personalities, but also of its history. The exquisite cinematography perfectly captures Mexico's inherent spirit of Magic Realism.

Que Viva Mexico is a little-known masterpiece by Russian filmmaker Sergei Eisenstein, who created a documentary of Mexican history, politics, and culture, out of a series of short *novellas*, which ultimately tie together. Although Eisenstein's budget ran out before he could complete the project, in 1979 this film was completed by Grigory Alexandrov, the film's original producer. It's an absolute must for anyone interested in Mexico or Mexican cinema.

Mexico's contemporary filmmakers are creating a sensation lately, and none more so than director Alfonso Cuarón. One of his early and highly acclaimed movies is the 2001 classic *Y Tu Mama También (And Your Mother Too)*, featuring current heartthrobs Gael Garcia Bernal and Diego Luna. This sexy, yet compelling, coming of age movie not only showcases both the grit and beauty of Mexico, but also the universality of love and life lessons.

Like Water for Chocolate is the 1993 film based on the book of the same name by Laura Esquivel, filmed by the author's husband, acclaimed contemporary Mexican director Alfonso Arau. Expect to be very hungry after watching this lushly visual film, which tells the story of a young woman who suppresses her passions under the watchful eye of a stern mother, and channels them into her cooking. In the process, we learn of the traditional norms of Mexican culture, and a great deal of the country's culinary treasures.

FAST FACTS: Mexico

Abbreviations Dept. (apartments); Apdo. (post office box); Av. (*avenida;* avenue); c/ (*calle;* street); Calz. (*calzada;* boulevard). "C" on faucets stands for *caliente* (hot), "F" for *fría* (cold). "PB" *(planta baja)* means ground floor; in most buildings the next floor up is the first floor (1).

Business Hours In general, businesses in larger cities are open between 9am and 7pm; in smaller towns many close between

2 and 4pm. Most close on Sunday. In resort areas it is common to find stores open at least in the mornings on Sunday, and for shops to stay open late, often until 8pm or even 10pm. Bank hours are Monday through Friday from 9 or 9:30am to anywhere between 3 and 7pm. Increasingly, banks open on Saturday for at least a half-day.

Cameras & Film Film costs about the same as in the United States. Tourists wishing to use a video or still camera at any archaeological site in Mexico or at many museums operated by the Instituto de Antropología e Historia (INAH) must pay $4 per camera at each site visited. (Listings for specific sites and museums note this fee.) Also, use of a tripod at any archaeological site requires a permit from INAH. It's courteous to ask permission before photographing anyone. It is never considered polite to take photos inside a church in Mexico. In some areas, there are other restrictions on photographing people and villages.

Car Rentals See "Getting Around," earlier in this chapter.

Climate See "When to Go," earlier in this chapter.

Currency See "Money," earlier in this chapter.

Doctors & Dentists Every embassy and consulate can recommend local doctors and dentists with good training and modern equipment; some of the doctors and dentists speak English. See the list of embassies and consulates under "Embassies & Consulates," below. Hotels with a large foreign clientele can often recommend English-speaking doctors.

Driving Rules See "Getting Around," earlier in this chapter.

Drug Laws It may sound obvious, but don't use or possess illegal drugs in Mexico. Mexican officials have no tolerance for drug users, and jail is their solution, with very little chance of release until the sentence (usually a long one) is completed or heavy fines or bribes are paid. Remember, in Mexico the legal system assumes you are guilty until proven innocent. *Note:* It isn't uncommon to be befriended by a fellow user, only to be turned in by that "friend," who collects a bounty. Bring prescription drugs in their original containers. If possible, pack a copy of the original prescription with the generic name of the drug.

U.S. Customs officials are on the lookout for diet drugs that are sold in Mexico but illegal in the U.S. Possession could land you in a U.S. jail. If you buy antibiotics over the counter (which you can do in Mexico) and still have some left, U.S. Customs probably won't hassle you.

Drugstores *Farmacias* (pharmacies) will sell you just about anything, with or without a prescription. Most pharmacies are open Monday through Saturday from 8am to 8pm. The major resort areas generally have one or two 24-hour pharmacies. Pharmacies take turns staying open during off hours; if you are in a smaller town and need to buy medicine during off hours, ask for the *farmacia de turno*.

Electricity The electrical system in Mexico is 110 volts AC (60 cycles), as in the United States and Canada. In reality, however, it may cycle more slowly and overheat your appliances. To compensate, select a medium or low speed on hair dryers. Many older hotels still have electrical outlets for flat two-prong plugs; you'll need an adapter for any plug with an enlarged end on one prong or with three prongs. Many better hotels have three-hole outlets (*trifásicos* in Spanish). Those that don't may have loan adapters, but to be sure, it's always better to carry your own.

Embassies & Consulates They provide valuable lists of doctors and lawyers, as well as regulations concerning marriages in Mexico. Contrary to popular belief, your embassy cannot get you out of jail, provide postal or banking services, or fly you home when you run out of money. Consular officers can provide advice on most matters and problems, however. Most countries have an embassy in Mexico City, and many have consular offices or representatives in the provinces.

The Embassy of the **United States** in Mexico City is at Paseo de la Reforma 305, next to the Hotel María Isabel Sheraton at the corner of Río Danubio (© **55/5080-2000** or 555/511-9980); hours are Monday through Friday from 8:30am to 5:30pm. Visit www.usembassy-mexico.gov for addresses of the U.S. consulates inside Mexico. There are U.S. Consulates General at López Mateos 924-N, Ciudad Juárez (© **656/611-3000**); Progreso 175, Guadalajara (© **333/268-2100**); Av. Constitución 411 Pte., Monterrey (© **818/345-2120**); and Tapachula 96, Tijuana (© **664/622-7400**). In addition, there are consular agencies in Acapulco (© **744/469-0556**); Cabo San Lucas (© **624/143-3566**); Cancún

(© 998/883-0272); Cozumel (© 987/872-4574); Hermosillo (© 662/217-2375); Ixtapa/Zihuatanejo (© 755/553-2100); Matamoros (© 868/812-4402); Mazatlán (© 669/916-5889); Mérida (© 999/925-5011); Nogales (© 631/313-4820); Nuevo Laredo (© 867/714-0512); Oaxaca (© 951/514-3054); Puerto Vallarta (© 322/222-0069); San Luis Potosí (© 444/811-7802); and San Miguel de Allende (© 415/152-2357).

The Embassy of **Australia** in Mexico City is at Rubén Darío 55, Col. Polanco (© 55/51101-2200). It's open Monday through Friday from 9am to 1pm.

The Embassy of **Canada** in Mexico City is at Schiller 529, Col. Polanco (© 555/724-7900); it's open Monday through Friday from 9am to 1pm. At other times, the name of a duty officer is posted on the door. Visit www.dfait-maeci.gc.ca for addresses of consular agencies in Mexico. There are Canadian consulates in Acapulco (© 744/484-1305); Cancún (© 998/883-3360); Guadalajara (© 333/615-6215); Mazatlán (© 669/913-7320); Monterrey (© 818/344-2753); Oaxaca (© 951/513-3777); Puerto Vallarta (© 322/293-0098); San José del Cabo (© 624/142-4333); and Tijuana (© 664/684-0461).

The Embassy of **New Zealand** in Mexico City is at José Luis Lagrange 103, 10th floor, Col. Los Morales Polanco (© 55/5283-9460; kiwimexico@compuserve.com.mx). It's open Monday through Friday from 8am to 3pm.

The Embassy of the **United Kingdom** in Mexico City is at Río Lerma 71, Col. Cuauhtémoc (© 55/5242-8500; www.embajada britanica.com.mx). It's open Monday through Friday from 8:30am to 3:30pm.

The Embassy of **Ireland** in Mexico City is at Bulevar Cerrada, Avila Camacho 76, 3rd floor, Col. Lomas de Chapultepec (© 55/5520-5803). It's open Monday through Friday from 9am to 5pm.

The **South African** Embassy in Mexico City is at Andrés Bello 10, 9th floor, Col. Polanco (© 55/5282-9260). It's open Monday through Friday from 8am to 3:30pm.

Emergencies In case of emergency, dial © **065** from any phone within Mexico. For police emergency numbers, turn to "Fast Facts" in the chapters that follow. The 24-hour **Tourist Help Line** in Mexico City is © **01-800/903-9200** or 555/250-0151. The operators don't always speak English, but they are always willing to help. The tourist legal assistance office

(Procuraduría del Turista) in Mexico City (℡ **555/625-8153** or 555/625-8154) always has an English speaker available. Though the phones are frequently busy, they operate 24 hours.

Holidays See "Holidays & Special Events," earlier in this chapter.

Internet Access In large cities and resort areas, a growing number of top hotels offer business centers with Internet access. You'll also find cybercafes in destinations that are popular with expats and business travelers. Even in remote spots, Internet access is common. Note that many ISPs automatically cut off your Internet connection after a specified period of time (say, 10 min.), because telephone lines are at a premium.

Language Spanish is the official language in Mexico. English is spoken and understood to some degree in most tourist areas. Mexicans are very accommodating with foreigners who try to speak Spanish, even in broken sentences. For basic vocabulary, refer to the appendix.

Legal Aid **International Legal Defense Counsel,** 111 S. 15th St., 24th floor, Packard Building, Philadelphia, PA 19102 (℡ **215/977-9982**), is a law firm specializing in legal difficulties of Americans abroad. See also "Embassies & Consulates" and "Emergencies," above.

Liquor Laws The legal drinking age in Mexico is 18; however, asking for ID or denying purchase is extremely rare. Grocery stores sell everything from beer and wine to national and imported liquors. You can buy liquor 24 hours a day, but during major elections, dry laws often are enacted for as much as 72 hours in advance of the election—and they apply to tourists as well as local residents. Mexico does not have laws that apply to transporting liquor in cars, but authorities are beginning to target drunk drivers more aggressively. It's a good idea to drive defensively.

It is not legal to drink in the street; however, many tourists do so. If you are getting drunk, you shouldn't drink in the street, because you are more likely to get stopped by the police.

Lost & Found To replace a **lost passport,** contact your embassy or nearest consular agent. You must establish a record of your citizenship and fill out a form requesting another FMT (tourist permit) if it, too, was lost. If your documents are stolen, get a police report from local authorities; having one *might* lessen the hassle of exiting the country without all your identification. Without the FMT, you can't leave the country, and without an affidavit affirming your passport request and citizenship, you may have problems at U.S. Customs when you get home. It's important to clear everything up *before* trying to leave. Mexican Customs may, however, accept the police report of the loss of the FMT and allow you to leave.

If you lose your **wallet** anywhere outside of Mexico City, before panicking, retrace your steps—you'll be surprised at how honest people are, and you'll likely find someone trying to find you to return your wallet.

If your wallet is stolen, the police probably won't be able to recover it. Be sure to notify all of your credit card companies right away, and file a report at the nearest police precinct. Your credit card company or insurer may require a police report number or record of the loss. Most credit card companies have an emergency toll-free number to call if your card is lost or stolen; these numbers are not toll-free within Mexico (see "Telephone & Fax," below, for instructions on calling U.S. toll-free numbers). The company may be able to wire you a cash advance off your credit card immediately, and, in many places, can deliver an emergency credit card in a day or two. **Visa**'s U.S. emergency number is ℭ **800/847-2911** or 410/581-9994. **American Express** cardholders and traveler's check holders should call ℭ **800/221-7282. MasterCard** holders should call ℭ **800/307-7309** or 636/722-7111. For other credit cards, call the toll-free number directory at ℭ **800/555-1212.**

If you need emergency cash over the weekend when all banks and American Express offices are closed, you can have money wired to you via **Western Union** (ℭ **800/325-6000;** www.westernunion.com).

Identity theft and fraud are potential complications of losing your wallet, especially if you've lost your driver's license along with your cash and credit cards. Notify the major credit-reporting bureaus immediately; placing a fraud alert on your records may protect you against liability for criminal activity. The three major U.S. credit-reporting agencies are **Equifax** (ℭ **800/766-0008;** www.equifax.com), **Experian**

((C) 888/397-3742; www.experian.com), and **TransUnion** ((C) 800/ 680-7289; www.transunion.com). Finally, if you've lost all forms of photo ID call your airline and explain the situation; they might allow you to board the plane if you have a copy of your passport or birth certificate and a copy of the police report you've filed.

Mail Postage for a postcard or letter is 1 peso; it may arrive anywhere from 1 to 6 weeks later. A registered letter costs $1.90. Sending a package can be quite expensive—the Mexican postal service charges $8 per kilo (2.2 lb.)—and unreliable; it takes 2 to 6 weeks, if it arrives at all. The recommended way to send a package or important mail is through FedEx, DHL, UPS, or another reputable international mail service.

Newspapers & Magazines There currently is no national English-language newspaper. Newspaper kiosks in larger cities carry a selection of English-language magazines.

Passports **For Residents of the United States:** Whether you're applying in person or by mail, you can download passport applications from the U.S. State Department website at **www.travel.state.gov**. To find your regional passport office, either check the U.S. State Department website or call the **National Passport Information Center's** toll-free number ((C) **877/487-2778**) for automated information.

For Residents of Canada: Passport applications are available at travel agencies throughout Canada or from the central Department of Foreign Affairs and International Trade, Ottawa, ON K1A 0G3 ((C) **800/567-6868**; www.ppt.gc.ca).

For Residents of the United Kingdom: To pick up an application for a standard 10-year passport (5-year passport for children under 16), visit your nearest passport office, major post office, or travel agency or contact the **United Kingdom Passport Service** at (C) **0870/521-0410** or search its website at www.ukpa.gov.uk.

For Residents of Ireland: You can apply for a 10-year passport at the **Passport Office,** Setanta Centre, Molesworth Street, Dublin 2 ((C) **01/671-1633**; www.irlgov.ie/iveagh). Those under age 18 and over 65 must apply for a €12 3-year passport. You can also apply at 1A South Mall, Cork ((C) **021/272-525**) or at most main post offices.

For Residents of Australia: You can pick up an application from your local post office or any branch of Passports Australia, but you must schedule an interview at the passport office to present your application materials. Call the **Australian Passport Information Service** at ⓒ **131-232,** or visit the government website at www.passports.gov.au.

For Residents of New Zealand: You can pick up a passport application at any New Zealand Passports Office or download it from their website. Contact the **Passports Office** at ⓒ **0800/ 225-050** in New Zealand or 04/474-8100, or log on to www.passports.govt.nz.

Pets Taking a pet into Mexico is easy but requires a little planning. Animals coming from the United States and Canada need to be checked for health within 30 days before arrival in Mexico. Most veterinarians in major cities have the appropriate paperwork—an official health certificate, to be presented to Mexican Customs officials, that ensures the pet's vaccinations are up-to-date. When you and your pet return from Mexico, U.S. Customs officials will require the same type of paperwork. If your stay extends beyond the 30-day time frame of your U.S.-issued certificate, you'll need an updated Certificate of Health issued by a veterinarian in Mexico. To check last-minute changes in requirements, consult the Mexican Government Tourist Office nearest you (see "Visitor Information," earlier in this chapter).

Police In Mexico City, police are to be suspected as frequently as they are to be trusted; however, you'll find many who are quite honest and helpful. In the rest of the country, especially in the tourist areas, most are very protective of international visitors. Several cities, including Puerto Vallarta, Mazatlán, Cancún, and Acapulco, have a special corps of English-speaking Tourist Police to assist with directions, guidance, and more.

Restrooms See "Toilets," below.

Safety See "Health & Safety," earlier in this chapter.

Smoking Smoking is permitted and generally accepted in most public places, including restaurants, bars, and hotel lobbies. Nonsmoking areas and hotel rooms for nonsmokers are becoming more common in higher-end establishments, but they tend to be the exception rather than the rule.

Taxes The 15% IVA (value-added) tax applies on goods and services in most of Mexico, and it's supposed to be included in the posted price. This tax is 10% in Cancún, Cozumel, and Los Cabos. There is a 5% tax on food and drinks consumed in restaurants that sell alcoholic beverages with an alcohol content of more than 10%; this tax applies whether you drink alcohol or not. Tequila is subject to a 25% tax. Mexico imposes an exit tax of around $18 on every foreigner leaving the country (see "Airport Taxes" under "Getting Around: By Plane," earlier in this chapter).

Telephone & Fax Mexico's telephone system is slowly but surely catching up with modern times. All telephone numbers have 10 digits. Every city and town that has telephone access has a two-digit (Mexico City, Monterrey, and Guadalajara) or three-digit (everywhere else) area code. In Mexico City, Monterrey, and Guadalajara, local numbers have eight digits; elsewhere, local numbers have seven digits. To place a local call, you do not need to dial the area code. Many fax numbers are also regular telephone numbers; ask whoever answers for the fax tone *("me da tono de fax, por favor")*. Cellular phones are very popular for small businesses in resort areas and smaller communities. To call a cellular number inside the same area code, dial 044 and then the number. To dial the cellular phone from anywhere else in Mexico, first dial 01, and then the three-digit area code and the seven-digit number. To dial it from the U.S., dial 011-52, plus the three-digit area code and the seven-digit number.

The **country code** for Mexico is **52.**

To call Mexico: If you're calling Mexico from the United States:
1. Dial the international access code: 011.
2. Dial the country code: 52.
3. Dial the two- or three-digit area code, then the eight- or seven-digit number. For example, if you wanted to call the U.S. consulate in Acapulco, the whole number would be 011-52-744-469-0556. If you wanted to dial the U.S. embassy in Mexico City, the whole number would be 011-52-55-5209-9100.

To make international calls: To make international calls from Mexico, first dial 00, then the country code (U.S. or Canada 1, U.K. 44, Ireland 353, Australia 61, New Zealand 64). Next, dial the area code and number. For example, to call the British embassy in Washington, you would dial 00-1-202-588-7800.

For directory assistance: Dial © **040** if you're looking for a number inside Mexico. *Note:* Listings usually appear under the owner's name, not the name of the business, and your chances of finding an English-speaking operator are slim to none.

For operator assistance: If you need operator assistance in making a call, dial © **090** to make an international call, and © **020** to call a number in Mexico.

Toll-free numbers: Numbers beginning with 800 within Mexico are toll-free, but calling a U.S. toll-free number from Mexico costs the same as an overseas call. To call an 800 number in the U.S., dial 001-880 and the last seven digits of the toll-free number. To call an 888 number in the U.S., dial 001-881 and the last seven digits of the toll-free number. For a number with an 887 prefix, dial 882; for 866, dial 883.

Time Zone Central Time prevails throughout most of Mexico. The states of Sonora, Sinaloa, and parts of Nayarit are on Mountain Time. The state of Baja California Norte is on Pacific Time, but Baja California Sur is on Mountain Time. All of Mexico observes **daylight saving time.**

Tipping Most service employees in Mexico count on tips for the majority of their income, and this is especially true for bellboys and waiters. Bellboys should receive the equivalent of 50¢ to $1 per bag; waiters generally receive 10% to 20%, depending on the level of service. It is not customary to tip taxi drivers, unless they are hired by the hour or provide touring or other special services.

Toilets Public toilets are not common in Mexico, but an increasing number are available, especially at fast-food restaurants and Pemex gas stations. These facilities and restaurant and club restrooms commonly have attendants, who expect a small tip (about 50¢).

Useful Phone Numbers **Tourist Help Line,** available 24 hours (© 01-800/903-9200 toll-free inside Mexico). **Mexico Hot Line** (© 800/44-MEXICO). **U.S. Dept. of State Travel Advisory,** staffed 24 hours (© 202/647-5225). **U.S. Passport Agency** (© 202/647-0518). **U.S. Centers for Disease Control and Prevention International Traveler's Hot Line** (© 404/332-4559).

Water Most hotels have decanters or bottles of purified water in the rooms, and the better hotels have either purified water from regular taps or special taps marked *agua purificada*. Some hotels charge for in-room bottled water. Virtually any hotel, restaurant, or bar will bring you purified water if you specifically request it but will usually charge you for it. Drugstores and grocery stores sell bottled purified water. Some popular brands are Santa María, Ciel, and Bonafont. Evian and other imported brands are also widely available.

2

Settling into Puerto Vallarta

by Lynne Bairstow

No matter how extensively I travel in Mexico, Puerto Vallarta remains my favorite part of this colorful country, for its unrivaled combination of simple pleasures and sophisticated charms. No other place in Mexico offers both the best of the country's natural beauty and an authentic dose of its vibrant culture.

Puerto Vallarta's seductive innocence captivates visitors, beckoning them to return—and to bring friends. Beyond the cobblestone streets, graceful cathedral, and welcoming atmosphere, Puerto Vallarta offers a wealth of natural beauty and man-made pleasures. Hotels of all classes and prices, over 250 restaurants, a sizzling nightlife, and enough shops and galleries to tempt even jaded consumers, make this town a perennial favorite.

Ecotourism activities flourish—from mountain biking the Sierra foothills to whale-watching, ocean kayaking, and diving with giant mantas in Banderas Bay. Forty-two kilometers (26 miles) of beaches, many in pristine coves accessible only by boat, extend around the bay. High in the Sierra Madre, the mystical Huichol Indians still live in relative isolation in an effort to protect their centuries-old culture from outside influences.

Vallarta (as locals refer to it) was never the "sleepy little fishing village" that many proclaim. It began life as a port for processing silver brought down from mines in the Sierra Madre—then was forever transformed by a movie director and two star-crossed lovers. In 1963, John Huston brought stars Ava Gardner and Richard Burton here to film the Tennessee Williams play *Night of the Iguana*. Burton's new love, Elizabeth Taylor, came along to ensure the romance remained in full bloom—even though both were married to others at the time. Titillated, the international paparazzi arrived, and when they weren't shooting photos of the famous couple—or of Gardner water-skiing back from the set, surrounded by a bevy of beach boys—they photographed the beauty of Puerto Vallarta.

Puerto Vallarta: Hotel Zone & Beaches

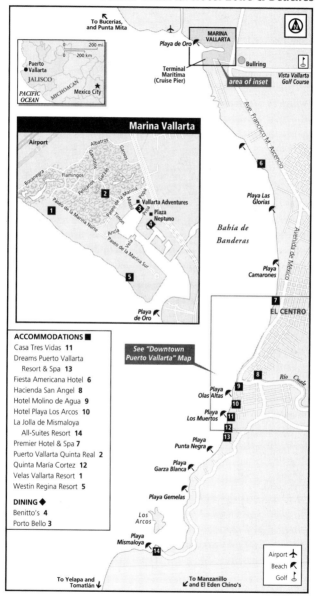

To Bucerias,
and Punta Mita

MARINA
VALLARTA

Playa de Oro

Terminal
Maritima
(Cruise Pier)

Bullring

Vista Vallarta
Golf Course

area of inset

Puerto
Vallarta

JALISCO

MICHOACAN

PACIFIC
OCEAN

Mexico City

0   200 mi
0   200 km

Marina Vallarta

Airport

Albatros

Garzas

Gaviotas

Pelicanos

Flamingos

Garza

Bocanegra

Paseo de la Marina Norte

Paseo de la Marina

Timón

Popa

Proa

Vallarta Adventures

Plaza
Neptuno

Ancia

Vela

Paseo de la Marina Sur

Mastil

Ave. Francisco M. Ascencio

Playa Las
Glorias

Bahía de
Banderas

Avenida de México

Playa
Camarones

Playa
de Oro

EL CENTRO

See "Downtown
Puerto Vallarta" Map

Río Cuale

Playa
Olas Altas

Playa
Los Muertos

Playa
Punta Negra

Playa
Garza Blanca

Playa Gemelas

Los
Arcos

Playa
Mismaloya

Airport ✈
Beach ⚓
Golf ⛳

To Yelapa and
Tomatlán ↓

To Manzanillo
and El Eden Chino's ↙

ACCOMMODATIONS ■

Casa Tres Vidas **11**
Dreams Puerto Vallarta
  Resort & Spa **13**
Fiesta Americana Hotel **6**
Hacienda San Angel **8**
Hotel Molino de Agua **9**
Hotel Playa Los Arcos **10**
La Jolla de Mismaloya
  All-Suites Resort **14**
Premier Hotel & Spa **7**
Puerto Vallarta Quinta Real **2**
Quinta María Cortez **12**
Velas Vallarta Resort **1**
Westin Regina Resort **5**

DINING ◆

Benitto's **4**
Porto Bello **3**

Luxury hotels and shopping centers have sprung up north and south of the original town, allowing Vallarta to grow into a city of 250,000 without sacrificing its considerable charms. It boasts the services and infrastructure of a modern city as well as the authenticity of a colonial Mexican village.

Cool breezes flow down from the mountains along the Río Cuale, which runs through the center of town. Fanciful public sculptures grace the boardwalk, or *malecón,* which is bordered by lively restaurants, shops, and bars. The *malecón* is a magnet for both residents and visitors, who stroll the main walkway to take in an ocean breeze, a multihued sunset, or a moonlit, perfect wave.

If I sound partial, it's not just because Puerto Vallarta is my favorite of Mexico's sunny resorts; this has been my home for the past 14 years. I live here in good company—there's a considerable colony of American, Canadian, and European residents. Perhaps they feel as I do: that the surrounding mountains offer the equivalent of a continual, comforting embrace, adding to that sense of welcome that so many visitors feel as well.

1 Puerto Vallarta Essentials

885km (553 miles) NW of Mexico City; 339km (212 miles) W of Guadalajara; 285km (178 miles) NW of Manzanillo; 447km (278 miles) SE of Mazatlán; 239km (149 miles) SW of Tepic

GETTING THERE & DEPARTING

By Plane   For a full list, of international carriers serving Mexico, see chapter 1. Local numbers of some international carriers serving Puerto Vallarta are **Alaska Airlines** (© **322/221-1350** or 322/221-1353), **American Airlines** (© **322/221-1799** or 322/221-1927), **America West** (© **322/221-1333,** or 01-880/235-9292 inside Mexico), and **Continental** (© **322/221-1025** or 322/221-2212), **Frontier** (© **800/432-1359**), and **Ted** (United's lower-cost carrier offers direct service from San Francisco and Denver; © **800/225-5833** in the U.S.).

Aeromexico (© **322/224-2777** or 322/221-1055) flies from Los Angeles, San Diego, Aguascalientes, Guadalajara, La Paz, León, Mexico City, Morelia, and Tijuana. **Mexicana** (© **322/224-8900** or 322/221-1266) has direct or nonstop flights from Chicago, Los Angeles, Guadalajara, Mazatlán, and Mexico City.

By Car   The coastal Highway 200 is the only choice from Mazatlán (6 hr. north) or Manzanillo (3½ hr. south). Highway 15 from Guadalajara to Tepic takes 6 hours; to save as much as 2 hours, take

Highway 15A from Chapalilla to Compostela, bypassing Tepic, then continue south on Highway 200 to Puerto Vallarta.

By Bus   The bus station, Central Camionera de Puerto Vallarta, is just north of the airport, approximately 11km (7 miles) from downtown. It offers overnight guarded parking and baggage storage. Most major first-class bus lines operate from here, with transportation to points throughout Mexico, including Mazatlán, Tepic, Manzanillo, Guadalajara, and Mexico City. Taxis into town are about $7.50 and readily available; public buses run from 7am to 11pm and regularly stop in front of the arrivals hall.

ORIENTATION

Arriving by Plane   The airport is close to the north end of town near the Marina Vallarta, about 10km (6 miles) from downtown. **Transportes Terrestres** minivans and **Aeromovil** taxis make the trip. They use a zone pricing system, with fares clearly posted at the ticket booths. Fares start at $10 for a ride to Marina Vallarta and go up to $30 for the south shore hotels. Federally licensed airport taxis exclusively provide transportation from the airport, and their fares are more than three times as high as city (yellow) taxi fares. A trip to downtown Puerto Vallarta costs $20, whereas a return trip using a city taxi costs only $6. Only airport cabs may pick up passengers leaving the airport. However, if you don't have too much baggage, you can cross the highway using the new overpass, and there you'll find yellow cabs lined up. Note that now when you arrive at the International Arrivals gate, after you collect your baggage, you enter into an enclosed area with colorful wall displays and an aggressive group of seemingly helpful greeters—beware—these are timeshare hustlers, and their goal, often in the guise of offering you free or discounted transportation, is to get you to attend a timeshare presentation. Keep walking, just outside this booth are the bona fide taxi and transportation alternatives.

VISITOR INFORMATION   Prior to arrival, a great source of general information is the **Puerto Vallarta Tourism Board** (C) **888/384-6822** in the U.S.; www.visitpuertovallarta.com. If you have questions after you arrive, visit the **Municipal Tourism Office** at Juárez and Independencia (C) **322/223-2500,** ext. 230), a corner of the white Presidencia Municipal building (city hall) on the northwest end of the main square. In addition to offering a listing of current events and promotional brochures for local activities and services, the employees can also assist with specific questions—there's usually an English speaker on staff. This is also the office of the tourist police. It's open Monday through Friday from 8am to 4pm. During low season it may close for lunch between 2 and 4pm.

The **State Tourism Office,** Plaza Marina L 144, second floor (© **322/221-2676** or -2677; fax 322/221-2678), also has brochures and can assist with specific questions about Puerto Vallarta and other points in the state of Jalisco, including Guadalajara, Costa Alegre, the town of Tequila, and the program that promotes stays in authentic rural haciendas. It's open Monday through Friday from 9am to 5pm.

CITY LAYOUT   The seaside promenade, the *malecón,* is a common reference point for giving directions. It's next to **Paseo Díaz Ordaz** and runs north-south through the central downtown area. From the waterfront, the town stretches back into the hills a half-dozen blocks. The areas bordering the **Río Cuale** are the oldest parts of town—the original Puerto Vallarta. The area immediately south of the river, called **Olas Altas** after its main street (and sometimes Los Muertos after the beach of the same name), is home to a growing selection of sidewalk cafes, fine restaurants, espresso bars, and hip nightclubs. In the center of town, nearly everything is within walking distance both north and south of the river. Bridges on Insurgentes (northbound traffic) and Ignacio Vallarta (southbound traffic) link the two sections of downtown.

AREA LAYOUT   Beyond downtown, Puerto Vallarta has grown along the beach to the north and south. **Avenida Francisco Medina Ascencio** links downtown to the airport. This main thoroughfare is lined with luxury hotels (in the **Zona Hotelera,** or Hotel Zone) and several shopping centers with casual restaurants.

Marina Vallarta, a resort city within a city, is at the northern edge of the Hotel Zone not far from the airport. It boasts modern luxury hotels, condominiums and homes, a huge marina with 450 yacht slips, a golf course, restaurants and bars, and several shopping plazas. Because it was originally a swamp, the beaches are the least desirable in the area, with darker sand and seasonal inflows of cobblestones. The Marina Vallarta peninsula faces the bay and looks south to the town of Puerto Vallarta.

Nuevo Vallarta is a planned resort north of the airport, across the Ameca River in the state of Nayarit (about 13km/8 miles north of downtown). It also has hotels, condominiums, and a yacht marina, with a limited selection of restaurants and shopping, although the new Paradise Plaza mall is bringing in new options. Most hotels there are all-inclusive, with some of the finest beaches in the bay, but guests usually travel into Puerto Vallarta (about a $13 cab ride) for anything other than poolside or beach action. Regularly scheduled public bus service costs about $1.50 and runs until 10pm.

Bucerías, a small beachside village of cobblestone streets, villas, and small hotels, is farther north along Banderas Bay, 30km (19 miles) beyond the airport. Past Bucerías, following the curved coastline of Banderas Bay to the end of the road is **Punta Mita.** Once a rustic fishing village, it is in the process of development as a luxury desti-nation. Five luxury boutique resorts, private villas, and three golf courses are in the works. The site of an ancient celestial observatory, it is an exquisite setting, with white-sand beaches and clear waters. The northern shore of Banderas Bay is emerging as the area's most exclusive address for luxury villas and accommodations.

In the other direction from downtown is the southern coastal highway, home to more luxury hotels. Immediately south of town lies the exclusive residential and rental district of **Conchas Chinas.** Ten kilometers (6 miles) south, on **Playa Mismaloya** (where *Night of the Iguana* was filmed), lies the Jolla de Mismaloya resort. There's no road on the southern shoreline of Banderas Bay, but three small coastal villages are popular attractions for visitors to Puerto Vallarta: **Las Animas, Quimixto,** and **Yelapa,** all accessible only by boat. The tiny, pristine cove of **Caletas,** site of John Huston's former home, is a popular day- or nighttime excursion (see "Boat Tours," in chapter 3).

GETTING AROUND

By Taxi Taxis are plentiful and relatively cheap. Most trips from downtown to the northern Hotel Zone and Marina Vallarta cost $3.50 to $7; to or from Marina Vallarta to Mismaloya Beach (to the south) costs $10. Rates are charged by zone and are generally posted in the lobbies of hotels. Taxis can also be hired by the hour or day for longer trips. Rates run $12 to $15 per hour, with discounts avail-able for full-day rates—consider this an alternative to renting a car.

Tips Steer Clear of the Rambo Bus!

Buses in Vallarta tend to be rather aggressive, and some even sport names—including "Terminator," "Rambo," and "Tor-nado." Don't tempt fate by assuming these buses will stop for pedestrians. Although Vallarta has an extremely low crime rate, bus accidents are frequent—and frequently fatal.

⌒Tips Don't Let Taxi Drivers Steer You Wrong

Beware of restaurant recommendations offered by taxi drivers—many receive a commission from restaurants where they discharge passengers. Be especially wary if a driver tries to talk you out of a restaurant you've already selected.

By Car Rental cars are available at the airport and through travel agencies, but unless you're planning a distant side trip, don't bother. Car rentals are expensive, averaging $66 per day, and parking around town is difficult. If you see a sign for a $10 jeep rental or $20 car rental, be aware that these are lures to get people to attend time-share presentations. Unless you are interested in a timeshare, stopping to inquire will be a waste of your time.

By Bus City buses, easy to navigate and inexpensive, will serve just about all your transportation needs. They run from the airport through the Hotel Zone along Morelos Street (1 block inland from the *malecón*), across the Río Cuale, and inland on Vallarta, looping back through the downtown hotel and restaurant districts on Insurgentes and several other downtown streets. To get to the northern hotel strip from old Puerto Vallarta, take the ZONA HOTELES, IXTAPA, or LAS JUNTAS bus. These buses may also post the names of hotels they pass, such as Krystal, Fiesta Americana, Sheraton, and others. Buses marked MARINA VALLARTA travel inside this area, stopping at the major hotels there.

Other buses operate every 10 to 15 minutes south to either Mismaloya Beach or Boca de Tomatlán (a sign in the front window indicates the destination) from Constitución and Basilio Badillo, a few blocks south of the river.

Buses run generally from 6am to 11pm, and it's rare to wait more than a few minutes for one. The fare is about 50¢.

By Boat The cruise ship pier *(muelle)*, also called Terminal Marítima, is where **excursion boats** to Yelapa, Las Animas, Quimixto, and the Marietas Islands depart. It's north of town near the airport, an inexpensive taxi or bus ride from town. Just take any bus marked IXTAPA, LAS JUNTAS, PITILLAL, or AURORA and tell the driver to let you off at the Terminal Marítima. **Note:** Odd though it may seem, you must pay a $1.50 fee (this is a federal tax) to gain access to the pier—and your departing excursion boat.

Water taxis to Yelapa, Las Animas, and Quimixto leave at 10:30 and 11am from the pier at Los Muertos Beach (south of downtown), on Rodolfo Rodríguez next to the Hotel Marsol. Another water taxi departs at 11am from the beachside pier at the northern edge of the *malecón*. A round-trip ticket to Yelapa (the farthest point) costs $25. Return trips usually depart between 3 and 4pm, but confirm the pickup time with your water taxi captain. Other water taxis depart from Boca de Tomatlán, about 30 minutes south of town by public bus. These water taxis are the better option if you want more flexible departure and return times from the southern beaches. Generally, they leave on the hour for the southern shore destinations, or more frequently if there is traffic. Prices run about $12 round-trip, with rates now clearly posted on a sign on the beach. A private water taxi costs $35 to $55 (depending on your destination) and allows you to choose your own return time. They'll take up to eight people for that price, so often people band together at the beach to hire one.

FAST FACTS: Puerto Vallarta

American Express The local office is at Morelos 660, at the corner of Abasolo (✆ 01-800/504-0400 and 01-800/333-3211 in Mexico, or 322/223-2955). Open Monday through Friday from 9am to 6pm, and Saturday from 9am to 1pm, it offers excellent, efficient travel agency services in addition to money exchange and traveler's checks.

Area Code The telephone area code is **322**.

Climate It's warm all year, with tropical temperatures; however, evenings and early mornings in the winter can turn quite cool. Summers are sunny, with an increase in humidity during the rainy season, between May and October. Rains come almost every afternoon in June and July, and are usually brief but strong—just enough to cool off the air for evening activities. In September, heat and humidity are least comfortable and rains heaviest.

Consumer Assistance Tourists with complaints about taxis, stores, abusive timeshare presentations, or other matters should contact **PROFECO**, the consumer protection office (✆ **322/225-0000**; fax 322/225-0018). The office is open Monday through Friday from 8:30am to 3:30pm and may not have fluent English-speaking staff.

Currency Exchange Banks are found throughout downtown and in the other prime shopping areas. Most banks are open Monday through Friday from 9am to 5pm, with shorter hours on Saturday. ATMs are common throughout Vallarta, including the central plaza downtown. They are becoming the most favorable way to exchange currency, with bank rates plus 24-hour convenience. Money exchange houses *(casas de cambio)*, located throughout town, offer longer hours than the banks with only slightly lower exchange rates.

Embassies & Consulates The consulates are in a building on the southern border of the central plaza (you'll see the U.S. and Canadian flags). The **U.S. Consular Agency** office (✆ 322/222-0069; fax 322/223-0074, 24 hr. a day for emergencies) is open Monday through Friday from 10am to 2pm. The **Canadian Consulate** (✆ 322/293-0099 or 322/293-0098; 24-hr. emergency line 01-800/706-2900) is open Monday through Friday from 9am to 3pm.

Emergencies **Police** emergency, ✆ 060; local police, ✆ 322/290-0513 or -0512; intensive care **ambulance**, ✆ 322/225-0386 (*Note:* English-speaking help is not always available at this number); **Red Cross**, ✆ 322/222-1533; **Global Life Ambulance Service** (provides both ground and air ambulance service), ✆ 322/226-1010, ext. 304.

Hospitals The following offer U.S.-standards service and are available 24 hours: **Ameri-Med Urgent Care,** Avenida Francisco Medina Ascencio at Plaza Neptuno, Local D-1, Marina Vallarta (✆ 322/221-0023; fax 322/221-0026; www.amerimed-hospitals. com); and **San Javier Marina Hospital,** Av. Francisco Medina Ascencio 2760, Zona Hotelera (✆ 322/226-1010).

Internet Access Puerto Vallarta is probably the most wired destination in Mexico. **The Net House,** Ignacio L. Vallarta 232 (✆ 322/222-6953; info@vallartacafes.com), 2 blocks past the southbound bridge, has 15 computers with fast connections and English keyboards. It's open daily from 8am to 2am and charges $3.50 per hour. **Café.com** (✆ 322/222-0092), Olas Altas 250, at the corner of Basilio Badillo, charges $2 for 30 minutes. It offers complete computer services, a full bar, and food service. It's open daily from 8am to 2am. Some hotels have lobby e-mail kiosks, but they're more expensive than the Net cafes.

Newspapers & Magazines Vallarta Today, a daily English-language newspaper (✆ **322/225-3323** or 322/224-2829), is a good source for local information and upcoming events. The bilingual quarterly city magazine *Vallarta Lifestyles* (✆ **322/221-0106**) is also very popular. Both are for sale at area newsstands and hotel gift shops. The weekly English-language *P.V. Tribune* (✆ **322/223-0585**) is distributed free throughout town and offers an objective local viewpoint.

Pharmacies **CMQ Farmacia,** Basilio Badillo 365 (✆ **322/222-1330**), is open 24 hours and makes free deliveries to hotels between 11am and 10pm with a minimum purchase of $20. **Farmacias Guadalajara,** Emiliano Zapata 232 (✆ **322/224-1811**), is also open 24 hours.

Post Office The *correo* is at Mina 188 (✆ **322/222-1888**). It's open Monday through Friday from 9am to 6pm, Saturday from 9am to 1pm. A second location, on Colombia St., behind Hidalgo park, is open the same hours.

Safety Puerto Vallarta enjoys a very low crime rate. Public transportation is safe to use, and Tourist Police (dressed in white safari uniforms with white hats) are available to answer questions, give directions, and offer assistance. Most encounters with the police are linked to using or purchasing drugs—so don't (see chapter 1). *Note:* The tourist police conduct random personal searches for drugs. Although there is some question about their right to do this, the best course of action if they want to frisk you is to comply—objecting will likely result in a free tour of the local jail. However, you are within your rights to request the name of the officer. Report any unusual incidents to the local consular office.

2 Where to Stay

Beyond a varied selection of hotels and resorts, Puerto Vallarta offers many alternative accommodations. Oceanfront or marina-view condominiums and elegant private villas can offer families and small groups a better value and more ample space than a hotel. For more information on short-term rentals, check out **www.virtualvallarta.com**. Prices start at $99 a night for nonbeachside condos and go to $1,000 for penthouse condos or private villas. Susan Weisman's **Bayside Properties,** Francisco Rodríguez 160, corner of Olas Altas

(© **322/223-4424;** www.puertovallartabayside.com), rents condos, villas, and hotels for individuals and large groups, including gay-friendly accommodations. She can arrange airport pickup and in-villa cooks. Another reputable option is the full-service travel agency, **Holland's** (© **415/841-1194** or 618/236-2787; www.PuertoVallartaVillas.com). For the ultimate, indulge in a Punta Mita Villa rental within this exclusive resort. Contact **Punta Mita Properties** (© **888-647-0979** or 329/291-6500; www.punta-mitaproperties.com). *Note:* This section lists hotels in directional order, moving south along Banderas Bay from the airport.

MARINA VALLARTA

Marina Vallarta is the most modern and deluxe area of hotel development in Puerto Vallarta. Located immediately south of the airport and just north of the cruise-ship terminal, it's a planned development whose centerpiece is a 450-slip modern marina.

The hotels reviewed below are on the beachfront of the peninsula. The beaches here are much less attractive than beaches in other parts of the bay; the sand is darker, firmly packed, and, during certain times of the year, quite rocky. These hotels compensate with oversize pool areas and exotic landscaping. This area suits families and those looking for lots of centralized activity. Marina Vallarta is also home to an 18-hole **golf course** designed by Joe Finger.

In addition to the hotels reviewed below, an excellent choice is the **Puerto Vallarta Quinta Real,** on the golf course at Pelicanos 311 (© **322/221-0800;** fax 322/221-0801; www.quintareal.com). The elegant, boutique-style hotel has extra-large rooms, an on-site spa, and a lovely pool. Although it is not on the beach, it has a beach club, with shuttle service for guests. High-season rates average $250.

Due to traffic (rather than distance), a taxi from the Marina to downtown takes 20 to 30 minutes.

Velas Vallarta Grand Suite Resort ⭑⭑⭑ (Kids)   The beachside Velas Vallarta is an excellent choice for families. Each suite offers a full-size, fully equipped kitchen, ample living and dining areas, separate bedroom or bedrooms, and a large balcony with seating. Following a complete makeover in 2003, the suites are now decorated in a sophisticated, modern design featuring jewel-tone colors, Huichol art and Mexican textiles, feather beds with goose down comforters, texturized wall coverings, new 27-inch flatscreen TVs, modern kitchen appliances, and teak wood furniture on balconies and terraces. Special extras include a pillow menu and luxury bathroom amenities. This property is part hotel, part full-ownership condominiums,

which means each suite is the size of a residential unit. The suites all have partial ocean views; they face a central area where three freeform swimming pools, complete with bridges and waterfalls, meander through tropical gardens. A full range of services means you'd never need to leave the place if you don't want to. The Marina Vallarta Golf Club is across the street, and special packages are available for Velas guests. Guests may pay an extra fee for the Gold Crown All-Inclusive option, which is one of the most premium all-inclusive programs in Mexico.

Paseo de la Marina 485, Marina Vallarta, 48354 Puerto Vallarta, Jal. © 800/659-8477 in the U.S. and Canada, or 322/221-0091. Fax 322/221-0755. www.velasvallarta.com. 361 units. High season $258 double; $325–$650 suite. All-inclusive option (per person, based on double occupancy) is an additional $170 studio; $215 suite. AE, DC, MC, V. Free indoor parking. **Amenities:** 2 restaurants; poolside snack bar; lobby bar; 3 pools; golf privileges at Marina Vallarta Golf Club; 3 lighted tennis courts; fitness center w/spa and massage; beach w/watersports equipment rental; bicycle rentals; activities program for children and adults; concierge; travel agency; car rental; salon; room service; laundry service; minimarket; deli. *In room:* A/C, TV, dataport, full kitchen w/coffeemaker, hair dryer, iron, safe.

Westin Regina Resort *📷📷*   Stunning architecture and vibrant colors are the hallmark of this award-winning property, considered Puerto Vallarta's finest. Although the grounds are large—over 8.4 hectares (21 acres) with 258m (850 ft.) of beachfront—the warm service and gracious hospitality create the feeling of an intimate resort. Hundreds of tall palms surround the spectacular central freeform pool. Hammocks are strung between the palms closest to the beach, which also has private beach cabañas. Rooms are contemporary, with oversize wood furnishings, tile floors, original art, and tub/shower combinations. Balconies have panoramic views. Eight junior suites and some double rooms have Jacuzzis, and the five grand suites and presidential suite are two-level, with ample living areas. Two floors of rooms make up the Royal Beach Club, with VIP services, including private concierge. The fitness center is one of the most modern, well-equipped facilities in Vallarta, with regularly scheduled spinning and yoga classes. **Nikki Beach** (www.nikkibeach.com), a renowned haven for the hip, opened an on-site, beachfront restaurant and club in 2004, with white bed-size lounges for sunbathing, or enjoying libations from noon until the wee hours. Their Sunday champagne brunch is especially popular.

Paseo de la Marina Sur 205, Marina Vallarta, 48321 Puerto Vallarta, Jal. © 800/228-3000 in the U.S., or 322/221-1100. Fax 322/221-1121. www.westinpv.com. 280 units. High season $258–$295 double, $585–$802 suite; low season $217–$234 double, $480–$600 suite. AE, DC, MC, V. Free parking. **Amenities:** 2 restaurants; 2 poolside bars; lobby bar; ocean-side pool; Nikki Beach Club; golf privileges at Marina Vallarta Golf Club; 3 lighted grass tennis courts; full-service, state-of-the-art health club w/treadmills, StairMasters, resistance equipment, sauna, steam room, solarium, whirlpool, massage, and salon; Kids' Club; travel agency; car rental; shopping arcade; 24-hr. room service; laundry service. *In room:* A/C, TV, dataport, minibar, coffeemaker, hair dryer, iron, safe-deposit box.

THE HOTEL ZONE

The main street running between the airport and town is Avenida Francisco Medina Ascencio. The hotels here offer excellent, wide beachfronts with generally tranquil waters for swimming. From here it's a quick taxi or bus ride to downtown.

Fiesta Americana Puerto Vallarta ✿ The Fiesta Americana's towering, three-story, thatched *palapa* lobby is a landmark in the Hotel Zone, and the hotel is known for its excellent beach and friendly service. An abundance of plants, splashing fountains, constant breezes, and comfortable seating areas in the lobby create a casual South Seas ambience. The nine-story terra-cotta-colored building embraces a large plaza with a pool facing the beach. Marble-trimmed rooms in neutral tones with pastel accents contain carved headboards and comfortable rattan and wicker furniture. All have private balconies with ocean and pool views.

Av. Francisco Medina Ascencio Km 2.5, 48300 Puerto Vallarta, Jal. ✆ 322/224-2010. Fax 322/224-2108. www.fiestaamericana.com. 291 units. High season $180 double; low season $120–$160 double. Year-round $256–$819 suite. AE, DC, MC, V. Limited free parking. **Amenities:** 3 restaurants; lobby bar w/live music nightly; large pool w/activities and children's activities in high season; travel agency; salon; room service; laundry service. *In room:* A/C, TV, minibar, hair dryer, safe.

Premier Hotel & Spa ✿✿ You couldn't ask for a better location to be close to all that Vallarta's vibrant *centro* has to offer. Located on a wide swathe of golden sand beach—and just a few blocks north of the start of the *malecón*—the Premier is easy walking distance or a quick taxi ride to the downtown restaurants, shops, galleries, and clubs. One of the newer hotels in Vallarta (opened 1999), the architecture is contemporary, but its size gives it an intimate feel. With a first-rate spa and a policy that restricts guests to ages 16 and older, it's a place that caters to relaxation. Four types of rooms are available, but all are decorated in warm colors with tile floors and light wood furnishings. Deluxe rooms have ocean views, a respectable seating area with comfortable chairs, plus a sizable private balcony—request one of several that has an outdoor whirlpool. There are also seven suites that have a separate living room plus a dining area with private bar, and a spacious terrace. These rooms also have a double whirlpool tub, and separate glass-enclosed shower. The top-of-the-line master suites have all that the above suites offer, plus an outdoor whirlpool on the spacious balcony. The stunning bi-level spa is the real attraction of this hotel—scented with aromatherapy and glowing with candlelight, it uses top-notch, 100% natural products, most based on Mexico's natural treasures like coconut, aloe, and papaya. If you're not tempted by the nearby and accessible dining choices in downtown Vallarta, the Premier also offers an all-inclusive option, with all meals and drinks included.

San Salvador 117, behind the Buenaventura Hotel, Col. 5 de Diciembre, 48350 Puerto Vallarta, Jal. © 877/886-9176 toll-free in the U.S., or 322/226-7001. Fax: 322/226-7043. www.premiereonline.com.mx. 83 rooms and suites. Room only rates: high season $135–$374 double; low season $121–$325 double. All-inclusive rates: high season $224–$299 per person, based on double occupancy; low season $167–$224 per person, double. For ages 16 and older only. AE, MC, V. **Amenities:** 3 restaurants; small pool; fitness center; full spa; travel agency; salon; 24-hr. room service; laundry service. *In room:* A/C, TV, minibar, coffeemaker, hair dryer, safe, bathrobes.

DOWNTOWN TO LOS MUERTOS BEACH

This part of town has recently undergone a renaissance; economical hotels and good-value guesthouses dominate. Several blocks off the beach, you can find numerous budget inns offering clean, simply furnished rooms; most offer discounts for long-term stays. Much of Vallarta's nightlife activity now centers in the areas south of the Río Cuale and along Olas Altas.

Hacienda San Angel ☆☆☆ *Finds*   This enchanting boutique hotel may not be on the beach, but you'll hardly miss it, you'll be so pampered in the stunning suites, or satisfied enjoying the view from the rooftop heated pool or Jacuzzi and sun deck. Once Richard Burton's home in Puerto Vallarta, it's located just behind Puerto Vallarta's famed church, making it easy walking distance to all of the restaurants, shopping, and galleries of downtown. The Hacienda is comprised of three villas; the first two are joined to the third villa by a path that winds through a lovely terraced garden filled with tropical plants, flowers, statuary, and a charming fountain. A large, heated pool and deck offer panoramic views of the city and Bay of Banderas, while a second sun deck with Jacuzzi literally overlooks the church's crown, across to the water beyond. Each of the Hacienda's nine elegant suites is individually decorated, accented with exquisite antiques and original art. Bed linens and coverings are of the finest quality, with touches like Venetian lace and goose-down pillows. Each morning, you'll awake to continental breakfast served outside your suite at your requested hour. From Monday through Saturday, guests are invited to a cocktail hour, where one of the Hacienda's signature drinks (like the Celestial Sin—a wicked blend of vodka and blue Curacao) are served, accompanied by snacks. Sophisticated style, coupled with casual Vallarta charm, make Hacienda San Angel the newest "find" in Mexico for the discriminating traveler.

Miramar 336, Col. Centro, 48300 Puerto Vallarta, Jal. © **322/222-2692.** www.haciendasanangel.com. 9 suites. High season $250–$475 double; low season $200–$370 double. All rates include daily continental breakfast. Rates for the entire Hacienda or separate villas consisting of 3 suites each are also available. MC, V. Very limited street parking available. **Amenities:** Menu of full breakfasts, lunches, and dinner, or private chef available; 2 pools; rooftop sun deck w/Jacuzzi; concierge; tour services; complimentary Internet access. *In room:* A/C, TV with DVD/CD player, hair dryer, safe-deposit box, bathrobes.

Hotel Molino de Agua 🐾
With an unrivaled location adjacent to both the Río Cuale and the ocean, this hotel is a mix of stone and stucco-walled bungalows and small beachside buildings, spread out among winding walkways and lush tropical gardens. It's immediately past the Río Cuale—after crossing the southbound bridge, it's on your right. Although it's centrally located on a main street, open spaces, big trees, birds, and lyrical fountains lend it tranquillity. The individual bungalows are in the gardens between the entrance and the ocean. They are well maintained and simply furnished, with a wooden desk and chair, Mexican tile floors, beamed ceilings, and beautiful tile bathrooms. Wicker rocking chairs grace the private patios. Rooms and suites in the two small two- and three-story buildings on the beach have double beds and private terraces, and are decorated in rustic Mexican style.

Vallarta 130 (Apdo. Postal 54), 48380 Puerto Vallarta, Jal. © **322/222-1957.** Fax 322/222-6056. www.molinodeagua.com. 60 units. High season garden bungalow $100 double, oceanfront room or suite $143–$175 double; low season bungalow $88 double, oceanfront room or suite $106–$132 double. AE, MC, V. Free secured parking. **Amenities:** Restaurant; bar; beachside pool; pool w/whirlpool; tour desk; car-rental desk. *In room:* A/C.

Hotel Playa Los Arcos 🐾🐾
This is one of Vallarta's perennially popular hotels and a favorite of mine, with a stellar location in the heart of Los Muertos Beach, central to the Olas Altas sidewalk-cafe action and close to downtown. The four-story structure is U-shaped, facing the ocean, with a small swimming pool in the courtyard. Rooms with private balconies overlook the pool. The 10 suites have ocean views; 5 of these have kitchenettes. The standard rooms are small but pleasantly decorated and immaculate, with carved wooden furniture painted pale pink. On the premises are a *palapa* beachside bar with occasional live entertainment, a gourmet coffee shop, and

the popular Kaiser Maximilian's gourmet restaurant. It's 7 blocks south of the river.

Olas Altas 380, 48380 Puerto Vallarta, Jal. ℂ **800/648-2403** in the U.S., or 322/222-1583. Fax 322/222-2418. www.playalosarcos.com. 175 units. High season $116–$140 double, $166 suite; low season $85 double, $127 suite. AE, MC, V. Limited street parking. **Amenities:** 2 restaurants; lobby bar; pool; tour desk; car-rental services; babysitting; laundry; safe-deposit boxes; money exchange at front desk. *In room:* A/C, TV.

SOUTH TO MISMALOYA

Casa Tres Vidas ⭐⭐ *Value*   Terraced down a hillside to Conchas Chinas Beach, Casa Tres Vidas is three individual villas that make great, affordable lodgings for families or groups of friends. Set on a stunning private cove, Tres Vidas gives you the experience of your own private villa, complete with service staff. It offers outstanding value for the location—close to town, with panoramic views from every room—as well as for the excellent service. Each villa has at least two levels and over 465 sq. m (5,000 sq. ft.) of mostly open living areas, plus a private swimming pool, heated whirlpool, and air-conditioned bedrooms. The Vida Alta penthouse villa has three bedrooms, plus a rooftop deck with pool and bar. Vida Sol villa's three bedrooms sleep 10 (two rooms have two king-size beds each). Directly on the ocean, Vida Mar is a four-bedroom villa, accommodating eight. The staff prepares gourmet meals in your villa twice a day—you choose the menu and pay only for the food. If you're planning a wedding, Tres Vidas and its adjacent sister property, Quinta María Cortez, do a stunning job.

Sagitario 134, Playa Conchas Chinas, 48300 Puerto Vallarta, Jal. ℂ **888/640-8100** or 801/531-8100 in the U.S., or 322/221-5317. Fax 322/221-53-27. www.casatresvidas.com. 3 villas. High season $625 villa; low season $450 villa. Rates include services. Special summer 1- or 2-bedroom rates available; minimum 3 nights. AE, MC, V. Very limited street parking. **Amenities:** 2 prepared daily meals; private pool; concierge; tour desk; car rental. *In room:* Kitchen facilities, safe-deposit box.

Dreams Puerto Vallarta Resort & Spa ⭐⭐   Formerly the Camino Real, this original luxury hotel in Puerto Vallarta was taken over by AMResorts in 2004 and turned into the premium all-inclusive Dreams Resort. It has the nicest beach of any Vallarta hotel, with soft white sand in a private cove. Set apart from other properties, with a lush mountain backdrop, it retains the exclusivity that made it popular from the beginning—yet it's only a 5- to 10-minute ride to town. The hotel consists of two buildings: the 250-room main hotel, which curves gently with the shape of the Playa Las Estacas, and the newer 11-story Club Tower, also facing the beach and ocean. An ample pool fronts the main building, facing the beach.

Standard rooms in the main building are large; some have sliding doors opening onto the beach, and others have balconies. Club Tower rooms (from the sixth floor up) feature balconies with whirlpool tubs. The top floor consists of six two-bedroom suites, each with a private swimming pool, and with special concierge services. All rooms feature ocean views, and are decorated in vibrant colors, with marble floors. In 2004, all rooms were completely renovated, with additions including two new swimming pools (including an adults-only tranquillity pool), a wedding gazebo, and upgraded health club and spa.

Carretera Barra de Navidad Km 3.5, Playa Las Estacas, 48300 Puerto Vallarta, Jal. © 866/237-3267 in the U.S. and Canada, or 322/221-5000. Fax 322/221-6000. www.dreamsresorts.com. 337 units. All-inclusive rates include all meals, premium drinks, activities, airport transfers, tips, and taxes. $298–$333 double; $598–$633 junior suite; $1,012–$1,500 suite. AE, DC, MC, V. Free secured parking. **Amenities:** 5 restaurants; lobby bar; pool bar; swimming pool; 2 lighted grass tennis courts; fully equipped health club and spa; children's program (Easter and Christmas vacations); travel agency; car rental; convenience store; 24-hr. room service; laundry service; beach *palapas* w/chair, towel, and dining service; nightly entertainment. *In room:* A/C, TV, dataport, minibar, hair dryer, iron, safe-deposit box.

Quinta María Cortez ★★★ *Finds* A sophisticated, imaginative B&B on the beach, this is Puerto Vallarta's most original place to stay—and one of Mexico's most memorable inns. Most of the seven large suites, uniquely decorated with antiques, whimsical curios, and original art, have a kitchenette and balcony. Sunny terraces, a small pool, and a central gathering area with fireplace and *palapa*-topped dining area (where an excellent full breakfast is served) occupy different levels of the seven-story house. A rooftop terrace offers another sunbathing alternative—and is among the best sunset-watching spots in town. The Quinta is on a beautiful cove on Conchas Chinas beach. A terrace fronting the beach accommodates chairs for taking in the sunset.

The Quinta María wins my highest recommendation (in fact, I enjoyed living here for a few years when it still accepted long-term stays), but admittedly it's not for everyone. Air-conditioned areas are limited, due to the open nature of the suites and common areas. Those who love it return year after year, charmed by this remarkable place and by the consistently gracious service.

A new and very popular specialty of QMC and its adjacent sister property Casa Tres Vidas (see above) is planning and hosting weddings.

Sagitario 132, Playa Conchas Chinas, 48300 Puerto Vallarta, Jal. © **888/640-8100** or 801/536-5850 in the U.S., or 322/221-5317. Fax 322/221-53-27. www.quinta-maria. com. 7 units. High season $100–$235 double; low season $85–$175 double. Rates include breakfast. AE, MC, V. Very limited street parking. Children not accepted.

Amenities: Small pool; concierge. *In room:* Dataport, minifridge, coffeemaker, hair dryer, safe-deposit box, CD player.

YELAPA

Verana ★★★ *Moments*   The magical Verana is my current favorite place to stay in Mexico. It has an unparalleled ability to inspire immediate relaxation and a deep connection with the natural beauty of the spectacular coast. Although Yelapa is 30 minutes by water taxi from town, even those unfamiliar with the village should consider it. Verana has six rustic yet sophisticated suites, set into a hillside with sweeping views of the mountains and ocean. Each is a work of art, hand-crafted with care and creativity by owners Heinz Leger, a former film production designer, and prop stylist Veronique Lieve. Each has a private terrace and two beds—but you won't find TVs, telephones, stereos, or other distractions. My favorite suite is the Studio; it's the most contemporary, with a wall of floor-to-ceiling windows that perfectly frame the spectacular view. The European-trained chef prepares scrumptious creations—global cuisine with a touch of Mexico. Compare this to the prices of the other rustic-chic resorts along Mexico's Pacific coast, and you'll find it's a true value. Adventurous travelers should not miss a stay at this unique place.

Domicilio conocido, 48300 Yelapa, Jal. ⓒ **800/677-5156** or 661/946-7477 in the U.S., or 322/222-2360; mobile 322/227-5420. www.verana.com. 6 villas. High season $200-$450 per night per villa, 5-night minimum; 3-bedroom Casa Grande $400 per night, all based on double occupancy; extra person $95 per night. Mandatory daily breakfast and dinner charge $65 per person. Lunch and beverages extra. Shorter stays based on availability. AE, MC, V. Management helps arrange transportation from Puerto Vallarta to Boca, where a private boat runs to Yelapa; from there, Verana is a gentle hike or mule ride. **Amenities:** Restaurant/bar; 2 prepared daily meals; pool; spa w/massage services; morning yoga classes; tours and excursions; library.

3 Where to Dine

Puerto Vallarta has the most exceptional dining scene of any resort town in Mexico. Over 250 restaurants serve cuisines from around the world, in addition to fresh seafood and regional dishes. Chefs from France, Switzerland, Germany, Italy, and Argentina have come for visits and stayed to open restaurants. In celebration of this diversity, Vallarta's culinary community hosts a 2-week-long gourmet dining festival each November.

Dining is not limited to high-end options—there are plenty of small, family-owned restaurants, local Mexican kitchens, and vegetarian cafes. Vallarta also has branches of the world food-and-fun chains: Hard Rock Cafe, Outback Steakhouse, and even Hooters. I won't bother to review these restaurants, where the quality and decor are so familiar.

Of the inexpensive local spots, one favorite is **El Planeta Vegetariano,** Iturbide 270, just down from the main church (© 322/222-3073), serving an inexpensive, bountiful, and delicious vegetarian buffet, which changes for breakfast and lunch/dinner. It's open Monday through Saturday. Breakfast ($3.50) is served from 8 to 11am; the lunch and dinner buffets ($5.50) are served from 11:30am to 10pm; no credit cards. A second location with the same prices and hours of service is now in Marina Vallarta (© **322/209-0555**), located in Marina del Rey, local L-4.

MARINA VALLARTA

Contrary to conventional travel wisdom, most of the best restaurants in the Marina are in hotels. Especially notable are **Andrea** (fine Italian cuisine), at Velas Vallarta, and **Nikki Beach** (fusion), on the beachfront of the Westin Regina Resort. (See "Where to Stay," earlier in this chapter, for more information.) Other choices are along the boardwalk bordering the marina yacht harbor. A notable stop is the **Café Max,** next to the Vallarta Adventures offices in Condominiums Marina Golf, Local 11 (© **322/221-0362**). It serves excellent

---

Moments Special Events in Puerto Vallarta

Each November, the annual **Gourmet Festival** (www.festival gourmet.com) is a standout reason to come here, with an agenda filled with culinary exhibitions, wine tastings, and guest chefs preparing special menus at area restaurants. In its second year, the **Film Festival of the Americas** (www.puertovallarta film.com) features film screenings, panel discussions with celebrity guests, and gala events. Dates vary; call the Tourism Board (© **888/384-6822** in the U.S.) for dates and schedule. From December 1 to December 12, the **Festival of the Virgin of Guadalupe** —Mexico's patron saint—inspires one of the most authentic displays of community and community in Mexico. Businesses, neighborhoods, associations, and groups make pilgrimages (called *peregrinaciones*) to the church, where they exchange offerings for a brief blessing by the priest. These processions, especially those created by hotels, often include floats, Aztec dancers, and mariachis, and are followed by fireworks. Hotels frequently invite guests to participate in the walk to the church. It's an event not to be missed.

coffee and espresso drinks, plus pastries and light snacks. Open Monday through Saturday from 8am to 1pm, and 4 to 10:30pm.

Benitto's ☆ CAFE   Wow! What a sandwich! Benitto's food would be reason enough to come to this tiny, terrific cafe inside the Plaza Neptuno—but added to that are the original array of sauces and the very personable service. This place is popular with locals for light breakfasts, filling lunches, and fondue and wine in the evenings. It's the best place in town to find pastrami, corned beef, or other traditional (gringo) sandwich fare, all served on your choice of gourmet bread. Draft beer and wine are available, as are the cafe's specialty infused waters.

Inside Plaza Neptuno. ⓒ **322/209-0287**. benittosdeli@prodigy.net.mx. Breakfast $3–$6; main courses $5–$7. No credit cards. Daily 8:30am–10:30pm.

Porto Bello ☆☆ ITALIAN   One of the first restaurants in the marina, Porto Bello remains a favorite for its authentically flavorful Italian dishes and exceptional service. For starters, fried calamari is delicately seasoned, and grilled vegetable antipasto could easily serve as a full meal. Signature dishes include fusilli prepared with artichokes, black olives, lemon juice, basil, olive oil, and Parmesan cheese, and sautéed fish filet with shrimp and clams in saffron tomato sauce. The elegant indoor dining room is air-conditioned, and there's also marina-front seating. The restaurant occasionally schedules live music in the evening.

Marina Sol, Local 7 (Marina Vallarta *malecón*). ⓒ **322/221-0003**. Main courses $7–$19. AE, MC, V. Daily noon–11pm.

DOWNTOWN
EXPENSIVE

Café des Artistes/Thierry Blouet Cocina del Autor ☆☆☆ FRENCH/INTERNATIONAL   This sophisticated restaurant is known as the place in town for that very special evening. Creative in its menu and innovative in design, the dinner-only restaurant rivals those in any major metropolitan city for its culinary sophistication, and may soon become a reason in itself to visit Vallarta. The award-winning chef and owner, Thierry Blouet, is both a member of the French Academie Culinaire and a Maitre Cuisinier de France. In late 2003, the singular dining experience of the Café evolved into a trio of special places, expanding to add the upscale Bar Constantini lounge, and separate, but connected Theirry Blouet, Cocina del Autor dining area. All are located in a restored house that resembles a castle. The interior of the original Café des Artistes combines murals, lush fabrics, and an array of original works of art, with both an interior dining area as well as a lushly landscaped terraced garden area, open only during the winter and spring. The menu of this section is a changing delight of French gourmet bistro fare, which draws heavily on Chef Blouet's French training, yet uses regional specialty ingredients. A few of the noteworthy entrees include sea bass filet served with polenta, and the renowned roasted duck glazed with honey, soy, ginger, and lime sauce, and served with a pumpkin risotto. At the Cocina del Autor, the atmosphere is sleek and stylish, and the fixed-priced tasting menu (prices depend on the number of plates you select, from three to six) offers you a choice of the chef's most creative and sumptuous creations, with each dish creatively combining ingredients to present one memorable "flavor"—choose any combination of starters, entrees, or desserts. They also provide perfect wine pairings, if desired. After, you're invited to the cognac and cigar room, an exquisite blend of old adobe walls, flickering candles, and elegant leather chairs. Or, move on to the adjacent Bar Constantini, with its live jazz music and plush sofas, for a fitting close to a memorable meal. It's without a doubt worth the splurge.

Guadalupe Sánchez 740. (ⓒ) **322/222-3228**, -3229, or -3230. www.cafedesartistes. com. Main courses $9–$31. Cocina del Autor tasting menu ranges $25–$68. AE, MC, V. Daily 6–11:30pm.

MODERATE

Daiquiri Dick's 🎭🎭 MODERN AMERICAN A Vallarta dining institution, Daiquiri Dick's has been around for over 20 years, evolving its winning combination of decor, service, and scrumptious cuisine. The menu is among Vallarta's most sophisticated, and the genuinely warm staff and open-air location fronting Los Muertos Beach add to the feeling of casual comfort. As lovely as the restaurant is, though, and as notorious as the fresh-fruit daiquiris are, the food is the main attraction. It incorporates touches of Tuscan, Thai, and Mexican. Start with grilled asparagus wrapped in prosciutto and topped with shaved Asiago cheese, then try an entree such as sesame-crusted tuna, grilled rare and served with wild greens; pistachio chicken served with polenta; or my favorite, simple yet indulgent lobster tacos. Chocolate banana bread pudding makes a perfect finish. Daiquiri Dick's is a great place for groups—as well as for a romantic dinner. It's one of the few places that is equally enjoyable for breakfast, lunch, or dinner.

Olas Altas 314. (ⓒ) **322/222-0566**. www.ddpv.com. Main courses $6.50–$21. AE, MC, V. Daily 9am–10:30pm. Closed Sept.

de Santos ⭐ MEDITERRANEAN   After it opened a few years ago, de Santos quickly became the hot spot in town for late-night dining and bar action. Although the food initially didn't live up to the atmosphere and music, now it does. It's Mediterranean-inspired; best bets include lightly breaded calamari, paella Valenciana, and excellent thin-crust pizza. Also ask about nightly specials. The cool, refined interior feels more urban than resort, and it boasts the most sophisticated sound system in town—including a DJ who spins to match the mood of the crowd. It probably helps that one of the partners is also a member of the wildly popular Latin group Mana. There's open-air terrace dining in the back. Prices are extremely reasonable for the quality and overall experience of an evening here. Be sure to stay and check out the adjacent club—simply the hottest nightspot in town (see "Puerto Vallarta After Dark," below). We hear an expansion is planned for summer 2005, adding even more dining tables in the club area during peak evening hours.

Morelos 771, Centro. ⓒ **322/223-3052**. www.desantos.com.mx. Reservations recommended during high season. Main courses $5–$20. AE, MC, V. Daily 5pm–1am; bar closes at 4am on weekends.

Las Palomas ⭐ MEXICAN   One of Puerto Vallarta's first restaurants, this is the power-breakfast place of choice—and a popular hangout for everyone else throughout the day. Authentic in atmosphere and menu, it's one of Puerto Vallarta's few genuine Mexican restaurants, with the atmosphere of a gracious home. Breakfast is the best value. The staff pours mugs of steaming coffee spiced with cinnamon as soon as you're seated. Try classic *huevos rancheros* or *chilaquiles* (tortilla strips, fried and topped with red or green spicy sauce, cream, cheese, and fried eggs). Lunch and dinner offer traditional Mexican specialties, plus a selection of stuffed crepes. The best places for checking out the *malecón* and watching the sunset while sipping an icy margarita are the spacious bar and upstairs terrace.

Paseo Díaz Ordaz 610. ⓒ **322/222-3675**. Breakfast $3.50–$10; lunch $8.50–$20; main courses $8.50–$22. AE, MC, V. Daily 8am–11pm.

Rito's Baci ⭐⭐ ITALIAN   If the food weren't reason enough to come here (and it definitely is!), then Rito himself would be. He directs gentle, devoted attention to every detail of this cozy trattoria. His grandfather emigrated from Italy, and the recipes and tradition of Italian food come naturally to him. So does his passion for food—it's obvious as he describes the specialties, which include lasagna (vegetarian, *verde,* or meat-filled); ravioli stuffed with spinach and ricotta; spaghetti with garlic, anchovy, and lemon zest; or a side of homemade Italian sausage. Everything is made by hand from fresh ingredients. Pizza-lovers favor the Piedmonte, with that famous sausage and mushrooms, and the Horacio, a cheeseless version with tomatoes, oregano, and basil. Sandwiches come hot or cold; arrive hungry—they're a two-handed operation. Because Rito offers home and hotel delivery, I enjoy his food more than any other restaurant's. It's 1½ blocks off the *malecón*.

Domínguez 181 (between Morelos and Juárez). © 322/222-6448. Pasta $7–$17; salads and sandwiches $2.50–$7; pizza $13–$17. MC, V. Daily 1–11pm.

Trio ⟨★★★⟩ *Finds* INTERNATIONAL   Trio is the darling of Vallarta restaurants, with diners beating a path to the modest but stylish cafe where chef-owners Bernhard Güth and Ulf Henricksson both share an undeniable passion for food, which imbues each dish. Trio is noted for its perfected melding of Mexican and Mediterranean flavors; memorable entrees include San Blas shrimp in a fennel-tomato vinaigrette served over broiled *nopal* cactus; herb risotto with toasted sunflower seeds and quail; and pan-roasted sea bass with glazed grapes, mashed potatoes, and sauerkraut in a white pepper sauce. These dishes may not be on the menu when you arrive, though— it's a constantly changing work of art. The atmosphere is always comfortable and welcoming, and the chefs regularly chat with guests at the end of the evening. The rooftop bar area allows for a more comfortable wait for a table or for after-dinner coffee. A real treat!

Guerrero 264. © 322/222-2196. Reservations recommended. Main courses $14– $26. AE, MC, V. Year-round daily 6pm–midnight; high season Mon–Fri noon–3:30pm.

Xitomates ⟨★★⟩ MEXICAN   Located in the heart of downtown, this creative Mexican restaurant has earned raves for its intimate atmosphere and chef/owner Luis Fitch's exceptionally creative versions of the country's culinary treasures. It's named for one of Mexico's contributions to gastronomy—the tomato (Xitomatl, in the ancient Aztec language of Náhuatl). The menu mixes Mexican with Caribbean, Asian, and Mediterranean influences, and the presentation is as creative as the preparation. Starters include their signature coconut shrimp in a tangy tamarind sauce, thinly sliced scallops with cucumber and jicama julienne, or mushrooms stuffed with shrimp or huitlacoche (a mushroom that grows on corn stalks). Main courses range from grilled salmon filet in a poblano chile sauce, to a tender rib-eye steak with mushrooms, delicately flavored with the Mexican herb, epazote. The house specialty dessert is a Toluca ice-cream cake.

Tapas Anyone?

Certainly, much of modern Mexico's culture draws on the important influence of Spain, so it only makes sense that culinary traditions would be evident as well. Within the last several years, dining on tapas has soared in popularity here. Of the many options, these are my favorites: the long-standing **Barcelona Tapas,** Matamoros and 31 de Octobre streets (② 322/222-0510), a large and lovely restaurant on a terrace built high on a hillside, with sweeping views of the Bay. They serve tapas and a selection of Spanish entrees, including paella, from 5pm to midnight. **La Taberna de San Pascual,** Corona 186 (② 322/223-9371; Mon–Sat 5pm–midnight, with bar service extending to 2am; closed Sun), is a cozy eatery, rich with brick walls and dark wood accents, located on popular Corona Street, in the center of downtown. All ingredients are imported from Spain, and there's a selection of excellent Spanish wines to accompany their flavorful tapas. **La Esquina de los Caprichos,** Miramar 402, corner of Iturbide (② 322/222-0911; Mon–Sat 1–11pm), is a tiny tapas place, known as having the most reasonably priced ($1.50–$6) tapas in town, and perhaps the tastiest.

The warmly decorated dining room is accented with tin star lamps and flickering candles. An excellent wine list and full bar complement the exquisite dining.

Morelos 570, across from Galería Uno. ② **322/222-1695.** www.losxitomates.com. Main courses $8–$22. AE, MC, V. Daily 7–11:30pm.

INEXPENSIVE

Adobe Grill 🐝 MEXICAN   Opening its doors in late 2004, Adobe Grill took over most of the space at the Casa de Tequila, where it's located in the back, in a beautiful garden setting, within this classic Hacienda-style building in central downtown. The space has been put to excellent use: This cafe serves modern, casual Mexican cuisine and is an ideal spot to stop for a snack or a margarita while shopping. Start with an order of chiles anchos, stuffed with cream cheese and raisins, or the *antijotos mexicana,* a sampler of Mexican snacks including sopes, quesadillas, a tamale, and guacamole. Favorite main courses include *mole poblano,* or the beef filet in a chile pasilla gravy, served with mashed sweet potatoes and grilled watermelon. For a sweet finish, don't miss their chocolate truffle with coconut foam in a strawberry salsa. All tortillas are handmade, as are the savory salsas. An elegant bar borders the room, serving undoubtedly Vallarta's most original selection of fine tequilas, many from small distilleries. In addition to the tequilas and fresh fruit margaritas, Adobe Grill also serves a selection of fine Mexican wines.

Morelos 589. ⓒ 322/222-2000. Main courses: $6–$17. MC, V. Mon–Sat noon–11pm.

Arrayán 🌟🌟🌟 *Finds* MEXICAN   The traditional but original Arrayán is the pot of gold at the end of the rainbow for anyone in search of authentic Mexican cuisine. Owner Carmen Porras enlisted Mexico City chef Carmen Titita (praised by James Beard for her culinary work) to assist in the design of the kitchen and creation of the restaurant's concise menu, which features genuine Mexican food of the region. The open-air (but covered) dining area surrounds a cozy courtyard, while its exposed brick walls, and funky-chic decor showcase a modern view of Mexican classics—tin tubs serve as sinks in the bathrooms, while colorful plastic tablecloths and primitive art enliven the dining room. Start with an order of sumptuous plantain fritters filled with black beans, or an unusual salad of diced *nopal* cactus paddles with fresh cheese. Favorite main courses include their tacos filled with prime beef filet, or a Mexican duck confit, served in an arrayán-orange sauce. (Arrayán—the namesake of the place—is a small bittersweet fruit native to the region.) Homemade, fresh-fruit ice creams are an especially tasty finish to your meal. The full bar offers an extensive selection of tequilas and regional liquors, while nonalcoholic beverages center around *aguas frescas,* a blended drink of fresh fruit and water. You can't miss the pink facade with the large bell at the entry. The excellent service is a plus to this can't-miss dining experience.

Allende 344, just past the corner with Matamoros. ⓒ 322/223-2963. carmyp@ prodigy.net.mx. Main courses $8–$12. No credit cards. Daily 1–11pm.

Vitea 🌟🌟🌟 *Finds* INTERNATIONAL   This beachfront bistro was opened in late 2004 by the chef/owners of Trio, and their recipe for success took hold from day one—the place is already bustling at any hour, and has become the new favorite among local residents. Due to strategically-placed mirrors on the back wall, every seat has a view of the ocean, while the eclectic interior is cheerful and inviting. Seating is at small bistro-style tables, along a banquette that runs the length of the back wall, or at the small but beautiful bar. The long, narrow bistro faces the waterfront between the central plaza and river, which is currently undergoing a restoration—the *malecón* is being extended and will soon pass by Viteo, certain to be joined by other cafes. But enough about looks—what counts here is the exceptional fare, which is both classic and original. Starters include a tomato and Roquefort salad with pecans, foie gras with Spanish plum sauce, and an exquisite bistro salad with bacon. Quiche is always on the menu, with changing selections, and main courses include chickpea ravioli with portobello mushrooms, Wiener schintzel with salad, or a traditional steak frites. Lunch offers lighter fare, including heavenly deli sandwiches. You won't be disappointed here, no matter what you order! There's a full bar with an excellent selection of wines, and the service is exceptional.

Libertad 24, at the *malecón*. ② **322/222-8703** or 322/222-8695. Reservations recommended during peak dining hours. Main courses $7–$19. MC, V. Daily noon–midnight.

SOUTH OF THE RIO CUALE TO OLAS ALTAS

South of the river is the densest restaurant area, where you'll find the street Basilio Badillo, nicknamed "Restaurant Row." A second main dining drag has emerged along Calle Olas Altas, with a variety of cuisines and price categories. Cafes and espresso bars, generally open from 7am to midnight, line its wide sidewalks.

EXPENSIVE

Café Kaiser Maximilian ★★ INTERNATIONAL   This bistro-style cafe has a casually elegant atmosphere with a genuinely European feel. It's the prime place to go if you want to combine exceptional food with great people-watching. Austrian-born owner Andreas Rupprechter is always on hand to ensure that the service is as impeccable as the food is delicious. Indoor, air-conditioned dining is at cozy tables; sidewalk tables are larger and great for groups of friends. The cuisine merges old-world European preparations with regional fresh ingredients. My favorite is filet of trout with watercress and beet sauce—so much so that I've never tried any other dish, although friends tell me mustard chicken with mashed potatoes is excellent, and the rack of lamb with polenta, endives, and lima beans is simply divine. The restaurant also offers northern European classics like *Rahmschnitzel* (sautéed pork loin and homemade noodles in creamy mushroom sauce). Desserts are especially tempting, as are gourmet coffees—Maximilian has an Austrian cafe and pastry shop next door.

Olas Altas 380-B (at Basilio Badillo, in front of the Hotel Playa Los Arcos), Zona Romántica. ② **322/223-0760.** Reservations recommended in high season. Main courses $16–$26. AE, MC, V. Mon–Sat 6–11pm.

Le Bistro ☆ MEXICAN/INTERNATIONAL   A long-standing favorite, Le Bistro is especially enjoyable for breakfast. I consider a morning meal here one of Vallarta's best values. Le Bistro is known for its elegant decor, great recorded jazz music, and open-air setting on the island in the midst of the Río Cuale—all creating a singular experience that blends sophistication with a typically Vallarta atmosphere. Favorite choices at breakfast are eggs Benedict and eggs *motuleño* style (sunny side up, smothered in tomato-based sauce and served with cheese, peas, and fried plantains). The specialty is crepes, which come in a variety of flavors for breakfast, lunch, or dinner. Especially scrumptious are those filled with chicken breast and squash blossoms (a Mexican delicacy) in hollandaise sauce. The menu also has an excellent selection of innovative Mexican cuisine, including duck in Oaxacan black *mole,* and rock Cornish hen stuffed with herbed rice, dried tropical fruits, and nuts, finished in mango cilantro sauce. The vegetarian offerings are more creative than most. An impressive wine list and ample selection of specialty coffees complement the menu.

Isla Río Cuale 16-A (just east of northbound bridge). ☎ **322/222-0283.** www.lebistro. com.mx. Reservations recommended in high season. Breakfast $5–$8; main courses $19–$25. AE, MC, V. Mon–Sat 9am–midnight.

MODERATE

Archie's Wok ☆☆☆ *Finds* ASIAN/SEAFOOD   Since 1986, Archie's has been legendary in Puerto Vallarta for serving original cuisine influenced by the intriguing flavors of Thailand, China, and the Philippines. Archie was Hollywood director John Huston's private chef during the years he spent in the area. Today his wife Cindy upholds his legacy at this tranquil retreat. The Thai mai tai and other tropical drinks, made from only fresh fruit and juices, are a good way to kick off a meal, as are the consistently crispy and delicious Filipino spring rolls. The popular Singapore fish filet features lightly battered filet strips in sweet-and-sour sauce; Thai garlic shrimp are prepared with fresh garlic, ginger, cilantro, and black pepper. Vegetarians have plenty of options, including broccoli, tofu, mushroom, and cashew stir-fry in black bean and sherry sauce. Finish with the signature Spice Islands coffee or a slice of lime cheese pie. Thursday through Saturday from 8 to 11pm, there's live classical harp and flute in Archie's Oriental garden.

Francisco Rodríguez 130 (½ block from the Los Muertos pier). ☎ **322/222-0411.** awok@pvnet.com.mx. Main courses $6–$21. AE, MC, V. Mon–Sat 2–11pm. Closed Sept–Oct.

Espresso ★★ ITALIAN   This popular eatery is Vallarta's best late-night dining option. The two-level restaurant is on one of the town's busiest streets—across from El Torito's sports bar, and cater-cornered from the lively Señor Frog's—meaning that traffic noise is a factor, though not a deterrent. The food is superb, the service attentive, and the prices more than reasonable. Owned by a partnership of lively Italians, it serves food that is authentic in preparation and flavor, from thin-crust, brick-oven pizzas to savory homemade pastas. My favorite pizza is the "Quattro Stagioni," topped with artichokes, black olives, ham, and mushrooms. Excellent calzones and panini (sandwiches) are also options. I prefer the rooftop garden area for dining, but many patrons gravitate to the pool table in the air-conditioned downstairs, which features major sports and entertainment events on satellite TV. Espresso also has full bar service and draft beer. Espresso is especially popular with *vallartenses* (locals).

Ignacio L. Vallarta 279. ✆ **322/222-3272**. Main courses $6.50–$13. AE, MC, V. Daily noon–4am.

La Palapa ★★ SEAFOOD/MEXICAN   This colorful, open-air, *palapa*-roofed restaurant on the beach is a decades-old local favorite, and with each recent visit, I have found the quality of both the food and service keeps improving. It's an exceptional dining experience, day or night. Enjoy a tropical breakfast by the sea, lunch on the beach, cocktails at sunset, or a romantic dinner (on a cloth-covered table in the sand). For lunch and dinner, seafood is the specialty; featured dishes include macadamia-and-coconut-crusted prawns, and poached red snapper with fresh cilantro sauce. Its location in the heart of Los Muertos Beach makes it an excellent place to start or end the day; I favor it for breakfast or, even better, a late-night sweet temptation and specialty coffee, while watching the moon over the bay. A particular draw is the all-you-can-eat Sunday brunch, which entitles you to a spot on popular Los Muertos beach for the day. A plus at lunch is you can enjoy the extra-comfortable beach chairs for postlunch sunbathing. A new classy bar area features acoustic guitars and vocals nightly from 8 to 11pm, generally performed by the owner, Alberto. La Palapa had a complete makeover in 2002 yet retained its charm and gracious service.

Pulpito 103. ✆ **322/222-5225**. Reservations recommended for dinner in high season. Breakfast $2.50–$12; main courses $7–$25; salad or sandwiches $5–$12. AE, MC, V. Daily 8am–11pm.

INEXPENSIVE

Café San Angel CAFE   This comfortable, classic sidewalk cafe is a local gathering place from sunrise to sunset. For breakfast, choose a burrito stuffed with eggs and *chorizo* sausage, a three-egg Western omelet, crepes filled with mushrooms, Mexican classics like *huevos rancheros* and *chilaquiles,* or a tropical fruit plate. Deli sandwiches, crepes, and pastries round out the small but ample menu. The cafe also serves exceptional fruit smoothies, like the Yelapa—a blend of mango, banana, and orange juice—and perfectly made espresso drinks. Note that the service is reliably slow and frequently frustrating, so choose this place if you have time on your side—and keep in mind that it offers the best people-watching in the area. Bar service and Internet access are available.

Olas Altas 449 (at Francisco Rodríguez). ℂ 322/223-1273. Breakfast $3.50–$6; main courses $3.50–$6. No credit cards. Daily 8am–1am.

Fajita Republic ☆☆ MEXICAN/SEAFOOD/STEAKS   Fajita Republic is consistently popular—and deservedly so. It has hit on a winning recipe: delicious food, ample portions, welcoming atmosphere, and low prices. The specialty is, of course, fajitas, grilled to perfection in every variety: steak, chicken, shrimp, combo, and vegetarian. All come with a generous tray of salsas and toppings. This "tropical grill" also serves sumptuous barbecued ribs, Mexican *molcajetes* with incredibly tender strips of marinated beef filet, and grilled shrimp. Starters include fresh guacamole served in a giant spoon and the ever-popular Maya cheese sticks (breaded and deep-fried). Try an oversize mug or pitcher of Fajita Rita Mango Margaritas—or another spirited temptation. This is a casual, fun, festive place in a garden of mango and palm trees. A new, second location in Nuevo Vallarta, across from the Grand Velas Resort is drawing equal raves, with the same menu and prices.

Pino Suárez 321 (at Basilio Badillo), 1 block north of Olas Altas. ℂ 322/222-3131. Breakfast $3.60–$4.70; main courses $9–$17. MC, V. Daily 9am–midnight.

Red Cabbage Café (El Repollo Rojo) ☆☆ *Finds* MEXICAN The tiny, hard-to-find cafe is worth the effort—a visit here will reward you with exceptional traditional Mexican cuisine and a whimsical crash course in contemporary culture. The small room is covered wall-to-wall and table-to-table with photographs, paintings, movie posters, and news clippings about the cultural icons of Mexico. Frida Kahlo figures prominently in the decor, and a special menu duplicates dishes she and husband Diego Rivera prepared for guests.

Specialties from all over Mexico include divine *chiles en nogada* (poblanos stuffed with ground beef, pine nuts, and raisins, topped with sweet cream sauce and served cold), intricate chicken *mole* from Puebla, and hearty *carne en su jugo* (steak in its juice). In addition, the vegetarian menu is probably the most diverse and tasty in town (the owner offers cooking classes for groups of four or more). This is not the place for an intimate conversation, however—the poor acoustics cause everyone's conversations to blend together, although generally what you're hearing from adjacent tables are raves about the food. Also, this is a nonsmoking restaurant—the only one I'm aware of in town.

Calle Rivera del Río 204A (across from Río Cuale). (*C*) 322/223-0411. Main courses $5–$20. No credit cards. Daily 5–10:30pm.

JUNGLE RESTAURANTS

One of the unique attractions of Puerto Vallarta is its "jungle restaurants," south of town toward Mismaloya. They offer open-air dining in a tropical setting by the sea or beside a mountain river. The many varieties of "jungle" and "tropical" tours (see "Organized Tours," in chapter 3) include a stop for swimming and lunch. If you travel on your own, a taxi is the best transportation—the restaurants are quite a distance from the main highway. Taxis are usually waiting for return patrons.

The most recommendable of the jungle restaurants is the ecologically sensitive **El Nogalito** (*C*)/fax 322/221-5225). Located beside a clear jungle stream, the exceptionally clean, beautifully landscaped ranch serves lunch, beverages, and snacks on a shady, relaxing terrace. Several hiking routes depart from the grounds, and the restaurant provides a guide (whom you tip) to point out the native plants, birds, and wildlife. It's much closer to town than the other jungle restaurants: To find it, travel to Punta Negra, about 8km (5 miles) south of downtown Puerto Vallarta. A well-marked sign points up Calzada del Cedro, a dirt road, to the ranch. It's open daily from noon to 5:30pm. No credit cards.

Just past Boca de Tomatlán, at Highway 200 Km 20, is **Chico's Paradise** (*C* 322/223-6005; chicosp@prodigy.net.mx). It offers spectacular views of massive rocks—some marked with petroglyphs—and the surrounding jungle and mountains. There are natural pools and waterfalls for swimming, plus a small *mercado* selling pricey trinkets. The menu features excellent seafood as well as Mexican dishes. The quality is quite good, and the portions are generous, although prices are higher than in town—remember, you're paying for the setting. Open daily from 10am to 6pm. No credit cards.

3

Exploring Puerto Vallarta & Beyond

by Lynne Bairstow

Beyond its cobblestone streets, graceful cathedral, and welcoming atmosphere, Puerto Vallarta offers a wealth of natural beauty and manufactured pleasures.

Ecotourism activities are gaining ground here—from mountain biking the Sierra foothills to whale-watching, ocean kayaking, and diving with giant mantas in Banderas Bay. Forty-two kilometers (26 miles) of beaches, many in pristine coves accessible only by boat, extend around the bay. High in the Sierra Madres, the mystical Huichol Indians still live in relative isolation in an effort to protect their centuries-old culture from outside influences.

Villages such as Rincon de Guayabitos, Barra de Navidad, and Melaque are laid-back and almost undiscovered. Starkly different from the spirited resort towns, they offer travelers a glimpse into local culture. Excursions to these smaller villages make easy day trips or extended stays.

1 Beaches, Activities & Excursions

Travel agencies can provide information on what to see and do in Puerto Vallarta and can arrange tours, fishing trips, and other activities. Most hotels have a tour desk on-site. Of the many travel agencies in town, I highly recommend **Tukari Servicios Turísticos,** Av. España 316 (© **322/224-7177;** fax 322/224-2350), which specializes in ecological and cultural tours. Another source is **Xplora Adventours** (© **322/223-0661**), in the Huichol Collection shop on the *malecón.* It has listings of all locally available tours, with photos, explanations, and costs. (A timeshare resort owns the company, though, so be prepared for them to invite you to a presentation, which you may decline.) **American Express Travel Services,** Morelos 660 (© **322/223-2955**), also has a varied selection of high-quality, popular tours. **Vallarta Adventures** ✸✸✸ (© **866/256-2739** toll-free in the U.S., or 322/297-1212, ext. 3; www.vallarta-adventures.com) has the largest and best selection of boat cruises and land tours. I can highly recommend any of their offerings. Book with them directly and get a 10% discount when you mention Frommer's.

THE BEACHES

For years, beaches were Puerto Vallarta's main attraction. Although visitors today are exploring more of the surrounding geography, the sands are still a powerful draw. Over 42km (26 miles) of beaches extend around the broad Bay of Banderas, ranging from action-packed party spots to secluded coves accessible only by boat.

IN TOWN   The easiest to reach is **Playa Los Muertos** (also known as Playa Olas Altas or Playa del Sol), just off Calle Olas Altas, south of the Río Cuale. The water can be rough, but the wide beach is home to a wide array of *palapa* restaurants that offer food, beverage, and beach-chair service. The most popular are the adjacent El Dorado and La Palapa, at the end of Pulpito Street. On the southern end of this beach is a section known as "Blue Chairs"—the most popular gay beach. Vendors stroll Los Muertos, and beach volleyball, parasailing, and jet-skiing are all popular pastimes. The **Hotel Zone** is also known for its broad, smooth beaches, accessible primarily through the hotel lobbies.

SOUTH OF TOWN   **Playa Mismaloya** is in a beautiful sheltered cove about 10km (6 miles) south of town along Highway 200. The water is clear and beautiful, ideal for snorkeling off the beach. Entrance to the public beach is just to the left of the **Jolla de Mismaloya All-Suites Resort** (© **322/226-0600**). The movie *Night of the Iguana* was filmed at Mismaloya, and the resort has a restaurant on the restored film set—**La Noche de la Iguana Set Restaurant,** open daily from noon to 11pm. The movie runs continuously in a room below the restaurant, and still photos from the filming hang in the restaurant. The restaurant is accessible by land on the point framing the south side of the cove. Just below the restaurant is **John Huston's Bar & Grill,** serving drinks and light snacks daily from 11am to 6pm.

The beach at **Boca de Tomatlán,** down the road, has numerous *palapa* restaurants where you can relax for the day—you buy drinks, snacks, or lunch, and you can use their chairs and *palapa* shade.

The two beaches are accessible by public buses, which depart from the corner of Basilio Badillo and Insurgentes every 15 minutes from 5:30am to 10pm and cost just 50¢.

Las Animas, Quimixto, and **Yelapa** beaches offer a true sense of seclusion; they are accessible only by boat (see "Getting Around," in chapter 2, for information about water-taxi service). They are larger than Mismaloya, offer intriguing hikes to jungle waterfalls, and are similarly set up, with restaurants fronting a wide beach. Overnight stays are available at Yelapa (see "Side Trips from Puerto Vallarta," later in this chapter).

NORTH OF TOWN   Marina Vallarta's beaches are the least desirable in the area, with darker sand and seasonal inflows of stones.

The entire northern coastline from Bucerías to Punta Mita is a succession of sandy coves alternating with rocky inlets. For years the beaches to the north, with their long, clean breaks, have been the favored locale for surfers. The broad, sandy stretches at **Playa Anclote, Playa Piedras Blancas,** and **Playa Destiladeras,** which all have *palapa* restaurants, have made them favorites with local residents looking for a quick getaway. At Playa Anclote you'll find a broad, sandy beach with protected swimming areas and a few great *palapa* (thatched roof) restaurants. Of the restaurants, El Anclote and El Dorado have been the long-standing favorites, but **Mañana,** by Chef Roger (© **329/291-6374**), is raising the culinary bar of this casual dining area. It's open Tuesday through Sunday 10am to 9pm, in summer 1 to 9pm. All have beach chairs available for your post-margarita nap in the sun.

You can also hire a *panga* (small motorized boat) at Playa Anclote, from the fisherman's cooperative on the beach, and have the captain take you to the **Marietas Islands** 🟊🟊🟊 offshore. These uninhabited islands are a great place for bird-watching, diving, snorkeling, or just exploring. Blue-footed booby birds (no joke) can be spotted all along the islands' rocky coast, and giant mantas, sea turtles, and colorful tropical fish swim among the coral cliffs. The islands are honeycombed with caves and hidden beaches—including the stunning Playa de Amor (beach of love) that only appears at low tide. You enter a shallow passageway to access this semicircular stretch of sand. There's also a cave 12m (40 ft.) below the surface with an air pocket where divers can dispose of their regulators and have an underwater conversation! Humpback whales congregate around these islands during the winter months, and *pangas* can be rented for a do-it-yourself whale-watching excursion. Trips cost about $20 per hour. You can also visit these islands aboard one of the numerous day cruises that depart from the cruise-ship terminal in Puerto Vallarta.

The stellar white-sand beach at **Punta Mita,** home of the Four Seasons, is closed to road access, except for guests of this residential resort development.

One option for visiting a north shore beach is to spend a day at the **Los Veneros Beach Club** (© **329/291-7082,** ext. 123 or 125, or 329/291-7085), 32km (20 miles) north of Puerto Vallarta, just past Destiladeras beach on the highway to Punta Mita. To get there, take a taxi or a public bus bound for Punta Mita. Two pools—one reserved for adults—and marble bathrooms with changing rooms and showers complement an exquisite beach. There's also a *palapa*-topped restaurant and bar, gym, kids' play area with water slides and splashes, and small shopping area. The entrance fee of $12 for adults, $8 for children includes towel service and the use of all the facilities for the day. Extra charges apply for food, drinks, horseback riding, or massage. It's open daily from 10am to 6pm.

ORGANIZED TOURS

BOAT TOURS   Puerto Vallarta offers a number of boat trips, including sunset cruises and snorkeling, swimming, and diving excursions. They generally travel one of two routes: to the **Marietas Islands,** a 30- to 45-minute boat ride off the northern shore of Banderas Bay, or to **Yelapa, Las Animas,** or **Quimixto** along the southern shore. The trips to the southern beaches make a stop at **Los Arcos,** an island rock formation south of Puerto Vallarta, for snorkeling. Don't base your opinion of underwater Puerto Vallarta on this, though—dozens of tour boats dump quantities of snorkelers overboard at the same time each day, so by now the fish know *not* to be there at that time. It is, however, an excellent site for night diving. When comparing boat cruises, note that some include lunch, while most provide music and an open bar on board. Most leave around 9:30am, stop for 45 minutes of snorkeling, and arrive at the beach destination around noon for a 2½-hour stay before returning around 3pm. At Quimixto and Yelapa, visitors can take a half-hour hike to a jungle waterfall or rent a horse for the ride. Prices range from $45 for a sunset cruise or a trip to one of the beaches with open bar, to $85 for an all-day outing with open bar and meals.

One boat, the *Marigalante* (© **322/223-0309;** www.marigalante. com.mx), is an exact replica of Columbus's ship the *Santa María,* built in honor of the 500th anniversary of his voyage to the Americas. It features a daytime "pirate's cruise" ($65 per person), complete with picnic barbecue and treasure hunt, and a sunset dinner cruise ($70 per person) with fireworks and dance music. Half-price for children ages 3 to 8.

One of the best trips is a day trip to **Caletas** 𝓕𝓕, the cove where John Huston made his home for years. **Vallarta Adventures** (🕾 **866/ 256-2739** toll-free in the U.S., or 322/297-1212, ext. 3; www.vallarta-adventures.com) holds the exclusive lease on the private cove and has done an excellent job of restoring Huston's former home, adding exceptional day-spa facilities and landscaping the beach, which is wonderful for snorkeling. They also have a colony of sea lions that play with the visiting divers! You'll have a hard time deciding whether to kayak, take a yoga class, hike through surrounding trails, or simply relax in the hammocks strung between palms on the beach. The facilities and relative privacy have made this excursion ($75 per person; $38 for children under 12) one of the most popular. The evening cruise includes dinner and a spectacular contemporary dance show, "Rhythms of the Night" (see "Puerto Vallarta After Dark," later in this chapter).

Travel agencies sell tickets and distribute information on all cruises. If you prefer to spend more time at Yelapa or Las Animas without snorkeling and cruise entertainment, see the information on travel by water taxis, in chapter 2, under "Getting Around."

Whale-watching tours become more popular each year. Viewing humpback whales is almost a certainty from mid- to late November to March. The majestic whales have migrated to this bay for centuries (in the 17th c. it was called "Humpback Bay") to bear their calves. The noted local authority is **Open Air Expeditions,** Guerrero 339 (🕾/fax **322/222-3310;** www.vallartawhales.com). It offers ecologically oriented, oceanologist-guided 4-hour tours on the soft boat *Prince of Whales,* the only boat in Vallarta specifically designed for whale-watching. Cost is $80, and travel is in a group of up to 12. Twice-daily departures (8:30am and 2:30pm) include a healthful snack. **Vallarta Adventures** (🕾 **866/256-2739** toll-free in the U.S., or 322/297-1212, ext. 3; www.vallarta-adventures.com) offers a variety of whale-watching excursions that may combine time for snorkeling, or focus on photographing these exquisite mammals. Prices range from $65 to $80, and offer a choice of boat, ranging from small boats to bring you closest for photos, to graceful sailboats. All trips include a predeparture briefing on whale behaviors.

LAND TOURS **Tukari Servicios Turísticos** (see "Beaches, Activities & Excursions," above) can arrange trips to the fertile birding grounds near **San Blas,** 3 to 4 hours north of Puerto Vallarta in the state of Nayarit, and shopping trips to **Tlaquepaque** and **Tonalá** (6 hr. inland, near Guadalajara). A day trip to **Rancho Altamira,** a

20-hectare (50-acre) working ranch, includes a barbecue lunch and horseback riding, then a stroll through **El Tuito,** a small nearby colonial-era village. The company can also arrange an unforgettable morning at **Terra Noble Art & Healing Center** 🌟🌟 (🕾 **322/223-3530** or 322/222-5400), a mountaintop day spa and center for the arts where participants can get a massage, *temazcal* (ancient, indigenous sweat lodge), or treatment, work in clay and paint, and have lunch in a heavenly setting overlooking the bay. Call ahead for reservations, and make sure to advise if you want to have lunch there.

Hotel travel desks and travel agencies, including Tukari and American Express, can also book the popular **Tropical Tour** or **Jungle Tour** ($25), a basic orientation to the area. These excursions are expanded city tours that include a drive through the workers' village of Pitillal, the affluent neighborhood of Conchas Chinas, the cathedral, the market, the Taylor-Burton houses, and lunch at a jungle restaurant. Any stop for shopping usually means the driver picks up a commission for what you buy.

The **Jeep Safari** is another excellent tour offered by **Vallarta Adventures** (🕾 **866/256-2739** toll-free in the U.S., or 322/297-1212, ext. 3; www.vallarta-adventures.com). The daily excursion travels in Mercedes all-terrain vehicles north of Puerto Vallarta through jungle trails, stops at a small town, ventures into a forest for a nature walk, and winds up on a pristine secluded beach for lunch and swimming. The $75 outing is worthwhile because it takes tourists on exclusive trails into scenery that would otherwise be off-limits.

AIR TOURS   Speaking of off-limits, you can explore some of the most remote and undiscovered reaches of the Sierra Madres in Vallarta Adventures' **San Sebastián Air Expedition** (🕾 **866/256-2739** toll-free in the U.S., or 322/297-1212, ext. 3; www.vallarta-adventures. com). A 15-minute flight aboard a 14-seat turbo-prop Cessna Caravan takes you into the heart of the Sierra Madre. The plane is equipped with raised wings, which allow you to admire—and photograph—the mountain scenery. The plane arrives on a gravel landing strip in the old mining town of San Sebastián, a beautiful village that dates from 1603. One of the oldest mining towns in Mexico, it reached its prosperous peak in the 1800s, with over 30,000 inhabitants. Today, San Sebastián remains an outstanding example of how people lived and worked in a remote Mexican mountain town—it's a living museum. The half-day adventure costs $130, which covers the flight, a walking tour of the town (including a stop at the old Hacienda Jalisco, a favored getaway of John Huston, Liz and Dick, and their friends), and brunch in town. Other excursions include overnight stays and return trips by bike or horseback. There's also a **Jeep tour** to San Sebastián, which costs $75 per person, for up to four people per jeep, and includes a guide. This tour departs at 9am and returns at 5pm. Call Pacific Travel (© **322/225-2270**) to make reservations.

Vallarta Adventures (© **866/256-2739** toll-free in the U.S., or 322/297-1212, ext. 3; www.vallarta-adventures.com) also offers a similar—yet different—air tour to the mountain villages of **Mascota** and **Talpa de Allende** *◈◈*, where you'll learn about the religious significance of these traditional towns. In Mascota, stroll the cobblestone streets lined with adobe houses and colonial haciendas, stopping at the majestic town church, dedicated to the Virgin de los Dolores (Virgin of Sorrows), which was completed in 1880 and took over 100 years to construct. You'll stop for lunch and tour a local raicilla distillery to sample this locally popular beverage before traveling on to Talpa. Talpa is known for being home to one of Mexico's most revered icons, the Virgin Rosario de Talpa, believed to grant miracles with her healing powers. Ask for one yourself, as you visit the Gothic church that bears her name, or simply wander around this pastoral village, set in a valley that is surrounded by pine-covered mountains. The 6-hour adventure includes airfare and lunch, for $140 per person. Departures are daily, except Wednesdays and Sundays, at 10:30am, from Aerotron.

Anyone up for a taste of Tequila? We're talking about the town, and a sampling of the best of the spirit of Mexico. Vallarta Adventures (see above) offers a trip that takes you to the classic town, where you visit one of the original haciendas and tequila (agave) fields. A comfortable 35-minute flight aboard a private 16-passenger plane takes you to the town of **Tequila.** This is the only region in the world where the legendary spirit is distilled. The visit centers around Herradura Tequila's impressive 18th-century Hacienda San José, where you learn about the myth and the tradition of producing tequila from the stately plants that line the hillsides of the town. From Tequila, you'll travel by plane on to Guadalajara, one of Mexico's largest cities, with a rich colonial heritage, for some time to shop at the world-renown markets of Tlaquepaque. Departures are every Thursday at 10am from the Aerotron private airport (adjacent to the Puerto Vallarta International Airport); the group returns to Puerto Vallarta by 8pm. Cost is $290, which includes all air and ground transportation, tours, lunch, and beverages.

Vallarta Adventures also offers air tours to remote mountain villages where the **Huichol Indians** live, as well as to the **Copper Canyon,** and the mystical village of **Mexcaltitan,** all departing from Puerto Vallarta. Details and online booking options are available at www.vallarta-adventures.com.

TOURS IN TOWN   Every Wednesday and Thursday in high season (late Nov to Easter), the **International Friendship Club (© 322/ 222-5466)** offers a **private home tour** of four villas in town. It costs $30 per person, with proceeds donated to local charities. Arrive early, because this tour sells out quickly. It starts at the Hotel Molino de Agua, Av. Ignacio L. Vallarta 130, adjacent to the southbound bridge over the Río Cuale. Get there at 10am, and you can buy breakfast while you wait for the group to gather. The tour departs at 11am and lasts approximately 2½ hours.

You can also tour the **Taylor/Burton villas** (Casa Kimberley; **© 322/222-1336**), at Calle Zaragoza 445. Tours of the two houses owned by Elizabeth Taylor and Richard Burton cost $8. Call ahead daily between 9am and 6pm, and if the manager is available, he will take you through the house.

STAYING ACTIVE

DIVING   Underwater enthusiasts from beginner to expert can arrange scuba diving through **Vallarta Adventures (© 866/256-2739** toll-free in the U.S., or 322/297-1212, ext. 3; www.vallarta-adventures.com), a five-star PADI dive center. Dives take place at Los Arcos, a company-owned site at Caletas Cove (where you'll dive in the company of sea lions!), Quimixto Coves, the Marietas Islands, or the offshore La Corbeteña, Morro, and Chimo reefs. The company also offers a full range of certification courses (through Instructor). **Chico's Dive Shop,** Díaz Ordaz 772–5, near Carlos O'Brian's **(© 322/222-1895;** www.chicos-diveshop.com), offers similar dive trips and is also a PADI five-star dive center. Chico's is open daily from 8am to 10pm and has branches at the Marriott, Las Palmas, Holiday Inn, Fiesta Americana, Krystal, San Marino, Villa del Palmar, Paradise Village, and Playa Los Arcos hotels.

ECOTOURS & ACTIVITIES   **Open Air Expeditions** (©/fax **322/222-3310;** www.vallartawhales.com) offers nature-oriented trips, including birding and ocean kayaking in Punta Mita. **Ecotours de México,** Ignacio L. Vallarta 243 (©/fax **322/222-6606**), has eco-oriented tours, including seasonal (Aug–Nov) trips to a turtle preservation camp where you can witness hatching baby Olive Ridley turtles.

Vallarta's newest adventure activity is **Canopy Tours.** You glide from treetop to treetop, getting an up-close-and-personal look at a tropical rainforest canopy and the trails far below. Expert guides assist you to the special platforms, and you move from one to another using pulleys on horizontal traverse cables, while the guides explain the tropical flora surrounding you. They also offer assistance—and moral support!—as you rappel back down to the forest floor. Tours depart from the **Vallarta Adventures** (© 866/256-2739 toll-free in the U.S., or 322/297-1212, ext. 3; www.vallarta-adventures.com) offices in both Marina Vallarta and Nuevo Vallarta at 8am, returning at 2pm. The price ($65 for adults, $33 for children 8–12) includes the tour, unlimited nonalcoholic beverages, and light snacks.

Canopy Tours de Los Veranos (© 322/223-6060; www.canopy tours-vallarta.com) run through the southern jungles of Vallarta, over the Orquidias River. This tour will pick you up at the Canopy office, near the south side Pemex station, and transport you to their facilities upriver from Mismaloya. Departures are at 9, 10, and 11am, noon, and 1 and 2pm. In addition to the 13 cables—the longest being a full 350m (115 ft.)—it also offers climbing walls, waterslides, and horseback riding. The guides here are noted for helping even the faint of heart propel through the treetops. Price is $80 for adults, or $46 for children. Use of the natural-granite climbing wall (helmets and climbing shoe use included) is $18; the 1½-hour jungle horseback riding tour is $35.

FISHING   Arrange fishing trips through travel agencies or through the **Cooperativa de Pescadores (Fishing Cooperative),** on the *malecón* north of the Río Cuale, next door to the Rosita Hotel (© 322/222-1202 or 322/224-7886). Fishing charters cost $90, for one to eight people; or select from other options where the price varies with the size of the boat. Although the posted price at the fishing cooperative is the same as you'll find through travel agencies, you may be able to negotiate a lower price at the cooperative, which does not accept credit cards. It's open Monday through Saturday from 7am to 10pm, but make arrangements a day ahead. You can also arrange fishing trips at the Marina Vallarta docks, or by calling **Fishing with Carolina** (© 322/224-7250; cell 044-322/292-2953; fishingwithcarolina@hotmail.com), which uses a 9m (30-ft.) Uniflite sportsfisher, fully equipped with an English-speaking crew. Fishing trips cost $350 for up to six people and include equipment and bait, but drinks, snacks, and lunch are optional, at $10 per person. If you mention Frommer's when you make your reservation, they'll offer a free lunch with your booking.

GOLF   Puerto Vallarta is an increasingly popular golf destination; five courses have opened in the past 4 years, bringing the total in the region to nine. The Joe Finger–designed private course at the **Marina Vallarta Golf Club** (© 322/221-0073) is an 18-hole, par-74 course that winds through the Marina Vallarta peninsula and affords ocean views. It's for members only, but most luxury hotels in Puerto Vallarta have memberships for their guests. Greens fees are $136 in high season, $115 in low season. Fees include golf cart, range balls, and tax. Hiring a caddy costs $8 to $10. Club rentals, lessons, and special packages are available.

North of town in the state of Nayarit, about 16km (10 miles) beyond Puerto Vallarta, is the 18-hole, par-72 **Los Flamingos Club de Golf** (© 329/296-5006). It features beautiful jungle vegetation and has just undergone a renovation and upgrade of the course. It's open from 7am to 5pm daily, with a snack bar (but no restaurant) and full pro shop. The greens fee is $95 and includes the use of a golf cart; hiring a caddy costs $12 plus tip, and club rental is $27 to $44. A free shuttle runs from downtown Puerto Vallarta; call for pickup times and locations.

The breathtaking Jack Nicklaus Signature course at the **Four Seasons Punta Mita** ✦✦✦ (© 329/291-6000; fax 329/291-6060) has 8 oceanfront holes and an ocean view from every hole. Its hallmark is the optional Hole 3B, the "Tail of the Whale," with a long drive to the only natural-island green in the Americas. It requires an amphibious cart to take you over when the tide is high, and there's an alternate hole for when the ocean or tides are not accommodating. It's open only to guests of the Four Seasons resort or to members of other golf clubs with a letter of introduction from their pro. Selected other area hotels also have guest privileges—ask your concierge. Greens fees for nonguests are $260, including cart, with (Calloway) club rentals for $60. Lessons are also available.

The **Vista Vallarta Golf Club** (© 322/290-0030) has a second Jack Nicklaus course, along with one designed by Tom Weiskopf. These courses, in the foothills of the Sierra Madre, behind the bull-ring in Puerto Vallarta, were the site of the 2002 PGA World Cup Golf Championship. A round is $167 per person, including cart.

The Robert von Hagge–designed **El Tigre** course at Paradise Village (© 322/297-0773; www.paradisevillage.com), in Nuevo Vallarta, opened in March 2002. The 7,239-yard course is on a relatively flat piece of land, but the design incorporates challenging bunkers, undulating fairways, and water features on several holes. El Tigre also offers lessons and has an expansive clubhouse. This seems to be the favored course of local pros. Greens fees are $185 a round, or $85 if you play after 2pm.

HORSEBACK-RIDING TOURS   Travel agents and local ranches can arrange guided horseback rides. **Rancho Palma Real,** Carretera Vallarta, Tepic 4766 (© 322/222-0501), has an office 5 minutes north of the airport; the ranch is in Las Palmas, approximately 40 minutes northeast of Vallarta. It is by far the nicest horseback-riding tour in the area. The horses are in excellent condition, and you enjoy a tour of local farms on your way to the ranch. The price ($62; American Express only) includes breakfast and lunch.

Another excellent option is **Rancho El Charro,** Av. Francisco Villa 895 (© 322/224-0114; cell 322/294-1689; www.ranchoelcharro. com), which has beautiful well-cared for horses, and a variety of rides for all levels, departing from their ranch at the base of the Sierra Madres. Rides range in length from 3 hours to 8 hours, and in price from $47 to $100. There's even the $60 Wild Ride, where you gallop along a ridge to a jungle waterfall—too often, riders are disappointed with only trotting along well-marked trails on these excursions, and this ride allows experienced riders much more freedom. Rancho El Charro also has multiple-day rides; check their website for details. **Rancho Ojo de Agua,** Cerrada de Cardenal 227, Fracc. Las Aralias (©/fax 322/224-0607), also offers high-quality tours, from its ranch located 10 minutes by taxi north of downtown toward the Sierra Madre foothills. The morning and sunset rides last 3 hours and take you up into the mountains overlooking the ocean and town. The cost is $52. Both of the ranches listed above have their own comfortable base camp for serious riders who want to stay out overnight.

SAILING   The newest addition to Vallarta's sailing scene is most impressive—**Coming About** 🎐🎐 (© 322/222-4119; www.coming-about.com) is a women-only sailing school that provides hands-on sailing instruction for day-sailing excursions, as well as week-long sailing classes at a variety of skill levels. Owned and operated by Pat Henry, who spent 8 years sailing around the globe, then wrote about it in her book *By the Grace of the Sea: A Woman's Solo Odyssey Around* *the World,* the classes are challenging, inspiring, and entertaining, as Pat shares her adventures with participants. Dubbed "any woman's sailing school," the goal is to take away the fear and the mystery, and make the skill of sailing accessible to everyone. Courses range from a 1-day introductory course to a 9-day bareboat charter captain course. Fees are $475 for four people for the 1-day course, $2,800 to $3,600 for the 9-day course, including hotel.

Vallarta Adventures (© **866/256-2739** toll-free in the U.S., or 322/297-1212, ext. 3; www.vallarta-adventures.com) offers two beautiful sailboats for charter or small-group sails (up to 12 people). Daytime sailing charters are priced at $80 per person; sunset sails are $60 per person. The service is superb, as is the quality of the food and beverages, making it, in my opinion, one of the very best ways to spend a Vallarta evening. These are known as the boats that are most frequently under sail—many other sailing charters prefer to motor around the bay.

SWIMMING WITH DOLPHINS   Ever been kissed by a dolphin? Take advantage of a unique opportunity to swim with Pacific bottlenose dolphins in one of two facilities—a clear lagoon or a special swim facility that's part of the Vallarta Adventures offices. **Dolphin Adventure** (© **866/256-2739** toll-free in the U.S., or 322/297-1212, ext. 3; www.vallarta-adventures.com) operates an interactive dolphin-research facility—considered the finest in Latin America—that allows limited numbers of people to swim with dolphins Monday through Saturday at scheduled times. Cost for the swim is $145. Reservations are required, and they generally sell out at least a week in advance. You may prefer the **Dolphin Encounter** ($60), which allows you to touch and learn about the dolphins in smaller pools, so you're ensured up-close-and-personal time with them. You can even be a **Trainer for a Day,** a special 7-hour program of working alongside the more experienced trainers and the dolphins, for a cost of $250. The new **Dolphin Kids** program, for children ages 4 to 8, is a gentle introduction to dolphins, featuring the Dolphin Adventure baby dolphins and their mothers interacting with

---

Tips A Spectator Sport

Bullfights are held December through April beginning at 5pm on Wednesday at the La Paloma bullring, across the highway from the town pier. Travel agencies can arrange tickets, which cost around $25.

the children participants ($60). I give this my highest recommendation. Not only does the experience leave you with an indescribable sensation, but it's also a joy to see these dolphins—they are well cared for, happy, and spirited. The program is about education and interaction, not entertainment or amusement, and is especially popular with children ages 10 and older.

TENNIS   Many hotels in Puerto Vallarta offer excellent tennis facilities; they often have clay courts. The full-service **Canto del Sol Tennis Club** (© **322/224-0123**) is at the Canto del Sol hotel in the Hotel Zone. It offers indoor and outdoor courts (including a clay court), full pro shop, lessons, clinics, and partner matches.

PARASAILING   Parasailing and other watersports are available at many beaches along the Bay of Banderas. The most popular spot is at Los Muertos Beach. WaveRunners, banana boats, and parasailing are available by the hour, half day, or full day. Be forewarned, however, that the swiftly shifting winds in Banderas Bay can make this a dangerous proposition. Fly at your own risk!

A STROLL THROUGH TOWN

Puerto Vallarta's cobblestone streets are a pleasure to explore; they're full of tiny shops, rows of windows edged with curling wrought iron, and vistas of red-tile roofs and the sea. Start with a walk up and down the *malecón*.

Among the sights you shouldn't miss is the **municipal building** on the main square (next to the tourism office), which has a large Manuel Lepe mural inside in its stairwell. Nearby, right up Independencia, sits the picturesque **Parish of Nuestra Señora de Guadalupe church,** Hidalgo 370 (© **322/222-1326**), topped with a curious crown held in place by angels—a replica of the one worn by Empress Carlota during her brief time in Mexico as Emperor Maximilian's wife. On its steps, women sell religious mementos; across the narrow street, stalls sell native herbs for curing common ailments. Services in English are held each Saturday at 5pm, and Sunday at 10am. Regular hours are Monday through Saturday from 7:30am to 8:30pm, Sunday from 6:30am to 8:30pm. Note that entrance is restricted to those properly attired—no shorts or sleeveless shirts allowed. Three blocks south of the church, head east on Libertad, lined with small shops and pretty upper windows, to the **municipal market** by the river. (It's the Río Cuale Mercado, but I recently overheard a tourist ask for the "real quality" market!) After exploring the market, cross the bridge to the island in the river; sometimes a painter is at work on its banks. Walk down the center

<hr>

Tips **A Spectacular Sight**

Performances of the **Papantla Flyers (Voladores de Papantla),** take place every Saturday and Sunday night at 6, 6:30, 8, 8:30, 9 and 10pm, on the *malecón,* adjacent to the "Boy on a Sea-horse" statue. In this pre-Columbian religious ritual four men are suspended from the top of a tall pole, circling around it (as if in flight), while another beats a drum and plays a flute while balancing himself at the top. It signifies the four cardinal points, and the mystic "center" of the self, a sacred direction for ancient Mexican cultures.

<hr>

of the island toward the sea, and you'll come to the tiny **Museo Río Cuale** (no phone; Mon–Sat 10am–4pm; free admission), which has a small but impressive permanent exhibit of pre-Columbian figurines.

Retrace your steps to the market and Libertad, and follow Calle Miramar to the brightly colored steps up to Zaragoza. Midway is a magnificent view over rooftops to the sea, plus a cute cafe, **Graffiti** (no phone), where you can break for a cappuccino and a snack. Up Zaragoza to the right 1 block is the famous **pink arched bridge** that once connected Richard Burton and Elizabeth Taylor's houses. In this area, known as **"Gringo Gulch,"** many Americans have houses.

2 Shopping

Shopping in Puerto Vallarta is generally concentrated in small, eclectic, independent shops rather than impersonal malls. You can find excellent **folk art,** original **clothing** designs, fine jewelry, and creative home accessories at great prices. Vallarta is known for having the most diverse and impressive selection of **contemporary Mexican fine art** outside Mexico City. It also has an abundance of tacky T-shirts and the ubiquitous **silver jewelry.**

THE SHOPPING SCENE

There are a few key shopping areas: central downtown, the Marina Vallarta *malecón,* the popular *mercados,* and on the beach—where the merchandise comes to you. Some of the more attractive shops are 1 to 2 blocks in **back of the *malecón.*** Start at the intersection of Corona and Morelos streets—interesting shops spread out in all directions from here. **Marina Vallarta** has two shopping plazas, Plaza Marina and Neptuno Plaza, on the main highway from the airport into town, which offer a limited selection of shops, with

Plaza Neptuno primarily featuring home decor shops. Although still home to a few interesting shops, the marina boardwalk *(marina malecón)* is dominated by real estate companies, timeshare vendors, restaurants, and boating services.

Puerto Vallarta's **municipal market** is just north of the Río Cuale, where Libertad and A. Rodríguez meet. The *mercado* sells clothes, jewelry, serapes, shawls, leather accessories and suitcases, papier-mâché parrots, stuffed frogs and armadillos, and, of course, T-shirts. Be sure to comparison-shop and dicker before buying. The market is open daily from 9am to 7pm. Upstairs, a **food market** serves inexpensive Mexican meals—for more adventurous diners, it's probably the best value and most authentic dining experience in Vallarta. An **outdoor market** is along Río Cuale Island, between the two bridges. Stalls sell crafts, gifts, folk art, and clothing. New to downtown is the **Small Vallarta** (© **322/222-7530**) on Paseo Díaz Ordaz 928, on the eastern side, just before the start of the *malecón*. It is a "small mall" with tourist-friendly shops and dining options, including Carl Junior's burgers, Häagen-Dazs ice cream, Swatch watch shop, El Mundo de Tequila, and a Diamonds International jewelry store.

Along any public beach, walking **vendors** will probably approach you. Their merchandise ranges from silver jewelry to rugs and T-shirts to masks. "Almost free!" they'll call out. If you're too relaxed to think of shopping in town, this can be an entertaining alternative for picking up souvenirs, and remember: Bargaining is expected. The most reputable beach vendors concentrate at Los Muertos Beach in front of the El Dorado and La Palapa restaurants (on Calle Pulpito).

In most of the better shops and galleries, shipping, packing, and delivery to Puerto Vallarta hotels are available. Some will also ship to your home address. Note that while bargaining is expected in the *mercados* and with beach vendors, stores generally charge fixed—and fair—prices for their wares.

Tips Beware the Silver Scam

Much of the silver sold on the beach is actually alpaca, a lower-quality silver metal (even though many pieces are stamped with the designation ".925," supposedly indicating true silver). Prices for silver on the beach are much lower, as is the quality. If you're looking for a more lasting piece of jewelry, you're better off in a silver shop.

Downtown Puerto Vallarta

ATTRACTIONS ●

Gringo Gulch
(neighborhood) **18**
Isla del Río Cuale **20**
Main Square **11**
Parish of Nuestra Señora
de Guadalupe **12**
Terra Noble Center
for the Arts **1**

ACCOMMODATIONS ■

Hacienda San Angel **13**
Hotel Molino de Agua **21**
Hotel Playa Los Arcos **26**

RESTAURANTS ◆

Adobe Grill **8**
Archie's Wok **28**
Arrayán **3**
Barcelona Tapas **2**
Bianca **22**
Café des Artistes **6**
Café Kaiser Maximilian **26**
Café San Angel **27**
Daiquiri Dick's **24**
de Santos **4**
Espresso **23**
Fajita Republic **25**
Kit-Kat **30**

La Esquina
de los Caprichos **15**
La Palapa **29**
La Taberna de
San Pascual **10**
Las Palomas **7**
Le Bistro **19**
Planeta Vegetariano **14**
Red Cabbage Café **31**
Rito's Baci **5**
Trío **17**
Xitomates **9**
Vitea **16**

THE LOWDOWN ON HUICHOL INDIAN ART

Puerto Vallarta has Mexico's best selection of Huichol art. The Huichol, descendants of the Aztec, are one of the world's last remaining indigenous cultures to remain true to ancient traditions, customs, language, and habitat. The Huichol live in adobe structures in the high Sierras (at an elevation of 1,394m/4,600 ft.) north and east of Puerto Vallarta. Due to the decreasing fertility (and therefore productivity) of the land surrounding their villages, they have come to depend more on the sale of their artwork for sustenance.

Huichol art has always been cloaked in a veil of mysticism— probably one of the reasons serious collectors seek out this form of *artesanía*. Colorful, symbolic yarn "paintings," inspired by visions experienced during spiritual ceremonies, characterize Huichol art. In the ceremonies, artists ingest peyote, a hallucinogenic cactus, which induces brightly colored visions; these are considered messages from their ancestors. The visions' symbolic and mythological imagery influences the art, which encompasses not only yarn paintings but also fascinating masks and bowls decorated with tiny colored beads.

The Huichol might be geographically isolated, but are learning the importance of good business, and have adapted their art to meet consumer demand. Original Huichol art, therefore, is not necessarily traditional. Iguanas, jaguars, sea turtles, frogs, eclipses, and eggs appear in response to consumer demand. For more traditional works, look for pieces that depict deer, scorpions, wolves, or snakes.

The Huichol have also had to modify their techniques to create more pieces in less time and meet increased demand. Patterned fill-work, which is faster to produce, sometimes replaces the detailed designs that used to fill the pieces. The same principle applies to yarn paintings. While some are beautiful depictions of landscapes and even abstract pieces, they are not traditional themes.

You may see Huichol Indians on the streets of Vallarta—they are easy to spot, dressed in white clothing embroidered with colorful designs. A number of fine Huichol galleries are in downtown Puerto Vallarta (see individual listings under "Crafts & Gifts" and "Decorative & Folk Art," below).

One place to learn more about them is **Huichol Collection,** Morelos 490, across from the sea-horse statue on the *malecón* (© **322/ 223-2141**). This shop offers an extensive selection of Huichol art in all price ranges, as well as a replica of a Huichol adobe hut, informational displays explaining more about their fascinating way of life and beliefs, and usually a Huichol artist at work. However, note that

Fun Fact **A Huichol Art Primer: Shopping Tips**

Huichol art falls into two main categories: yarn paintings and beaded pieces. All other items you might find in Huichol art galleries are either ceremonial objects or items used in everyday life.

Yarn paintings are made on a wood base covered with wax and meticulously overlaid with colored yarn. Designs represent the magical vision of the underworld, and each symbol gives meaning to the piece. Paintings made with wool yarn are more authentic than those made with acrylic; however, acrylic yarn paintings are usually brighter and have more detail because the threads are thinner. It is normal to find empty spaces where the wax base shows. Usually the artist starts with a central motif and works around it, but it's common to have several independent motifs that, when combined, take on a different meaning. A painting with many small designs tells a more complicated story than one with only one design and fill-work on the background. Look for the story of the piece on the back of the painting. Most Huichol artists write in pencil in Huichol and Spanish.

Beaded pieces are made on carved wooden shapes depicting different animals, wooden eggs, or small bowls made from gourds. The pieces are covered with wax, and tiny *chaquira* beads are applied one by one to form designs. Usually the beaded designs represent animals; plants; the elements of fire, water, or air; and certain symbols that give a special meaning to the whole. Deer, snakes, wolves, and scorpions are traditional elements; other figures, such as iguanas, frogs, and any animals not indigenous to Huichol territory are incorporated by popular demand. Beadwork with many small designs that do not exactly fit into one another is more time-consuming and has a more complex symbolic meaning. This kind of work has empty spaces where the wax shows.

this is a timeshare sales location, so don't be surprised if you're hit with a pitch for a "free" breakfast and property tour.

CLOTHING

Vallarta's single true department store is **LANS,** with branches at Juárez 867 (② **322/226-9100;** www.lans.com.mx), and in Plaza Caracol, next door to the supermarket Gigante, in the Hotel Zone (② **322/226-0204**). Both offer a wide selection of name-brand clothing, accessories, footwear, cosmetics, and furnishings. Along with the nationally popular **LOB, Carlos 'n' Charlie's,** and **Bye-Bye** brands, Vallarta offers original designs.

de Santos Boutique   Hip and sultry fashions, direct from South America are the specialties of this small but well-stocked boutique. It's open Monday to Saturday 11am to 9:30pm. Morelos 771, adjacent to the de Santos Club and restaurant. ② **322/223-5326** or 322/223-3052.

Laura López Labra Designs   The most comfortable clothing you'll ever enjoy. LLL is renowned for her trademark all-white (or natural) designs in 100% cotton or lace. Laura's fine gauze fabrics float in her designs of seductive skirts, romantic dresses, blouses, beachwear, and baby dolls. Men's offerings include cotton drawstring pants and lightweight shirts. Other designs include a line of precious children's clothing and some pieces with elaborate embroidery based on Huichol Indian designs. Personalized wedding dresses are also available. Open Monday through Saturday from 10am to 3:30pm; Fridays and Saturdays also from 5 to 9pm. Basilio Badillo 329. ② **322/222-3074.**

Mar de Sueños ⭐⭐   This small shop carries stunning swimsuits and exquisite lingerie. Without a doubt, it's the best place in Vallarta for fine women's beachwear, intimate apparel, and evening wear. The shop also stocks a selection of fine linen clothing—and it's one of the few places in Mexico that carries the renowned Italian line La Perla. Other name brands include Gottex, D&G, and DKNY. Open Monday through Saturday from 10am to 2pm and 5 to 9pm. Leona Vicario 220-C. ② **322/222-2662.**

CONTEMPORARY ART

Known for sustaining one of the stronger art communities in Latin America, Puerto Vallarta has an impressive selection of fine galleries featuring quality original works. Several dozen galleries get together to offer art walks almost every week between November and April.

Corsica   Among the newest and best of Vallarta's galleries, Corsica features an exquisite collection of sculptures, installations, and paintings from world-renown contemporary artists from Mexico.

They offer professional packing and worldwide shipping with purchases. There are three locations—all within a few blocks of one another—at Guadalupe Sanchez 735, Leona Vicario 230, and Pipila 268. Open Monday through Saturday 11am to 2pm, and by appointment 5 to 11pm. ℂ **322/223-1821** or 322/222-9260. www.galeriacorsica.com.

Galería AL (Arte Latinoamericano)   This gallery showcases contemporary works created by young, primarily Latin American artists, as well as Vallarta favorite Marta Gilbert. Feature exhibitions take place every 2 weeks during high season. The historic building (one of Vallarta's original structures) has exposed brick walls; small rooms of exhibition spaces on the second and third floors surround an open courtyard. It's also rumored to have a friendly resident ghost, who partner Susan Burger says has been quite welcoming. Open Monday through Saturday from 10:30am to 9pm. Josefa Ortiz Domínguez 155. ℂ/fax **322/222-4406**.

Galería des Artistes   This stunning gallery features contemporary painters and sculptors from throughout Mexico, including the renowned original "magiscopes" of Feliciano Bejar. Paintings by Vallarta favorite Evelyn Boren, as well as a small selection of works by Mexican masters, including Diego Rivera and Orozco, can be found here, among the exposed brick walls and stylish interior spaces. It's open Monday to Saturday 11am to 10pm. Leona Vicario 248; ℂ **322/223-0006**.

Galleria Omar Alonso   Across the street from Galería des Artistes, Galería Omar Alonso exhibits photography by internationally renowned artists. Leona Vicario 249. ℂ **322/222-5587**. www.galeriaomaralonso.com.

Galería Pacífico   Since opening in 1987, Galería Pacífico has been considered one of the finest in Mexico. On display is a wide selection of sculptures and paintings in various media by midrange masters and up-and-comers alike. The gallery is 1½ blocks inland from the fantasy sculptures on the *malecón.* Among the artists whose careers Galería Pacífico has influenced are rising talents Rogelio Diaz and Brewster Brockman, internationally renowned sculptor Ramiz Barquet, and Patrick Denoun. Open Monday through Saturday from 10am to 8pm, Sunday by appointment. Between May and October, check for reduced hours or vacation closings. Aldama 174, 2nd floor. ℂ **322/222-1982**. Fax 322/222-5502. galeriapacifico@prodigy.net.mx.

Galería Uno   One of Vallarta's first galleries, the Galería Uno features an excellent selection of contemporary paintings by Latin American artists, plus a variety of posters and prints. During high season, exhibitions change every 2 weeks. In a classic adobe building with open courtyard, it's also a casual, *salón*-style gathering place for friends of owner Jan Lavender. Open Monday through Saturday from 10am to 10pm. A branch, **Arte de las Américas** (© 322/221-1985), is at Marina Vallarta between La Taberna and the Yacht Club. It exhibits some of the same artists but has a decidedly more abstract orientation. It's open Monday through Saturday from 10am to 2pm and 5 to 9pm. Morelos 561 (at Corona). © 322/222-0908.

Galleria Dante   This gallery-in-a-villa showcases contemporary art as well as sculptures and classical reproductions of Italian, Greek, and Art Deco bronzes—against a backdrop of gardens and fountains. Located on the "Calle de los cafés," the gallery is open during the winter Monday through Saturday from 10am to 5pm, and by appointment. Basilio Badillo 269. © 322/222-2477. Fax 322/222-6284. www. galleriadante.com.

Studio Cathy Von Rohr   This lovely studio showcases the work of Cathy Von Rohr, one of the most respected artists in the area. For years, Cathy lived in the secluded cove of Majahuitas, on the bay's southern shore, and much of her work reflects the tranquillity and deep connection with the natural world that resulted. Paintings, prints, and sculptures are featured. It's open by appointment and does not accept credit cards. Manuel M. Diéguez 321. © 866/256-2739 toll-free in the U.S., or 322/222-5875. www.cathyvonrohr.com.

CRAFTS & GIFTS

Alfarería Tlaquepaque   Opened in 1953, this is Vallarta's original source for Mexican ceramics and decorative crafts, all at excellent prices. Talavera pottery and dishware, colored glassware, birdcages, baskets, and wood furniture are just a few of the many items in this warehouse-style store. Open Monday through Saturday, 9am to 9pm, and Sundays from 9am to 3pm. Av. México 1100. © 322/223-2121.

La Casa del Feng Shui   I am enchanted by this shop's selection of crystals, candles, talismans, fountains, and wind chimes—along with many more items designed to keep the good energy flowing in your home, office, or personal space. Why not take home something to add more harmony to your life? Open Monday through Saturday, 10am to 7pm. Corona 165, around the corner from Morelos. © 322/222-3300.

Safari Accents   Flickering candles glowing in colored-glass holders welcome you to this highly original shop overflowing with creative gifts, one-of-a-kind furnishings, and reproductions of paintings by Frida Kahlo and Botero. Open daily from 10am to 11pm. Olas Altas 224, Local 5. ☎ **322/223-2660**.

DECORATIVE & FOLK ART

Banderas Bay Trading Company 🅐   This shop features fine antiques and one-of-a-kind decorative objects for the home, including contemporary furniture, antique wooden doors, religious-themed items, *retablos* (painted scenes on tin backgrounds depicting the granting of a miracle), original art, beeswax candles in grand sizes, hand-loomed textiles, glassware, and pewter. This unique selection is handpicked by one of the area's most noteworthy interior designers, Peter Bowman. Open Monday to Saturday 9am to 9pm. Cárdenas 263 (near Ignacio L. Vallarta). ☎ **322/223-4352**.

Lucy's CuCu Cabaña and Zoo *(Finds*   Owners Lucy and Gil Givens have assembled an exceptionally entertaining, eclectic, and memorable collection of Mexican folk art—about 70% of which is animal-themed. Each summer they travel Mexico and personally select the handmade works created by over 100 indigenous artists and artisans. Items include metal sculptures, Oaxacan wooden animals, *retablos,* and fine Talavera ceramics. Open Monday through Saturday from 10am to 10pm. The store is closed from May 15 to October 15. Basilio Badillo 295. No phone.

Olinala   Two floors of fine indigenous Mexican crafts and folk art, including an impressive collection of museum-quality masks and original contemporary art by gallery owner Brewster Brockman. Open Monday through Friday from 10am to 2pm and 5 to 8pm, Saturday from 10am to 2pm. Cárdenas 274. ☎ **322/222-4995**.

Puerco Azul   Set in a space that actually has a former pig-roasting oven, Puerco Azul features a whimsical and eclectic selection of art and home accessories, much of it created by owner and artist Lee Chapman (aka Lencho). You'll find many animal-themed works in bright colors, including his signature "blue pigs" *(puercos azules).* Open Monday to Saturday from 10am to 8pm, closed on Sunday. Constitución 325, just off Basilio Badillo's "restaurant row." ☎ **322/222-8647**.

Querubines *(Finds*   This is my personal favorite for the finest-quality artisanal works from throughout Mexico. Owner Marcella García travels across the country to select the items, which include exceptional artistic silver jewelry, embroidered and hand-woven clothing, bolts of loomed fabrics, tin mirrors and lamps, glassware, pewter frames and trays, high-quality wool rugs, straw bags, and Panama hats. Open Monday through Saturday from 9am to 9pm. Under the same ownership and open the same hours, **Serafina,** Basilio Badillo 260 (② 322/223-4594), features a more extensive selection of cotton clothing and handmade jewelry. Juárez 501A (corner of Galeana,). ② 322/ 223-1727.

JEWELRY & ACCESSORIES

Mosaique   It's a potpourri of global treasures—an extensive selection of silk, cotton, and cashmere pareos and shawls, plus resort bags, jewelry, and home decor items. You'll also see blouses, tops, and wrap skirts in mix-and-match colors. The emphasis here is on handmade and hand-dyed, richly colored natural fabrics. There's a second location at Juárez 279 (② 322/223-3183). Both are open Monday through Saturday from 10am to 9pm, Sunday from 10am to 6pm. Basilio Badillo 277. ② 322/223-3146.

Viva ✦✦✦ (Finds   At Viva, both the shop and the jewelry are stunning. You enter through a long corridor lined with displays showcasing exquisite jewelry from over 450 international designers, including Mexico's finest silversmiths. The main room, under a large pyramid-shaped skylight, holds comfy couches surrounded by memorable jewelry displays. Viva also features the largest selection of authentic French espadrilles and ballet slippers in Latin America, plus an inspired selection of beach hats, sunglasses, and accessories. Open daily from 10am to 11pm. Basilio Badillo 274. ② 322/222-4078. www.vivacollection.com.

TEQUILA & CIGARS

La Casa del Habano   This fine tobacco shop has certified quality cigars from Cuba, Mexico, and the Dominican Republic, along with humidors, cutters, elegant lighters, and other smoking accessories. It's also a local cigar club, with a walk-in humidor for regular clients. In the back, you'll find comfy leather couches, TV sports, and full bar service—in other words, a manly place to take a break from shopping. Open Monday through Saturday from noon to 9pm. Aldama 170. ② 322/223-2758.

La Casa del Tequila ✦   Here you'll find an extensive selection of premium tequilas, plus information and tastings. Also available are cigars from Cuba and Veracruz, books, tequila glassware, humidors, and other tequila-drinking and cigar-smoking accessories. The shop has recently been downsized to accommodate the **Adobe Grill** (see "Where to Dine," in chapter 2) in the back, but now you can enjoy tasty Mexican fare and margaritas while you shop! Open Monday through Saturday from noon to 11pm. Morelos 589. ℂ 322/222-2000.

3 Puerto Vallarta After Dark

Puerto Vallarta's spirited nightlife reflects the town's dual nature: part resort, part colonial town. In years past, Vallarta was known for its live music scene, but in recent years the nocturnal action has shifted to DJ clubs, spinning an array of eclectic, contemporary music. A concentration of nightspots lies along Calle Ignacio L. Vallarta (the extension of the main southbound road) after it crosses the Río Cuale. Along one 3-block stretch you'll find a live blues club, sports bar, live mariachi music, a gay dance club, a steamy live salsa dance club, and the obligatory **Señor Frog's.** Walk from place to place and take in a bit of it all!

The *malecón,* which used to be lined with restaurants, is now known more for hip dance clubs and a few more relaxed options, all of which look out over the ocean. You can first stroll the broad walkway by the water's edge and check out the action at the various clubs, which extend from **Bodeguita del Medio** on the north end to **Hooters** just off the central plaza.

Marina Vallarta's clubs offer a more upscale, indoor, air-conditioned atmosphere. South of the Río Cuale, the **Olas Altas** zone's small cafes and martini bars buzz with action. In this zone, there's also an active gay and lesbian club scene.

PERFORMING ARTS & CULTURAL EVENTS

Cultural nightlife beyond the **Mexican Fiesta** is limited. Culture centers on the visual arts; the opening of an exhibition has great social and artistic significance. Puerto Vallarta's gallery community comes together to present almost weekly **art walks,** with new exhibits, featured artists, and complimentary cocktails. These social events alternate between the galleries along the Marina Vallarta *malecón* and those in the central downtown area. Check listings in the daily English-language newspaper, *Vallarta Today,* or the events section of www.virtualvallarta.com, to see what's on the schedule during your stay. Also of note are the free musical performances in the downtown plaza's gazebo—check with the municipal tourism office for current schedule.

FIESTA NIGHTS

Major hotels in Puerto Vallarta feature frequent fiestas for tourists—extravaganzas with open bars, Mexican buffet dinners, and live entertainment. Some are fairly authentic and make a good introduction for first-time travelers to Mexico; others can be a bit cheesy. Shows are usually held outdoors but move indoors when necessary. Reservations are recommended.

NH Krystal Vallarta   One of the best fiesta nights is here on Tuesday and Saturday at 7pm. These things are difficult to quantify, but Krystal's program is probably less tacky than those at most of its counterparts. Av. de las Palmas, north of downtown off the airport road. ⓒ 322/224-1041. kvallart@krystal.com.mx. Cover $48.

Rhythms of the Night (Cruise to Caletas) 🕼🕼🕼 *Moments* This is an unforgettable evening under the stars at John Huston's former home at the pristine cove called Las Caletas. The smooth, fast Vallarta Adventures catamaran travels here, entertaining guests along the way. Tiki torches and native drummers greet you at the dock. There's no electricity—you dine by the light of candles, the stars, and the moon. The buffet dinner is delicious—steak, seafood, and generous vegetarian options. Everything is first-class. The entertainment showcases indigenous dances in contemporary style. The cruise departs at 6pm and returns by 11pm. Departs from Terminal Marítima. ⓒ 866/256-2739 toll-free in the U.S., or 322/297-1212, ext 3. www.vallarta-adventures.com. Cost $70 (includes cruise, dinner, open bar, and entertainment).

THE CLUB & MUSIC SCENE
RESTAURANT/BARS

Bar Constantini 🕼🕼   The newest and most sophisticated lounge in Vallarta is set in the elegant eatery, Café des Artistes. Opened in late 2003, it's become a popular option for those looking for a lively yet sophisticated option for after dinner drinks. The plush sofas are welcoming, and the list of champagnes by the glass, signature martinis, and specialty drinks are suitably tempting. Live jazz and blues in an intimate atmosphere are drawing crowds. An ample appetizer and dessert menu make it appropriate for a late-night dining-and-drinks option. Open from 6pm to 2am. Guadalupe Sánchez 740. ⓒ 322/222-3229.

Bianco 🕼   Among the more popular choices for sophisticated nightlife in Vallarta is the sleek Bianco. It has a long glass-top bar and cozy seating areas where conversation is possible. This is the spot—finally—for anyone over 30 who wants to enjoy an evening out, listening to contemporary music. The air-conditioned lounge also features occasional live music, notably salsa on Thursday nights. You can't miss the dramatic entrance, and the lounge even has valet parking—a first in Vallarta. Open daily from 5pm to 4am. Insurgentes 109, Col. Emiliano Zapata. ✆ 322/222-2748.

Carlos O'Brian's Vallarta's original nightspot was once the only place for an evening of revelry. Although the competition is stiffer nowadays, COB's still packs them in—especially the 20-something set. The late-night scene resembles a college party. Open daily from noon to 2am; happy hour is from noon to 6pm. Paseo Díaz Ordaz (malecón) 786, at Pipila. ✆ 322/222-1444 or 322/222-4065. Weekend cover $11 (includes 2 drinks).

Kit Kat Club ☞ It's swank and sleek and reminiscent of a New York club, but don't be fooled—the Kit Kat Club also has a terrific sense of humor. In the golden glow of candlelight, lounge around on cushy leopard-patterned chairs or cream-colored overstuffed banquettes, listening to swinging tunes while you sip a martini. Not only does the place attract a very hip, generally gay crowd, but it also serves good food, with especially tasty appetizers—which can double as light meals—and scrumptious desserts. Michael, the owner, describes his air-conditioned lounge and cafe as cool, crazy, wild, jazzy, and sexy. Often, in high season, you'll be treated to a cabaret-style floorshow performed by a cross-dressing songstress. Open daily from 6pm to 2am. Pulpito 120, Playa Los Muertos. ✆ 322/223-0093.

La Bodeguita del Medio This authentic Cuban restaurant and bar is known for its casual energy, terrific live music, and mojitos. It is a branch of the original Bodeguita in Havana (reputedly Hemingway's favorite restaurant there), which opened in 1942. If you can't get to that one, the Vallarta version has successfully imported the essence—and has a small souvenir shop that sells Cuban cigars, rum, and other items. The downstairs has large wooden windows that open to the *malecón* street action, while the upstairs offers terrific views of the bay. Walls throughout are decorated with old photographs and patrons' signatures—if you can, find a spot and add yours! I feel the food is less memorable here than the music and atmosphere, so I recommend drinks and dancing, nothing more. Open daily from 11:30am to 2am. Paseo Díaz Ordaz (malecón), at Allende. ✆ 322/223-1585.

La Cantina de los Remedios   Cantinas are a centuries-old Mexican tradition, and this one has retained the fundamentals while updating the concept to a hip club. Cantinas serve little complimentary plates of food as your table orders drinks. La Cantina does this from 1 to 5pm; dishes might include *carne con chile* (meat in chile sauce), soup of the day, or quesadillas. In the evenings, recorded music alternates between sultry boleros and the hottest in Mexican rock, at a volume that permits conversation, creating a romantic, clubby atmosphere. If you require more stimulation, play a board game in one of the smaller rooms or on the larger open-air patio. Beers cost $1.50, bar drinks $2.50. Open Sunday through Wednesday from noon to 2am, Thursday through Saturday from noon to 4am. No credit cards. Morelos 709, downtown. ℂ 322/222-7701.

ROCK, JAZZ & BLUES

Club Roxy   A popular live-music club in Vallarta, Club Roxy features a hot house band led by club owner Pico, playing a mix of reggae, blues, rock, and anything by Santana. Live music jams between 10pm and 2am Monday through Saturday nights. It's open daily from 6pm to 2am. Ignacio L. Vallarta 217 (between Madero and Cárdenas, south of the river). No phone.

El Faro Lighthouse Bar ⟲   A circular cocktail lounge at the top of the Marina lighthouse, El Faro is one of Vallarta's most romantic nightspots. Live or recorded jazz plays, and conversation is manageable. Drop by at twilight for the magnificent panoramic views, but don't expect anything other than a drink and, if you get lucky, some popcorn. Open daily from 5pm to 2am. Royal Pacific Yacht Club, Marina Vallarta. ℂ 322/221-0541 or 322/221-0542. elfaropv@pvnet.com.mx.

Mariachi Loco   This lively mariachi club features singers belting out boleros and ranchero classics. The mariachi show begins at 9pm—the mariachis stroll and play as guests join in impromptu singing—and by 10pm it gets going. After midnight the mariachis play for pay, which is around $10 for each song played at your table. There's Mexican food from 7 to 10:30pm. Open daily from 1pm to 4am. Cárdenas 254 (at Ignacio Vallarta). ℂ 322/223-2205.

DANCE CLUBS

A few of Vallarta's dance clubs charge admission, but generally you pay just for drinks—$4 for a margarita, $2.50 for a beer, more for whiskey and mixed drinks. Keep an eye out for discount passes frequently available in hotels, restaurants, and other tourist spots. Most clubs are open from 10pm to 4am.

Christine This dazzling club draws a crowd with an opening laser-light show, pumped-in dry ice, flashing lights, and a dozen large-screen video panels. Once a disco—in the true sense of the word—it received a needed face-lift in 2003, and is now a more modern dance club, with techno, house, and hip-hop the primary tunes played. The sound system is truly amazing, and the mix of music can get almost anyone dancing. Dress code: No shorts for men, tennis shoes, or thongs. Open daily from 10pm to 4am; the light show begins at 11pm. In the Krystal Vallarta hotel, north of downtown off Av. Francisco Medina Ascencio. ✆ 322/224-0202. Cover free–$6.

de Santos ✮✮✮ Vallarta's chicest dining spot is known more for the urban, hip crowd the bar draws—it is *the* local hot spot. In 2003 it added a stunning state-of-the-art club, which quickly became the place for the superchic to party. The lower level holds an air-conditioned bar and dance floor, where a DJ spins the hottest of house and techno. Upstairs, there's an open-air rooftop bar with chill-out music and acid jazz. Enjoy the tunes and the fresh air while lounging around on one of the several oversize beds. One partner, a member of the superhot Latin rock group Mana, uses Vallarta as a home base for writing songs. The crowd, which varies in age from 20s on up, shares a common denominator of cool style. The restaurant bar is open daily from 5pm to 1am; the club is open Wednesday through Saturday from 10pm to 6am, and often waives the cover charge for women. Wednesday nights—Ladies' Night—draws a particularly large crowd. Morelos 771. ✆ 322/223-3052 or -3053. Cover usually $10 (includes 1 drink).

Emporium by Collage A multilevel monster of nighttime entertainment, Collage includes a pool salon, video arcade, bowling alley, and the always-packed Disco Bar, with frequent live entertainment. It's just past the entrance to Marina Vallarta, air-conditioned, and very popular with a young, mainly local crowd. Open daily from 10am to 6am. Calle Proa s/n, Marina Vallarta. ✆ 322/221-0505 or 322/221-0861. Cover $5.50–$25, but call ahead as cover varies depending on the theme—Mardi Gras, Foam Party, Black Light party, and so on.

Hilo You'll recognize Hilo by the giant-sized sculptures that practically reach out the front entrance and pull you into this high-energy club, which has become a favorite with the 20-something set. Music ranges from house and electronic to rock. It seems the later the hour, the more crowded the place becomes. Open daily from 10am to 6am. Malecon, between Aldama and Abasolo sts. ✆ 322/223-5361. Cover $7, weekends and holidays.

J & B Salsa Club This is the locally popular place to go for dancing to Latin music—from salsa to samba, the dancing is hot! On Fridays, Saturdays, and holidays the air-conditioned club features live bands. Open Monday through Saturday from 10pm to 6am. Av. Francisco Medina Ascencio Km 2.5 (Hotel Zone). ℭ **322/224-4616**. Cover $9.

Nikki Beach This haven of the hip hails from South Beach, Miami, and St. Tropez, and has brought its ultracool vibe to Vallarta. White-draped bed-size lounges scatter the outdoor lounge area, under a canopy of tall palms and umbrellas. Indoor dining and lounge areas are also available. The music is the latest in electronic, house, and chill, with visiting DJs often playing on weekend nights. Sundays feature their signature beach brunch, and Thursday evenings feature "Beautiful People" night. It's a great choice for catching rays during the day while sipping tropical drinks, but its real appeal is the nocturnal action. Open Sunday to Wednesday from 11am to 1am (food service stops at 11pm); Thursday to Saturday from 11am to 3am (food service stops at 1am.). On the beach at the Westin Regina Resort, Marina Vallarta. ℭ **322/221-0252** or 322/226-1150. www.nikkibeach.com.

The Palm Video & Show Bar The big screen above the dance floor of this colorful, lively club plays the most danceable videos in town. They're certain to get you moving. The pool table is regularly in play, and the air-conditioned club frequently books live shows featuring female impersonators. This is a gay-friendly but not exclusively gay club, with a spirited, festive atmosphere. Open daily from 7pm to 2am. Olas Altas 508. ℭ **322/223-4813**. www.thepalmbar.com. Cover $5 on show nights only.

Señor Frog's The sheer size of this outpost of the famed Carlos 'n' Charlie's chain is daunting, but it fills up and rocks until the early morning hours. Cute waiters are a signature of the chain, and one never knows when they'll assemble on stage and call on a bevy of beauties to join them in a tequila-drinking contest. Occasionally live bands appear. Although mainly popular with the 20s set, all ages will find the air-conditioned club fun. There's food service, but it's better known for its dance-club atmosphere. Open daily from 11am to 4am. Ignacio L. Vallarta and Venustiano Carranza. ℭ **322/222-5171** or 322/222-5177. Cover–$11 (includes 2 drinks).

Zoo Your chance to be an animal and get wild in the night. The Zoo even has cages to dance in if you're feeling unleashed. This popular club has a terrific sound system and a great variety of dance music, including techno, reggae, and rap. Every hour's happy hour, with two-for-one drinks. It opens daily at noon and closes in the wee hours. Paseo Díaz Ordaz (malecón) 630. © **322/222-4945.** Cover $11 (includes 2 drinks).

A SPORTS BAR

Micky's No Name Cafe   With umpteen TVs and enough sports memorabilia to start a minimuseum, Micky's is a great place to catch your favorite game. It shows all NBA, NHL, NFL, and MLB broadcast events, plus pay-per-view. Mickey's also serves great barbecued ribs and USDA imported steaks. It's open daily from 9am to midnight. Morelos 460 (malecón), at Mina. © **322/223-2508.**

GAY & LESBIAN CLUBS

Vallarta has a vibrant gay community with a wide variety of clubs and nightlife options, including special bay cruises and evening excursions to nearby ranches. The free *Gay Guide Vallarta* (© **322/299-0936;** www.gayguidevallarta.com) specializes in gay-friendly listings, including weekly specials and happy hours.

Club Paco Paco   This combination dance club, cantina, and rooftop bar stages a spectacular "Trasvesty" transvestite show every Thursday, Friday, Saturday, and Sunday night at 1:30am. It's open daily from 1pm to 6am and is air-conditioned. Ignacio L. Vallarta 278. © **322/222-1899.** www.pacopaco.com. Cover $6 (includes 1 drink) after 10pm or start of 1st show, whichever is earlier.

Garbos   This small, cozy club is gay friendly, but not exclusively gay, and features great recorded music and occasional live music on weekends. It's open daily from 6pm to 2am and is air-conditioned. Pulpito 142. © **322/229-7309.**

Los Balcones   One of the original gay clubs in town, this air-conditioned bi-level space boasts several dance floors and an excellent sound system. It earned a few chuckles when *Brides* magazine listed it as one of the most romantic spots in Vallarta. It posts nightly specials, including exotic male dancers. Open from 9pm to 4am daily November through March, closed Sunday in the off season. Juárez 182. © **322/222-4671.**

Ranch Disco Bar   This place is known for the nightly "Ranch Hand's Show," at 11:30pm and 2am. The club also has a new dance floor. Open daily from 9pm to 6am. Venustiano Carranza 239 (around the corner from Paco Paco, and can also be accessed directly from Paco Paco). © **322/223-0537.** Cover $6 (includes 1 drink).

4 Side Trips from Puerto Vallarta

YELAPA: ROBINSON CRUSOE
MEETS JACK KEROUAC *ʁ*

It's a cove straight out of a tropical fantasy, and only a 45-minute trip by boat from Puerto Vallarta. Yelapa has no cars, has one sole paved (pedestrian-only) road, and got electricity only in the past 3 years. It's accessible only by boat. Its tranquillity, natural beauty, and seclusion have made it a popular home for hippies, hipsters, artists, writers, and a few expats (looking to escape the stress of the world, or perhaps the law). A seemingly strange mix, but you're unlikely to ever meet a stranger—Yelapa remains casual and friendly.

To get there, travel by excursion boat or inexpensive water taxi (see "Getting Around," in chapter 2). You can spend an enjoyable day here, but I recommend a longer stay—it provides a completely different perspective.

Once you're in Yelapa, you can lie in the sun, swim, snorkel, eat fresh grilled seafood at a beachside restaurant, or sample the local moonshine, *raicilla*. The local beach vendors specialize in the most amazing pies you've ever tasted (coconut, lemon, or chocolate). Equally amazing is how the pie ladies walk the beach while balancing the pie plates on their heads; they sell crocheted swimsuits, too. You can also tour this tiny town or hike up a river to see one of two waterfalls. The closest to town is about a 30-minute walk from the beach. *Note:* If you use a local guide, agree on a price before you start out. Horseback riding, guided birding, fishing trips, and paragliding are also available.

For overnight accommodations, local residents frequently rent rooms, and there's also the rustic **Hotel Lagunita** *ʁ* (© **322/ 209-5056** or -5055; www.hotel-lagunita.com). Its 32 cabañas have private bathrooms, and the hotel has electricity, a saltwater pool, primitive spa with massage, an amiable restaurant and bar, as well as the Barrcuda Beach lounge and brick-oven pizza cafe, plus a gourmet coffee shop. Though the prices are high for what you get, it is the most accommodating place for most visitors. Double rates run $95 during the season and $75 in the off season (MasterCard and Visa are accepted). Lagunita has become a popular spot for yoga retreats, and regularly features yoga classes.

A stylish alternative is the fashionable **Verana** *ʁʁʁ* (© **800/ 677-5156** or 322/222-2360; www.verana.com). See "Where to Stay," in chapter 2, for details.

If you stay over on a Wednesday or Saturday during the winter, don't miss the regular dance at the **Yelapa Yacht Club** (no phone). Typically tongue-in-cheek for Yelapa, the "yacht club" consists of a cement dance floor and a disco ball, but the DJ spins a great range of tunes, from Glenn Miller to Eminem, attracting all ages and types. Dinner ($5–$12) is a bonus—the food may be the best anywhere in the bay. The menu changes depending on what's fresh. Ask for directions; it's in the main village, on the beach.

NUEVO VALLARTA & NORTH OF VALLARTA: ALL-INCLUSIVES

Many people assume Nuevo Vallarta is a suburb of Puerto Vallarta, but it's a stand-alone destination over the state border in Nayarit. It was designed as a megaresort development, complete with marina, golf course, and luxury hotels. Although it got off to a slow start, it is finally coming together, with a collection of mostly all-inclusive hotels on one of the widest, most attractive beaches in the bay. The biggest resort, Paradise Village, has a growing marina and an 18-hole golf course inland from the beachside strip of hotels. The Mayan Palace also recently opened an 18-hole course. The Paradise Plaza shopping center, next to Paradise Village, adds much to the area's shopping, dining, and services. It's open daily from 10am to 10pm. To get to the beach, you travel down a lengthy entrance road from the highway, passing by fields (great for birding) and nearby lagoons (great for kayaking).

Etc. Beach Club, Paseo de los Cocoteros 38, Nuevo Vallarta (© 322/297-0174), is worth a day trip. This beach club has a volleyball net, showers, restroom facilities, and food and drink service on the beach, both day and night. To get there, take the second entrance to Nuevo Vallarta coming from Puerto Vallarta and turn right on Paseo de los Cocoteros; it is past the Vista Bahía hotel. It's open daily during the winter from 11am to 10:30pm, summer from 11am to 7pm. Drinks cost $2.50 to $7, entrees $4.50 to $17; cash only.

A trip into downtown Puerto Vallarta takes about 30 minutes by taxi (about $15, available 24 hr. a day). The ride is slightly longer by public bus, which costs $1.20 and operates from 7am to 11pm.

Marival Grand & Club Suites   This all-inclusive hotel sits almost by itself at the northernmost end of Nuevo Vallarta. Done in Mediterranean style, it offers a complete vacation experience, from its beautiful beach to adjacent dance club. There are a large variety of room types, ranging from standard units with no balconies to large master suites with whirlpools. The master suites have minibars and hair dryers. The broad white-sand beach is one of the real assets here—it stretches over 450m (1,500 ft.). There is also an extensive activities program, including fun for children.

Paseo de los Cocoteros and Bulevar Nuevo Vallarta s/n, 63735 Nuevo Vallarta, Nay. ☎ 322/297-0100. Fax 322/297-0262. www.gomarival.com. 495 units. High season $246 double; low season $230 double. Upgrade to junior suite $50 per day, to master suite with whirlpool $300 per day. Rates are all-inclusive. Ask for seasonal specials. AE, MC, V. From the Puerto Vallarta airport, enter Nuevo Vallarta from the 2nd entrance; Club Marival is the 1st resort to your right on Paseo de los Cocoteros. **Amenities:** 6 restaurants; 8 bars; 3 pools and a whirlpool for adults; 2 pools and a water park for children; 4 lighted tennis courts; spa; business center; salon. *In room:* A/C, TV, safe-deposit boxes.

Paradise Village 🏝🏝   Truly a village, this self-contained resort on an exquisite stretch of beach offers a full array of services, from an on-site dance club to a full-service European spa and health club. The collection of pyramid-shaped buildings, designed in Maya-influenced style, houses well-designed all-suite accommodations in studio, one-bedroom, and two-bedroom configurations. All have sitting areas and kitchenettes, making the resort ideal for families or groups of friends. The Maya theme extends to both oceanfront pools, with mythical creatures forming water slides and waterfalls. The exceptional spa is reason enough to book a vacation here, with treatments, hydrotherapy, massage (including massage on the beach), and fitness and yoga classes. Special spa packages are always available. A new and compelling attraction is their El Tigre golf course (details earlier in this chapter, under "Golf"), and their on-site marina continues to draw a growing number of boats and yachts.

Paseo de los Cocoteros 001, 63731 Nuevo Vallarta, Nay. ☎ 800/995-5714 in the U.S., or 322/226-6770. Fax 322/226-6713. www.paradisevillage.com. 490 units. High season $164–$308 junior or 1-bedroom suite; $340–$388 2-bedroom suite; $565–$599 3-bedroom suite; low season $137–$246 junior or 1-bedroom suite; $246–$267 2-bedroom suite, $514–$546 3-bedroom suite. AE, DC, MC, V. **Amenities:** 2 restaurants; 2 beachside snack bars; theme nights; nightclub; 2 beachside swimming pools; lap pool; championship golf club w/18-hole course; 4 tennis courts; European spa and complete fitness center; watersports center; Kid's Club; travel services desk; guests-only rental-car fleet; basketball court; beach volleyball; petting zoo; full marina. *In room:* A/C, TV, dataport, minibar, coffeemaker, hair dryer, iron, safe-deposit box.

BUCERIAS: A COASTAL VILLAGE 🏝

Only 18km (11 miles) north of the Puerto Vallarta airport, Bucerías ("boo-seh-*ree*-ahs," meaning "place of the divers") is a small coastal fishing village of 10,000 people in Nayarit state on Banderas Bay. It's caught on as an alternative to Puerto Vallarta for those who find the

pace of life there too invasive. Bucerías offers a seemingly contra-
dictory mix of accommodations—trailer-park spaces and exclusive
villa rentals tend to dominate, although there's a small selection of
hotels as well.

To reach the town center by car, take the exit road from the
highway and drive down the shaded, divided street that leads to the
beach. Turn left when you see a line of minivans and taxis (which
serve Bucerías and Vallarta). Go straight 1 block to the main plaza.
The beach, lined with restaurants, is a half-block farther. You'll see
cobblestone streets leading from the highway to the beach, and hints
of villas and town homes behind high walls. Second-home owners
and about 1,500 transplanted Americans have already sought out
this peaceful getaway; tourists have discovered its relaxed pace as well.

If you take the bus to Bucerías, exit when you see the line of minivans and taxis on the street that leads to the beach. To use public
transportation from Puerto Vallarta, take a minivan or bus marked
BUCERIAS (they run from 6am–9pm). The last minivan stop is
Bucerías's town square. There's also 24-hour taxi service.

Exploring Bucerías   Come here for a day trip from Puerto Vallarta
just to enjoy the long, wide, uncrowded beach, along with the fresh
seafood served at the beachside restaurants or at one of the unusually
great cafes listed below. If you are inclined to stay a few days, you can
relax inexpensively and explore more of Bucerías. Sunday is street-
market day, but it doesn't get going until around noon, in keeping
with the town's casual pace.

The **Coral Reef Surf Shop,** Heroe de Nacozari 114-F (© 329/
298-0261), sells a great selection of surfboards and gear, and offers
surfboard and boogie board rentals, surf lessons, and ATV and other
adventure tours to surrounding areas.

Where to Stay   Unfortunately, I cannot recommend any of the
hotels in Bucerías; they're run-down, and most people who choose to
stay here opt for a private home rental. Check out the villa rental bul-
letin board at **www.sunworx.com**. **Las Palmas** in Bucerías (© 329/
298-0060; fax 329/298-1100) will book accommodations, including
villas, houses, and condos. Call ahead, or ask for directions to the
office when you get to Bucerías. It's open Monday through Friday
from 9am to 2pm and 4 to 6pm, Saturday from 9am to 2pm.

Where to Dine   Many seafood restaurants, besides those listed
below, front the beach. The local specialty is *pescado zarandeado,* a
whole fish smothered in tasty sauce and slow-grilled.

Cafe Magaña *(*(* BARBECUED RIBS   Famous for its ribs and chicken, Cafe Magaña makes 10 original homemade sauces, including the "legendary" Salsa Magaña. Flavors have mythological names and contain creative ingredients like ginger, garlic, oranges, apples, cinnamon, and chiles. The sauces have been such a hit that British owner Jeff Rafferty also sells bottled versions and says to look for them commercially soon. This casual, colorful cafe and take-out restaurant also features TV sports and an occasional live band.

Calle Lázaro Cárdenas 40. ✆ **329/298-1761**. www.sunworx.com/salsa. Main courses $7–$12. No credit cards. Daily 5–11pm.

Karen's Place *(* INTERNATIONAL/MEXICAN   This casual oceanside restaurant offers classic cuisine, plus Mexican favorites in a style that appeals to North American appetites. Known for Sunday Champagne brunch (9am–3pm), it is a perfect place to enjoy a light beach lunch, or a romantic dinner. The best-selling entree is a Parmesan herb-crusted fish filet with a salad of baby greens. The casual, comfortable restaurant features live music on Tuesday and Thursday. It also has a terrace dining area with spectacular views, and a sushi menu.

On the beach at the Costa Dorada, Calle Lázaro Cárdenas. ✆ **329/229-6892** or 329/298-0832. www.all.at/karens. Breakfast $4.50–$5.50; Sun brunch (9am–3pm) $12; main courses $5.50–$13. No credit cards. Tues–Sun 9am–9pm.

Le Fort *(*(*(* FRENCH   What an unforgettable dining experience! It's more than dinner—the evening consists of watching as Chef Gilles Le Fort prepares your gourmet meal and teaches you how to re-create it. The U-shaped bar in the intimate kitchen accommodates diners, who sip fine wines and nibble on pâté while the master works. Chef Le Fort has won many culinary awards, but his warm conviviality is the key ingredient of this unusual experience. Once dinner is served, the chef and his wife, Margarita, will join the table, entertaining with stories of their experiences in Mexico. The first group of six to book for the evening chooses the menu; the maximum class size is 16, so groups often blend together. Le Fort has probably the most extensive wine cellar in the bay—some 4,000 bottles. Hand-rolled Cuban cigars, homemade sausages, pâtés, and more delicacies are available in the adjoining shop.

Calle Lázaro Cárdenas 71, 1 block from the Hotel Royal DeCameron. ✆ **329/298-1532**. www.lefort.com.mx. Reservations required. 3-course dinner, wines, and recipes $45 per person. No credit cards. Daily 8–10:30pm; cooking classes available 10am–1:30pm.

Mark's ★★ *Finds* ITALIAN/STEAK/SEAFOOD   It's worth a special trip to Bucerías just to eat at this covered-patio restaurant. The most popular American hangout in town, Mark's offers a great assortment of thin-crust pizzas and flatbread, baked in its brick oven and seasoned with fresh herbs grown in the garden. Everything has exquisite flavorings—some favorites include shrimp in angel-hair pasta, pesto-crusted fish filet, Ahi tuna served rare, and filet mignon with bleu-cheese ravioli. Multitalented chef Jan Marie (Mark's charming wife and partner) runs an adjacent boutique, featuring elegant home accessories and unique gift items. The bar televises all major sporting events.

Calle Lázaro Cárdenas 56, ½ block from the beach. © **329/298-0303.** Pasta $8.70–$19; main courses $13–$22. MC, V. High season daily 5–11pm; low season daily 5–10pm. From the highway, turn left just after bridge, where there's a small sign for Mark's. Double back left at next street (immediately after you turn left) and turn right at next corner. Mark's is on the right.

PUNTA MITA: EXCLUSIVE SECLUSION ★★★

At the northern tip of the bay is an arrowhead-shaped, 600-hectare (1,500-acre) peninsula bordered on three sides by the ocean, called Punta Mita. Considered a sacred place by the Indians, this is the point where Banderas Bay, the Pacific Ocean, and the Sea of Cortez come together. It's magnificent, with white-sand beaches and coral reefs just offshore. Stately rocks jut out along the shoreline, and the water is a dreamy translucent blue. Punta Mita is evolving into one of Mexico's most exclusive developments. The master plan calls for a total of five luxury hotels, several high-end residential communities, and three championship golf courses. It is the first luxury residential development in Mexico intended for the foreign market. Today, all you'll find is the elegant Four Seasons Resort and its Jack Nicklaus Signature golf course, but by next year, a new 68-unit all-suite Rosewood resort will open, and shortly after that, a St. Regis resort will open, along with Punta Mita's second Jack Nicklaus golf course.

Four Seasons Resort Punta Mita ★★★   The Four Seasons Resort has brought a new standard of luxury to Mexico's Pacific Coast. The boutique hotel combines seclusion and pampering service with a welcoming sense of comfort. Accommodations are in three-story *casitas* surrounding the main building, which holds the lobby, cultural center, restaurants, and pool. Every guest room offers views of the ocean from a large terrace or balcony. Most suites also offer a private plunge pool, a separate sitting room, a bar, and a powder room. Room interiors are typical Four Seasons—plush and spacious, with a king-size or two double beds, a seating area, and an oversize bathroom with a deep soaking tub, separate glass-enclosed shower, and dual vanity sink. More than the stylish luxury, this hotel boasts unerring service that is both warm and unobtrusive. At least 45 minutes from Puerto Vallarta's activities, it's the perfect get-away— but then, most guests feel so relaxed and at ease, it's hard to think of venturing beyond the resort at all. The full-service spa, tennis center, and private championship golf course seem to be options enough.

63734 Bahía de Banderas, Nay. ⓒ 800/332-3442 in the U.S., or 329/291-6000. Fax 329/291-6060. www.fourseasons.com. 140 units. High season $691–$796 double, $1,814–$2,048 suite; low season $457–$656 double, $1,170–$1,287 suite. AE, DC, MC, V. Free valet parking. **Amenities:** 2 restaurants; lobby bar; heated infinity pool surrounded by private cabañas; tennis center w/4 courts of various surfaces; full-service fitness center; European-style spa; *temazcal;* watersports equipment including sea kayaks, Windsurfers, surfboards, and sunfish sailboats; Kids for All Seasons children's activity program; game room, 24-hr. concierge service; tour desk; 24-hr. room service; daily activity agenda; cultural center w/lectures and activities; complimentary video library. *In room:* A/C, TV/VCR, dataport, minibar, coffeemaker, hair dryer, iron, safe-deposit box, high-speed Internet access.

Casa Las Brisas ☆☆ *(Finds)*   Although it's not technically in Punta Mita, Casa Las Brisas is near enough to convey the relaxed seclusion of this area, in an intimate setting. It's on the back road that runs from Punta Mita to Sayulita, on the small, pristine Careyerros Bay. The six rooms are set in a villa, overlooking the beach. The villa itself is a work of white stucco walls, tile floors and patios, thatch and tile roofs, and guayaba wood balcony detailing. Patios and intimate indoor-outdoor seating areas on varying levels are ideal for an afternoon read or an evening cocktail. Interiors of the guest rooms are simple and elegant, with touches such as carved armoires, headboards, and doors from Michoacan. The colorful bathrooms feature large showers lined with hand-painted tiles. Private balconies with ocean views surround the pool, which features submerged sunning chairs and a small fountain. There are no TVs or telephones, but a cellphone in the lobby is available for guests. A big plus here is the delicious dining, included in the price of your stay.

Playa Careyero, 63734 Punta de Mita, Nay. ⓒ 877/278-8018 in the U.S., 322/306-2122, or 322/225-4364. www.mexicoboutiquehotels.com/casalasbrisas/index.html. 7 suites. High season $385–$445 suite; low season $335–$395 suite. Rates include all meals and drinks; minimum 3-night stay required. Credit cards for deposit only; cash payment upon booking. **Amenities:** Restaurant; small pool; universal gym station; spa services; tour services; entertainment room w/TV, DVD, and VCR. *In room:* Remote-controlled A/C, minibar, safe-deposit box, bathrobes.

SAYULITA: MUCH MORE THAN A GREAT SURF SPOT

Sayulita is only 40km (25 miles) northwest of Puerto Vallarta, on Highway 200 to Tepic, yet it feels a world apart. It captures the simplicity and tranquillity of beach life long since gone from Vallarta—but hurry, because this place is on the verge of exploding in popularity. For years, Sayulita was first and foremost a surfers' destination—the main beach in town is known for its consistent break and long, rideable waves. Recently, visitors and locals who find Vallarta too cosmopolitan have also started flocking here.

An easygoing attitude seems to permeate the air in this beach town. Yet despite its simplicity, niceties are popping up all over among the basic accommodations, inexpensive Mexican food stands, and handmade, hippie-style baubles. It's quickly becoming gentrified with new restaurants, cafes, and elegant villas for rent.

Sayulita is a popular stage for surfing tournaments; on any given weekend you might encounter perfect-swell-seeking surfers—or a Huichol Indian family that has come down to sell their wares. This eclectic mix of the cool, the unusual, and the authentic Mexican makes Sayulita such a special place.

To get to Sayulita, you can rent a car, or take a taxi from the airport or downtown Vallarta. The rate is about $50 to get to the town plaza. You can also take a taxi back to Vallarta. The stand is on the main square, or you can call for pickup at your hotel. The trip from the airport to Sayulita costs $55. Guides also lead tours to Puerto Vallarta, Punta Mita, and other surrounding areas, including a Huichol Indian community.

Where to Stay   Sayulita offers several private homes for rent. Your best option is to contact **Upi Viteri** (upiviteri@prodigy.net.mx), who has access to some of the nicest rental properties.

Villa Amor   Villa Amor is a collection of inviting, airy, perfectly appointed guest rooms—think of it as your private villa by the sea. Owner Rod Ingram and his design team have carefully crafted each space and individual suite into something truly special. The exterior walls curve invitingly and open up to breathtaking views all around. The one- and two-bedroom suites have fully equipped kitchenettes, plus open-air seating or dining areas (or both), and some have plunge pools. TVs are available on request. Construction of 24 new villas is under way; it makes the place a bit unsightly from the road, but once you're there, you'll find the peace and beauty you came for.

Camino Playa Los Muertos s/n, 63732 Sayulita, Nay. ℂ **329/291-3010**. Fax 329/291-3018. www.villaamor.com. 21 units. $85 double; $135–$195 1-bedroom villa;

$275–$350 2-bedroom villa. No credit cards. **Amenities:** Restaurant; kayaks; boogie boards; surfboards; bicycles; concierge; tour desk; room service; massage. *In room:* Fan.

Where to Dine   If you are in Sayulita, chances are you heard about it because of **Don Pedro's,** the most popular restaurant in town, in the heart of the main beach.

Don Pedro's INTERNATIONAL   Many say it's Don Pedro's that has brought so much attention to Sayulita in recent years—Vallarta area visitors came for the food, then booked their next vacation in this funky town. Choose between a two-level indoor dining area, or shaded tables on the beach for breakfast, lunch, or dinner. Starters include calamari, spring rolls, and fresh salads. Main courses include thin-crust pizzas, fresh fish artfully prepared, and a changing selection of savory pasta and chicken dishes, such as chicken Provençal, a whole chicken marinated in garlic and herbs, served with sautéed spinach and roasted tomatoes and white beans. Grilled Ahi tuna with mashed potatoes is also a favorite. In the bar area, TVs broadcast sporting events of any relevance, from the Super Bowl to Mexican soccer. I enjoy a relaxing lunch here, then staying for the beach action. Full bar service also available.

Marlin 2, on the beachfront. ⓒ 329/291-3090. www.donpedros.com. Main courses $4–$14. MC, V. Daily 8am–11pm.

L'Ultima Spiaggia ITALIAN   Paolo, an Italian chef, runs this tiny restaurant by the seashore. The menu is simple and classic, with salads, pizzas, and pastas. Paolo picks the freshest ingredients at the market every morning for his daily specials. They usually include fresh fish and seafood pasta dishes. Start with dorado carpaccio. The pizzas, baked in a wood-burning oven, have thin, crispy crusts. Don't miss the gnocchi, homemade fresh every day. The restaurant has a table out by the sea, which is perfect for romantic dinners. Breakfast features European-style offerings, including light omelets and fresh fruit. The espressos and cappuccinos are by far the best in Sayulita.

Camino Playa Los Muertos s/n, downstairs from Villa Amor. ⓒ 322/100-6879. Breakfast $3–$8; pizza $7–$11; main courses $8–$17. No credit cards. Tues–Sun 8:30–11am and 6–11pm.

Rollie's 🅡🅡 *(Finds* BREAKFAST   Breakfast heaven! This family restaurant emanates a happy aura that puts its patrons in a good mood. The menu reflects the tone of the place, with options such as Rollie's Delight (blended fresh orange and banana), Adriana's Rainbow (an omelet with cheese, tomatoes, green peppers, and onions), and my personal favorite, Indian Pipe Pancakes. All dishes come with Rollie's famous potatoes (lightly seasoned pan-fried new potatoes).

Av. Revolución, 2 blocks west of the main square. ✆ **329/291-3053**. Breakfast $3–$8. No credit cards. Daily Nov–Apr 8am–noon. Closed May–Oct.

SAN SEBASTIAN: AN AUTHENTIC MOUNTAIN HIDEAWAY 🐸🐸🐸

If you haven't heard about San Sebastián yet, it probably won't be long—its remote location and historic appeal have made it the Mexican media's new darling destination. Originally discovered in the late 1500s and settled in 1603, the town peaked as a center of mining operations, swelling to a population of over 30,000 by the mid-1800s. Today, with roughly 600 year-round residents, San Sebastián retains all the charm of a village locked in time, with an old church, a coffee plantation, an underground tunnel system—and wholly without a T-shirt shop.

Getting There   By car, it's a 2½-hour drive up the Sierra Madre from Puerto Vallarta on an improved road, but it can be difficult during the summer rainy season, when the road washes out frequently. **Vallarta Adventures** (✆ **866/256-2739** toll-free in the U.S., or 322/297-1212, ext. 3; www.vallarta-adventures.com) runs a daily plane service for half-day tours and can occasionally accommodate overnight visitors. The small private airport can arrange flights. **Aerotrón** (✆ **322/221-1921**) charges about $130 round-trip, **Aéro Taxis de la Bahía** (✆ **322/221-1990**) about $92 round-trip, depending on the type of plane and number of passengers. For more information on air tours and horseback-riding excursions, see the "Organized Tours" section, earlier in this chapter.

Where to Stay   There are two places to stay in San Sebastián. The first is the very basic **El Pabellón de San Sebastián,** which faces the town square. Its nine simply furnished rooms surround a central patio. Don't expect extras here; rates run $40 per double. The town's central phone lines handle reservations—you call (✆ **322/297-0200**) and leave a message or send a fax, and hopefully the hotel will receive it. More reliable is e-mail: ssb@pvnet.com.mx. Except on holidays, there is generally room at this inn. No credit cards.

A more enjoyable option is the stately **Hacienda Jalisco** 🐸🐸 (✆ **322/223-1695;** www.haciendajalisco.com), built in 1850 and once the center of mining operations in this mining town. The beautifully landscaped, old hacienda is near the airstrip, a 15-minute walk from town. Proprietor Bud Acord has welcomed John Huston, Liz Taylor, Richard Burton, Peter O'Toole, and a cast of local characters over the years.

The 10 clean rooms have wood floors, rustic furnishings and antiques, and working fireplaces; some are decorated with pre-Columbian reproductions. The ample bathrooms are tiled and have skylights. Hammocks grace the upstairs terrace, while a sort-of museum on the lower level attests to the celebrity guests and importance the hacienda has enjoyed over the years. Because of its remote location, all meals are included. The rate is $80 per person per night, and includes full breakfast and dinner; alcoholic beverages are extra. Reserve through e-mail (pmt15@hotmail.com or info@hacienda jalisco.com), through the town telephone listed above, or on their website. Group rates and discounts for longer stays are available. No credit cards. Guided horseback, walking, or mine tours can be arranged through the Hacienda.

4

Costa Alegre: From Puerto Vallarta to Barra de Navidad

by Lynne Bairstow

Costa Alegre is one of Mexico's most spectacular coastal areas, a 232km (145-mile) stretch that connects tropical forests with a series of dramatic cliff-lined coves. Tiny outpost towns line the coast, and dirt roads trail down to a succession of magical coves with pristine, exclusive beaches. This area is a favored hideaway for publicity-fatigued celebrities and those in search of natural seclusion.

The area is known as **Costa Alegre (Happy Coast)**—the marketer's term—and **Costa Careyes (Turtle Coast),** after the many sea turtles that nest here. It is home to an eclectic array of the most captivating and exclusive places to stay in Mexico, with a selective roster of activities that includes championship golf and polo. Along the line, however, you will encounter the funky beach towns that were the original lure for travelers who discovered the area.

EXPLORING COSTA ALEGRE   Costa Alegre is more an ultimate destination than a place to rent a car and take a drive. Most of the beaches are tucked into coves accessible by dirt roads that can extend for miles inland. If you do drive along this coast, Highway 200 is safe, but it's not lit and it curves through the mountains, so travel only during the day. A few buses travel this route, but they stop only at the towns that line the highway; many of them are several kilometers inland from the resorts along the coast.

1 Along Costa Alegre (from North to South)

CRUZ DE LORETO'S LUXURY ECORETREAT

Hotelito Desconocido *Moments*   The fact that the Hotelito Desconocido ("little unknown hotel") is ecologically minded is a bonus, but it's not the principal appeal. A cross between *Out of Africa* and *Blue Lagoon,* it is among my favorite places in Mexico. Think camping out with luxury linens, romantic candles everywhere, and a symphony performed by cicadas, birds, and frogs.

The rustic, open-air rooms, called *palafitos,* are in cottages perched on stilts over a lagoon. A grouping of suites is on the ample sand bar that separates the tranquil estuary from the Pacific Ocean. However, these are the least desirable units, and are often damp from the ocean air. Also here is a saltwater pool—the ocean is too aggressive for even seasoned swimmers.

The rooms have cotton sheets, oversize bath towels, and gauzy mosquito nets. Ceiling fans cool the air, and water is solar-heated. It's easy to disconnect here. In fact, it's mandatory: There's no electricity, no phones, no neighboring restaurants, nightclubs, or shopping— only delicious tranquillity. What the service lacks in polish it makes up for in enthusiasm. Rates do not include meals or drinks; a meal plan is mandatory, because there are no other options nearby (making the whole package somewhat pricey)—but it's a unique experience.

Playón de Mismaloya s/n, Cruz de Loreto, 48360 Tomatlán, Jal. 𝄐 **800/851-1143** in the U.S. and Canada. Reservations 𝄐 **01-800/013-1313** in Mexico, 322/281-4010, or 322/222-2546. Fax 322/281-4130. www.hotelito.com. 30 units. High season *palafito* double $370–$450, *palafito* suite $490–$670; low season *palafito* double $290–$340, *palafito* suite $390–$530. Mandatory daily meal plan $90 per person. AE, MC, V. Take Hwy. 200 south for 1 hr., turn off at exit for Cruz de Loreto, and continue on clearly marked route on unpaved road for about 25 min. Not appropriate for children. **Amenities:** 2 restaurant/bars; primitive-luxury spa w/massage and spa treatments, sauna, and whirlpool; windsurfing; kayaking; mountain biking; birding tours; hiking; horseback riding; billiards; beach volleyball. All activities are subject to an extra charge.

LAS ALAMANDAS: AN EXCLUSIVE LUXURY RESORT

Las Alamandas 𝄐𝄐𝄐 Almost equidistant between Manzanillo (1½ hr.) and Puerto Vallarta (1¾ hr.) lies Mexico's original ultra-exclusive resort. A dirt road winds for about a mile through a tiny village to the guardhouse of Las Alamandas, on 28 hectares (70 acres) set against low hills that are part of a 600-hectare (1,500-acre) estate. The resort, owned by Isabel Goldsmith, daughter of British financier Sir James Goldsmith, consists of villas and *palapas* spread among four beaches, gardens, lakes, lagoons, and a bird sanctuary. It's designed for privacy—to the point that guests rarely catch a glimpse of one another. The resort has air-conditioning, telephones, and a new beachside massage *palapa,* yet manages to keep the experience as natural as possible. The resort accommodates only 22 guests.

The six spacious villas have tiled verandas with ocean views. They have several bedrooms (each with its own bathroom) and can be rented separately; guests who rent whole villas have preference for reservations. Some villas are on the beach, others across a

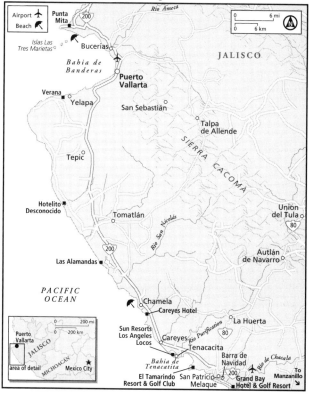

cobblestone plaza. TVs with VCRs are available on request, but there's no outside reception. Van transportation to and from Manzanillo ($293 one-way) and Puerto Vallarta ($289 one-way) can be arranged when you reserve your room. Air transport from Puerto Vallarta is also available; call for details.

Hwy. 200, 48800 Manzanillo–Puerto Vallarta, Jal. Mailing address: Domicilio Conocido Costa Alegre QUEMARO Jalisco, Apdo. Postal 201, 48980 San Patricio Melaque, Jal. ℭ **888/882-9616** in the U.S. and Canada, or 322/285-5500. Fax 322/285-5027. www.alamandas.com. 14 units. High season $567–$1,998 double, $2,039–$4,235 villa; low season $495–$1,312 double, $1,496–$2,978 villa. Meal plans available. AE, MC, V. **Amenities:** Restaurant; 18m (60-ft.) pool; lighted tennis court; weight room; mountain bikes; concierge; tour desk; room service; horses; hiking trails; boogie boards; birding boat tours; book and video library; landing strip (make advance arrangements). *In room:* A/C, dataport, minibar.

CAREYES

The Careyes Hotel 🐢🐢   The Careyes is a gem of a resort nestled on a small, pristine cove between dramatic cliffs that are home to the exclusive villas of Careyes. This area has practically defined the architectural style that defines Mexico beach chic—bold washes of vibrant colors, open spaces, and gardens that showcase the tropical flowers and palms indigenous to the area.

The hotel, a Starwood Luxury Collection property, recently completed significant upgrades in services and facilities. The pampering accommodations all face the ocean and are stylishly simple. Although guests come here for isolation, you can enjoy many services, including a full European spa and polo. It's both rustic and sophisticated, with the room facades awash in scrubbed pastels forming a U around the center lawn and freeform pool. Rooms have a dramatic feel, from the plantation shutters and white-tile floors to the handsome loomed bedspreads and colorful pillows. Some units have balconies; all have ocean views. Twenty rooms have private pools, and villas are available for rent. The hotel is popular for weddings and small corporate retreats.

The hotel offers a number of special-interest activities for guests. Named after the hawksbill turtle (*carey* in Spanish), the hotel sponsors a Save the Turtle program in which guests can participate between July and December.

The hotel is roughly 160km (100 miles) south of Puerto Vallarta. It's about a 2-hour drive north of Manzanillo on Highway 200, and about a 1-hour drive from the Manzanillo airport. Taxis from the Manzanillo airport charge around $100 one-way. There are car-rental counters at the Manzanillo and Puerto Vallarta airports. A car would be useful only for exploring the coast—Barra de Navidad and other resorts, for example—and the hotel can make touring arrangements.

Hwy. 200 Km 53.5, 48970 Careyes, Jal. CP. Mailing address: Apdo. Postal 24, 48970 Cihuatlán, Jal. ✆ **800/525-4800** in the U.S. and Canada, 315/351-0000, or 315/351-0606. Fax 315/351-0100. www.elcareyesresort.com or www.luxurycollection.com. 51 units. High season $265 double, $415–$485 suite; low season $225 double, $350–$450 suite. AE, MC, V. **Amenities:** Restaurant; bar; deli; large beachside pool; privileges at exclusive El Tamarindo resort (40km/25 miles south), w/18-hole mountaintop golf course; 2 tennis courts; fully equipped, state-of-the-art spa w/massage, hot and cold plunge pools, steam, sauna, weight equipment; kayaks; windsurf boards; Aquafins; "Just for Kids" children's activity program (during Christmas and Easter vacations); room service; laundry service; paddle court; book and video library, Internet access room. *In room:* A/C, TV/VCR, minibar, small fridge, hair dryer, bathrobes.

TENACATITA BAY

Located 60 minutes (53km/33 miles) north of the Manzanillo airport, this jewel of a bay is accessible by an 8km (5-mile) dirt road that passes through a small village set among banana plants and coconut palms. Sandy, serene beaches dot coves around the bay (frolicking dolphins are a common sight), and exotic birds fill a coastal lagoon. Swimming and snorkeling are good, and the bay is a popular stop for luxury yachts. Just south of the entrance to Tenacatita is a sign for the all-inclusive **Sun Resorts Los Angeles Locos,** as well as the exclusive **El Tamarindo** resort and golf club. There is no commercial or shopping area, and dining options outside hotels are limited to a restaurant or two that may emerge during the winter months (high season). Relax—that's what you're here for.

El Tamarindo ★★★ *Finds*   A personal favorite, El Tamarindo is a gem that combines stunning jungle surroundings with exquisite facilities, gracious service, and absolute tranquillity. The area's most luxurious resort, part of Starwood Hotels' Luxury Collection, it comes complete with its own golf course.

The bungalows exude exclusivity—each thatched-roof villa has a splash pool and whirlpool, hammock, plus lounging and dining areas that overlook a private lawn and complement the stunning bedrooms. What they don't have are televisions. Service throughout the resort is exceptional. The bedrooms—with dark hardwood floors and furnishings—can be closed off for air-conditioned comfort, but the remaining areas are open to the sea breezes and heady tropical air.

The categories of bungalows denote their location—Beachfront (on a calm cove, but not as private as the others), Palm Tree, Garden, and Forest. The non-beachside bungalows all have similar decor and amenities but feature more closed-in areas. Anyone squeamish about creepy-crawlies may be uncomfortable in the beginning, but listening to the life around you is a spectacular sensation. On 800 hectares (2,000 acres) of tropical rainforest bordering the Pacific Ocean, you'll feel as if you've found your own personal bit of heaven.

El Tamarindo has a championship 18-hole golf course; the approach to the first hole is through a forest of palms so tall they block the sun. The course has seven oceanside holes and dramatic views. Equally exceptional is their spa services, with most massages and treatments provided in beachfront *cabañas.* Their twice-weekly *temazcal,* a 2½-hour indigenous purification ritual, gets my highest recommendation—a combination of steam bath and spiritual experience, it's generally led by their spa director, Reto. Swiss-born, Reto has studied with Mexican shamans and other soulful teachers, and brings a unique and highly gifted approach to rejuvenating experiences.

The resort restaurant is the only dining option, but you won't be disappointed. The menu, which changes daily, has ample selections of fresh seafood selections, as well as pastas and beef, and all are artfully prepared. You can't leave without trying the resort's Tamarind Margarita.

Carretera Melaque–Puerto Vallarta Km 7.5, 48970 Cihuatlán, Jal. ℂ **315/351-5032**. Fax 315/351-5070. www.eltamarindoresort.com or www.luxurycollection.com. 29 bungalows. High season Ocean Front Villa $695, Palm Tree Villa $559, 2-bedroom Palm Tree Villa $805, Mountain Villa $589; low season Ocean Front Villa $485, Palm Tree Villa $485, 2-bedroom Palm Tree bungalow $685, Mountain Villa $375. AE, MC, V. From Puerto Vallarta (3 hr.) or the Manzanillo airport (40 min.), take Hwy. 200, then turn west at the clearly marked exit for El Tamarindo. Follow signs for about 25 min. **Amenities:** Restaurant; bar; large beachside pool w/whirlpool; 2 clay tennis courts; spa services; windsurfing; kayaking; aquafin sailboats; mountain biking; horseback riding; estuary bird-watching tours; hiking; en-suite dining; yoga classes; *temazcal* (pre-Hispanic sweat lodge), TV and Internet-access room below Lobby. *In room:* A/C, dataport, hair dryer, safe, bathrobes.

Sun Resorts Los Angeles Locos 𝕲
On a 4.8km (3-mile) stretch of sandy beach, Los Angeles Locos offers an abundance of activities and entertainment. An extensive activities program and an ample selection of dining and entertainment options offer guests excellent value. It's a good choice for families and groups of friends. All rooms have ocean views, with either balconies or terraces. The three-story hotel is basic in decor and amenities, but comfortable. The attraction here is the wide array of on-site activities, plus a "Jungle River" cruise excursion (included in the room rate). **La Lagarta Disco** is a little on the dark and smoky side but can really rock, depending on the crowd—it's basically the only option on the bay.

Carretera Federal 200 Km 20, Tenacatita 48989, Municipio de la Huerta, Jal. ℂ **315/351-5020** or 315/351-5100. Fax 315/351-5020. www.losangeleslocos.com. 204 units. High season $140 double; low season $95 double. Children 5–12 $30 year-round. Rates are all-inclusive. Ask about family specials. AE, MC, V. **Amenities:** 2 restaurants and snack bar (w/buffets and a la carte dining); 3 bars; dance club; nightly shows and entertainment; adult pool; kids' pool adjacent to the beach; 3 tennis courts; exercise room; windsurfing; kayaks; Hobie cats; Kid's Club; massage; babysitting; laundry service; pool tables; horseback riding; basketball court. *In room:* A/C, TV.

2 Barra de Navidad & Melaque

This pair of rustic beach villages (only 5km/3 miles apart) has been attracting travelers for decades. Only 30 minutes north of Manzanillo's airport, and 104km (65 miles) north of downtown Manzanillo, Barra has a few brick or cobblestone streets, good budget hotels and restaurants, and funky beach charm. All of this lies incongruously next to the superluxurious Grand Bay Hotel, which sits on a bluff across the inlet from Barra. Melaque offers budget hotels on and off the beach, fewer restaurants, and little in the way of charm, although the beach is as wide as and more beautiful than Barra's. Both villages appeal to those looking for a quaint, quiet, inexpensive retreat rather than a modern, sophisticated destination.

In the 17th century, Barra de Navidad was a harbor for the Spanish fleet; from here, galleons first set off in 1564 to find China. Located on a crescent-shaped bay with curious rock outcroppings, Barra de Navidad and neighboring Melaque are connected by a continuous beach on the same wide bay. It's safe to say that the only time Barra and Melaque hotels are full is during Easter and Christmas weeks. **Barra de Navidad** has more charm, more tree-shaded streets, better restaurants, more stores, and more conviviality between locals and tourists. Barra is very laid-back; faithful returnees adore its lack of flash. Other than the Grand Bay Hotel, on the cliff across the waterway in what is called Isla Navidad (although it's not on an island), nothing is new or modern. But there's a bright edge to Barra, with more good restaurants and limited—but existent—nightlife.

Melaque, on the other hand, is larger, rather sun-baked, treeless, and lacking in attractions. It does, however, have plenty of cheap hotels available for longer stays, and a few restaurants. Although the beach between the two is continuous, Melaque's beach, with deep sand, is more beautiful than Barra's.

Isla Navidad Resort has a manicured 27-hole golf course and the super-luxurious Grand Bay Hotel, but the area's pace hasn't quickened as fast as expected. The golf is challenging and delightfully uncrowded, with another exceptional course at nearby El Tamarindo. It's a serious golfer's dream.

ESSENTIALS

Getting There Buses from Manzanillo frequently run up the coast along Highway 200 on their way to Puerto Vallarta and Guadalajara. The fare is about $3.50. Most stop in the central villages of

Barra de Navidad and Melaque. From the Manzanillo airport, it's only around 30 minutes to Barra, and taxis are available. The fare from Manzanillo to Barra is around $40; from Barra to Manzanillo, $30. From Manzanillo, the highway twists through some of the Pacific Coast's most beautiful mountains. Puerto Vallarta is a 3-hour (by car) to 5-hour (by bus) ride north on Highway 200 from Barra.

Visitor Information　The **tourism office** for both villages is at Jalisco 67 (between Veracruz and Mazatlán), Barra (©/fax **315/ 355-5100;** www.barradenavidad.com). The office is open daily from 9am to 5pm. The **Travel Agency Isla Navidad Tours,** Veracruz 204-A, Barra de Navidad (© **315/355-5666** or 315/355-5667), can handle arrangements for plane tickets and sells bus tickets from Manzanillo to Puerto Vallarta and Guadalajara. It's open Monday through Friday from 11am to 8pm and Saturday from 11am to 6pm.

Orientation　In Barra, hotels and restaurants line the main beachside street, **Legazpi.** From the bus station, beachside hotels are 2 blocks straight ahead, across the central plaza. Two blocks behind the bus station and to the right is the lagoon side. More hotels and restaurants are on its main street, **Morelos/Veracruz.** Few streets are marked, but 10 minutes of wandering will acquaint you with the village's entire layout. There's a taxi stand at the intersection of Legazpi and Sinaloa streets. Legazpi, Jalisco, Sinaloa, and Veracruz streets border Barra's **central plaza.**

ACTIVITIES ON & OFF THE BEACH

Swimming and enjoying the attractive beach and views of the bay take up most tourists' time. You can hire a small boat for a coastal ride or fishing in two ways. Go toward the *malecón* on Calle Veracruz until you reach the tiny boatmen's cooperative, with fixed prices posted on the wall, or walk two buildings farther to the water taxi ramp. The water taxi is the best option for going to Colimilla (5 min., $2) or across the inlet (3 min., $1) to the Grand Bay Hotel. Water taxis make the rounds regularly, so if you're at Colimilla, wait, and one will be along shortly. At the cooperative, a 30-minute **lagoon tour** costs $20, and a **sea tour** costs $25. **Sportfishing** is $80 for up to four people for a half day in a small *panga* (open fiberglass boat, like the ones used for water taxis).

　Surfing along Costa Alegre is gaining ground, thanks in large part to Germaine Badke, and the **South Swell Mex Surf Shop** (© **314/338-7152;** www.southswellmex.com), which he owns and operates. The shop offers boogie board and surfboard rentals,

Barra de Navidad Bay Area

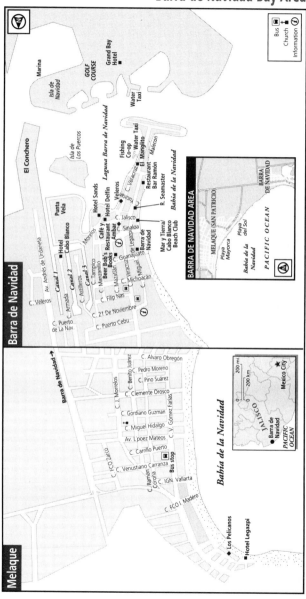

Bus
Church
Information

Marina

Isla de Navidad

GOLF COURSE

Grand Bay Hotel

Water Taxi

El Conchero

Isla de Los Puercos

Laguna Barra de Navidad

Fishing Co-op

Water Taxi

El Manglito

Malecón

Restaurant Bar Ramón

R. Seamaster

Bahía de la Navidad

Av. Andrés de Urdaneta

Hotel Cabo Blanco

Punta Vela

Hotel Sands

Hotel Delfín

Veleros

C. Veracruz

Morelos

Café y Beer Bob's Restaurant Books

Ambar

C. Jalisco

C. Sinaloa

Mar y Tierra Cabo Blanco Beach Club

Barra de Navidad

Canal 1

Canal 2

Canal 3

C. Armada

C. Veleros

C. Astilleros

C. Manzanillo

C. Tampico

C. Mazatlán

Guadalajara

C. Miguel Legazpi

C. Miguel

Guanajuato

C. Michoacán

C. Filip Nas

C. 21 De Noviembre

C. Puerto de La Nav.

C. Puerto Cebu

BARRA DE NAVIDAD AREA

MELAQUE (SAN PATRICIO)

Playa Mayorca

Playa del Sol

Bahía de la Navidad

PACIFIC OCEAN

BARRA DE NAVIDAD

Melaque

Barra de Navidad →

C. Alvaro Obregón

C. Benito Juárez

C. Pedro Moreno

C. Pino Suárez

C. I. Morelos

C. Clemente Orosco

C. Gordiano Guzmán

C. Miguel Hidalgo

Av. Lòpez Mateos

C. V. Gómez Farías

C. Carrillo Puerto

Bus stop

C. FCO Tarco

C. Venustiano Carranza

C. Ramón Corona

C. IGN. Vallarta

C. FCO I. Madero

Bahía de la Navidad

200 mi

200 km

JALISCO

Mexico City

Barra de Navidad

PACIFIC OCEAN

Los Pelicanos

Hotel Legazpi

surfboard and surf supply sales, and will also create a custom-designed board. Surf lessons are also available. They're located in Suite 2 of the Hotel Alondra.

The Grand Bay Hotel's beautiful and challenging 27-hole, 7,053-yard, par-72 **golf course** is open to the public. Hotel guests pay greens fees of $166 for 18 holes, $192 for 27 holes; nonguests pay $216 and $240, respectively. Prices include a motorized cart. Caddies are available, as are rental clubs. The Crazy Cactus (see below) can arrange golf at El Tamarindo's gorgeous mountaintop course, about 32km (20 miles) north of Barra.

Beer Bob's Books, Ave. Tampico, between Sinaloa and Guanajuato, is a book-lover's institution in Barra and a sort of community service that the rather grouchy Bob does for fun. His policy of "leave a book if you take one" allows vacationers to select from hundreds of neatly shelved paperbacks, as long as they leave a book in exchange. It's open Monday through Friday from noon to 3pm and occasionally in the evenings. "Beer Bob" got his name because in earlier days, when beer was cheap, he kept a cooler stocked, and book browsers could sip and read. (When beer prices went up, Bob put the cooler away.)

WHERE TO STAY

Low season in Barra is any time except Christmas and Easter weeks. Except for those 2 weeks, it doesn't hurt to ask for a discount at the inexpensive hotels. To arrange **real estate rentals,** contact **The Crazy Cactus,** Jalisco 8, a half-block inland from the town church on Legazpi (©/fax **315/355-6099;** crazycactusmx@yahoo.com). The store may be closed May through October.

VERY EXPENSIVE

Grand Bay Hotel Wyndham Resort 𝄐 *Overrated* Across the yacht channel from Barra de Navidad, this luxurious hotel opened in 1997 on 480 hectares (1,200 acres) next to its 27-hole golf course. Now operated by Wyndham Resorts, it overlooks the village, bay, Pacific Ocean, and Navidad lagoon. The hotel's beach is narrow and on the lagoon. A better beach is opposite the hotel on the bay in Barra de Navidad. The spacious rooms are sumptuously outfitted with marble floors, large bathrooms, and hand-carved wood furnishings. Prices vary according to view and size of room, but even the modest rooms are large; all have cable TV. Each comes with a king-size or two double beds, a glass-top desk, ceiling fans plus air-conditioning, and a balcony. All suites have a steam sauna and telephones in the bathroom as well as a sound system. The hotel is a short water-taxi ride across the inlet from Barra de Navidad; it is also on a paved road from Highway 200. Although the hotel bills itself as being on the Island of Navidad at Port Navidad, the port is the marina, and the hotel is on a peninsula.

Isla Navidad, Col. 45110. ℂ 01-800/996-3426, 315/355-5050, or 314/331-0500 in Mexico, or 310/536-9278 in the U.S. Fax 315/355-6070. www.islaresort.com.mx; www.wyndham.com. 199 units. High season $220–$460 double; $550–$680 suite; low season $160–$321 double, $468–$614 suite. Ask about tennis, golf, fishing, and honeymoon packages. Rates include round-trip transportation to and from Manzanillo airport. AE, DC, DISC, MC, V. **Amenities:** 2 restaurants; 2 bars; golf club w/food and bar service; swimming pool w/water slides and swim-up bar; 27-hole, par-72 golf course designed by Robert Von Hagge; golf club w/pro shop and driving range; 3 lighted grass tennis courts w/stadium seating; small but sufficient workout room; Kid's Club w/activity program; 24-hr. concierge; business center; salon; room service; babysitting; laundry service; dry cleaning; 150-slip marina w/private yacht club; fishing, boat tours, and other excursions can be arranged. *In room:* A/C, TV, dataport, minibar, hair dryer, iron, safe-deposit box, bathrobes.

MODERATE

Hotel Cabo Blanco 👁👁   Located on the point where you cross over to Isla Navidad, the Cabo Blanco is an outstanding option for family vacations or longer-term stays. Rooms are pleasantly rustic, with tile floors, large tile tubs, separate dressing areas, and stucco walls. The hotel overlooks the bay, but it's a 5-minute walk to the beach. The beamed-ceiling lobby is in its own building; rooms are in hacienda-style buildings surrounded by gardens. The atmosphere is generally tranquil, except during weekends and Mexican holidays, when this hotel tends to fill up. Because the Cabo Blanco doesn't front the beach, it has an affiliated beach club and restaurant, Mar y Tierra (see "Where to Dine," below).

Armada y Bahía de la Navidad s/n, 48987 Barra de Navidad, Jal. ℂ 315/355-5103 or 315/355-5136. Fax 315/355-6494. 101 units. $130 double; $256 suite with kitchenette. All-inclusive plans also available. AE, MC, V. **Amenities:** 2 restaurants; 4 pools (2 adults only); 2 tennis courts; concierge; tour desk; car-rental desk; laundry service. *In room:* A/C, TV.

INEXPENSIVE

Hotel Barra de Navidad 👁   At the northern end of Legazpi, this popular, comfortable beachside hotel is among the nicest in the town. It has friendly management, and some rooms with balconies overlooking the beach and bay. Other, less expensive rooms afford only a street view. Only the oceanview rooms have air-conditioning. A nice swimming pool is on the street level to the right of the lobby.

Legazpi 250, 48987 Barra de Navidad, Jal. ℂ 315/355-5122. Fax 315/355-5303. 59 units. $50–$72 double. MC, V. **Amenities:** Pool.

Hotel Delfín One of Barra's better-maintained hotels, the four-story (no elevator) Delfín is on the landward side of the lagoon. It offers pleasant, basic, well-maintained, and well-lit rooms. Each has red-tile floors and a double, two double, or two single beds. The tiny courtyard, with a small pool and lounge chairs, sits in the shade of an enormous rubber tree. From the fourth floor, there's a view of the lagoon. A breakfast buffet is served from 8:30 to 10:30am (see "Where to Dine," below).

Morelos 23, 48987 Barra de Navidad, Jal. ✆ **315/355-5068.** Fax 315/355-6020. 24 units. $49 double; ask about low-season discounts. MC, V. Free parking. **Amenities:** Restaurant; pool.

Hotel Sands The colonial-style Sands, across from the Hotel Delfín (see above) on the lagoon side at Jalisco, offers small but homey rooms with red-tile floors and windows with both screens and glass. The remodeled bathrooms have new tiles and fixtures. Lower rooms look onto a public walkway and wide courtyard filled with greenery and singing birds; upstairs rooms are brighter. Twelve rooms (suites or bungalows) have air-conditioning and kitchenette facilities. The hotel is known for its warm hospitality and high-season happy hour (2–6pm) at the pool terrace bar beside the lagoon. On weekends from 9pm to 4am, an adjacent patio "disco" plays recorded music for dancing. Breakfast is served from 7:30am to noon. Fishing trips can be arranged, and tours to nearby beaches are available.

Morelos 24, 48987 Barra de Navidad, Jal. ✆/fax **315/355-5018.** 42 units. High season $61 double; low season $42 double. Rates include breakfast. Room-only rates $10 less. Discounts for stays of 1 week or more. MC, V (6% surcharge). **Amenities:** Restaurant; bar; pool w/whirlpool overlooking lagoon beach; children's play area; tour desk.

WHERE TO DINE

El Manglito ★ SEAFOOD/INTERNATIONAL On the placid lagoon, with a view of the palatial Grand Bay Hotel, El Manglito serves home-style Mexican food to a growing number of repeat diners. The whole fried fish accompanied by drawn garlic butter, boiled vegetables, rice, and french fries, is a crowd-pleaser. Other enticements include boiled shrimp, chicken in orange sauce, and shrimp salad.

Veracruz, near the boatmen's cooperative. No phone. Main courses $5–$10. No credit cards. Daily 9am–11pm.

Hotel Delfín INTERNATIONAL The second-story terrace of this small hotel is a pleasant place to begin the day. The self-serve buffet offers an assortment of fresh fruit, juice, granola, yogurt, milk, pastries, and unlimited coffee. The price includes made-to-order eggs and delicious banana pancakes—for which the restaurant is known.

Morelos 23. 🅒 **315/355-5068.** Breakfast buffet $4. No credit cards. Daily 8:30am–noon.

Mar y Tierra INTERNATIONAL   Hotel Cabo Blanco's beach club is also a popular restaurant and bar, and a great place to spend a day at the beach. On the beach, there are shade *palapas* and beach chairs, and a game of volleyball seems constantly in progress. The colorful restaurant is decorated with murals of mermaids. Perfectly seasoned shrimp fajitas come in plentiful portions.

Legazpi s/n (at Jalisco). 🅒 **315/355-5028.** Main courses $10–$17. AE, MC, V. Wed–Sun 2–10pm; closes at 6pm on Sun (opens at 10am Wed–Mon for hotel guests).

Restaurant Bar Ambar CREPES/SPANISH/FRENCH   This cozy, thatched-roof, upstairs restaurant is open to the breezes. The crepes are named after towns in France; the delicious *crêpe Paris,* for example, is filled with chicken, potatoes, spinach, and green sauce. Sweet dessert crepes are also available. International main dishes include imported (from the U.S.) rib-eye steak in Dijon mustard sauce, mixed brochettes, quiche, and Caesar salad. Ambar serves Spanish-style tapas from noon until 6pm, and adds French specialties during dinner.

Av. Veracruz 101-A (at Jalisco). No phone. Crepes $5–$13; main courses $5–$15. No credit cards. Daily noon–midnight (happy hour 1pm–midnight). Closed July–Oct.

Restaurant Bar Ramón 🅖 *Value* SEAFOOD/MEXICAN   It seems that everybody eats at Ramón's, where the chips and fresh salsa arrive unbidden, and service is prompt and friendly. The food is especially good—however, most options are fried. Try fresh fried shrimp with french fries, or any daily special that features vegetable soup or chicken-fried steak. Great value!

Legazpi 260. 🅒 **315/355-6435.** Main courses $6–$10. MC, V. Daily 7am–11pm.

Seamaster SEAFOOD/INTERNATIONAL   This cheery, colorful restaurant on the beach facing the ocean is a great place for sunsets and margaritas, or a meal anytime. Specialties include steamed shrimp (peeled or unpeeled), fried calamari, barbecue chicken, ribs, steak, chicken wings, hamburgers, and other sandwiches. During high season, it turns into a popular dance club at night.

Legazpi (at Yucatán). No phone. Main courses $5–$15. No credit cards. Daily noon–midnight.

BARRA DE NAVIDAD AFTER DARK

When dusk arrives, visitors and locals alike find a cool spot to sit outside, sip cocktails, and chat. Many outdoor restaurants and stores in Barra accommodate this relaxing way to end the day, adding extra tables and chairs for drop-ins.

During high season, the **Hotel Sands** poolside and lagoon-side bar has happy hour from 2 to 6pm. The colorful **Sunset Bar and Restaurant,** facing the bay at the corner of Legazpi and Jalisco, is a favorite for sunset watching, and then a game of oceanside pool or dancing to live or taped music. It's most popular with travelers ages 20 to 30. In the same vein, **Chips Restaurant,** on the second floor facing the ocean at the corner of Yucatán and Legazpi near the southern end of the *malecón,* has an excellent sunset vista. Live music follows the last rays of light, and patrons stay for hours. **Piper's Lover Bar & Restaurant,** Legazpi 254 (© **315/355-6747;** www.piperlover.com), is done in the style of the Carlos Anderson's chain—but it's not one of them. Still, it is lively, with pool tables and occasional live music.

At the **Disco El Galeón,** in the Hotel Sands on Calle Morelos, cushioned benches and cement tables encircle the round dance floor. It's all open-air, and about as stylish as you'll find in Barra. It serves drinks only. Admission is $6, and it's open Friday and Saturday from 9pm to 4am.

5

Manzanillo

by Lynne Bairstow

Manzanillo has long been known as a resort town with wide, curving beaches, legendary sportfishing, and a celebrated wealth of dive sites. Golf is also an attraction here, with two popular courses in the area.

One reason for Manzanillo's popularity could be its enticing tropical geography—with vast groves of tall palms, abundant mango trees, and successive coves graced with smooth sand beaches. To the north, mountains blanketed with palms rise alongside the shoreline. And the weather is near perfect, with balmy temperatures and year-round sea breezes. Even the approach by plane into Manzanillo showcases the promise—you fly in over the beach and golf course. Once on the ground, you exit the airport through a palm grove.

Manzanillo is a dichotomous place—it is Mexico's busiest commercial seaport and a tranquil town of multicolor houses cascading down the hillsides to meet the central commercial area of simple seafood restaurants, shell shops, and salsa clubs. The activity in Manzanillo divides neatly into two zones: the downtown commercial port and the luxury Santiago Peninsula resort zone to the north. The busy harbor and rail connections to Mexico's interior dominate the downtown. The town's waterfront *zócalo* provides a glimpse into local life. The exclusive Santiago Peninsula, home to the resorts and golf course, separates Manzanillo's two golden sand bays.

1 Manzanillo Essentials

256km (160 miles) SE of Puerto Vallarta; 267km (167 miles) SW of Guadalajara; 64km (40 miles) SE of Barra de Navidad

ORIENTATION
GETTING THERE & DEPARTING
By Plane Alaska Airlines (© 800/426-0333 in the U.S., or 314/334-2211) offers service from Los Angeles; **America West** (© 800/235-9292 in the U.S.) flies from Phoenix; and **Aero California** (© 800/237-6225 in the U.S. and Canada, or 314/334-1414) has

flights from Los Angeles. Ask a travel agent about the numerous **charters** from the States in the winter.

The **Playa de Oro International Airport** is 40km (25 miles; 45 min.) northwest of town. *Colectivo* (minivan) airport service is available from the airport; hotels arrange returns. Make reservations for return trips 1 day in advance. The *colectivo* fare is based on zones and runs $8 to $10 for most hotels. Private taxi service between the airport and downtown area is around $25. **Budget** (℃ 800/527-0700 in the U.S., or 314/333-1445) and **AutoRentas** (℃ 314/333-2580) run airport counters during flight arrivals; they will also deliver a car to your hotel. Daily rates run $58 to $78. You need a car only if you plan to explore surrounding cities and the Costa Alegre beaches.

By Car **Coastal Highway 200** leads from Acapulco (south) and Puerto Vallarta (north). From Guadalajara, take Highway 54 through Colima into Manzanillo. Outside Colima you can switch to a toll road, which is faster but less scenic.

By Bus Buses run to Barra de Navidad (1½ hr. north), Puerto Vallarta (5 hr. north), Colima (1½ hr. east), and Guadalajara (4½ hr. north), with deluxe service and numerous daily departures. Manzanillo's **Central Camionera** (bus station) is about 12 long blocks east of town. If you follow Hidalgo east, the station will be on your right.

VISITOR INFORMATION

The **tourism office** (℃ **314/333-2277** or 314/333-2264; fax 314/333-2264) is on the Costera Miguel de la Madrid 4960, Km 8.5. It's open Monday through Thursday from 9am to 3pm and 5 to 7pm, Friday from 9am to 3pm, and Saturday from 10am to 2pm.

CITY LAYOUT

The town lies at one end of an 11km-long (7-mile) beach facing Manzanillo Bay and its commercial harbor. The beach has four sections—**Playa Las Brisas, Playa Azul, Playa Salahua,** and **Playa Las Hadas.** At the other end of the beaches is the high, rocky **Santiago Peninsula.** Santiago is 11km (7 miles) from downtown; it's the site of many beautiful homes, the best hotel in the area (Las Hadas), and the Mantarraya Golf Course. The peninsula juts out into the bay, separating Manzanillo Bay from Santiago Bay. Playa Las Hadas is on the south side of the peninsula, facing Manzanillo Bay, and **Playa Audiencia** is on the north side, facing Santiago Bay. The inland town of **Santiago** is opposite the turnoff to Las Hadas.

Manzanillo Area

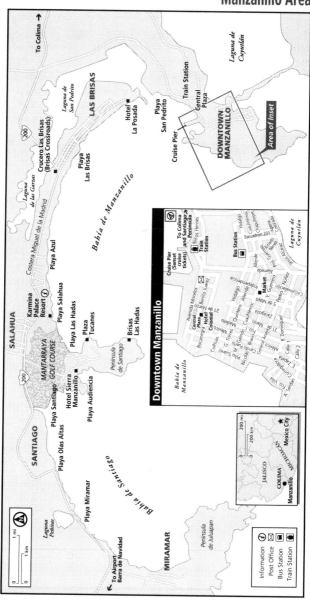

163

Activity in downtown Manzanillo centers on the **central plaza,** or *zócalo,* officially known as the Jardín Alvaro Obregón. A railroad, shipyards, and a basketball court with constant pickup games separate it from the waterfront. The plaza has flowering trees, a fountain, twin kiosks, and a view of the bay. It is a staple of local life, where people congregate on park benches to swap gossip and throw handfuls of rice to the ever-present *palomas* (doves—really just pigeons). Large ships dock at the pier nearby. **Avenida México,** the street leading out from the plaza's central gazebo, is the town's principal commercial thoroughfare. This area is currently undergoing a government-funded renaissance, so look for new improvements.

Once you leave downtown, the highway (the **Costera Miguel de la Madrid,** or just Costera Madrid) runs through the neighborhoods of Las Brisas, Salahua, and Santiago to the **hotel zones** on the Santiago Peninsula and at Miramar. Shell shops, minimalls, and several restaurants are along the way.

There are two main lagoons and two bays. **Laguna de Cuyutlán,** almost behind the city, stretches south for miles, paralleling the coast. **Laguna de San Pedrito,** north of the city, parallels the Costera Miguel de la Madrid; it's behind Playa Las Brisas beach. (Both are good birding sites.) **Manzanillo Bay** encompasses the harbor, town, and beaches. The Santiago Peninsula separates it from the second bay, **Santiago.** Between downtown and the Santiago Peninsula, **Las Brisas** is a flat peninsula with a long stretch of golden sand, a lineup of inexpensive but run-down hotels, and a few good restaurants.

GETTING AROUND

By Taxi   Taxis in Manzanillo are plentiful. Fares are fixed by zones; rates for trips within town and to more distant points should be posted at your hotel. Daily rates can be negotiated for longer drives outside the Manzanillo area.

By Bus   Local buses *(camionetas)* run a circuit from downtown in front of the train station, along the Bay of Manzanillo, to the Santiago Peninsula and the Bay of Santiago to the north; the fare is 10¢. The ones marked LAS BRISAS go to the Las Brisas crossroads, to the Las Brisas Peninsula, and back to town; MIRAMAR, SANTIAGO, and SALAHUA buses go to outlying settlements along the bays and to most restaurants mentioned below. Buses marked LAS HADAS go to the Santiago Peninsula and pass the Las Hadas resort and the Sierra Manzanillo and Plaza Las Glorias hotels. This is an inexpensive way to see the coast as far as Santiago and to tour the Santiago Peninsula.

FAST FACTS: Manzanillo

American Express There is no local office for American Express in Manzanillo. However, a highly recommendable agency (and American Express's former representative) is **Bahías Gemelas Travel Agency,** Km 10 Costera Miguel de la Madrid (© **314/333-1000;** fax 314/333-0649). It's open Monday through Friday from 10am to 2pm and 4 to 6pm, Saturday from 10am to 2pm.

Area Code The telephone area code is **314.**

Bank **Banamex,** just off the plaza on Avenida México, downtown (© **314/332-0115**), is open Monday through Friday from 9am to 4pm.

Hospital Call the **Cruz Roja (Red Cross)** at © **314/336-5770,** or **General Hospital** at © **314/332-1903.**

Internet Access **Digital Center,** Blvd. Miguel de la Madrid 96-B (© **314/333-9191**), is in the hotel zone, near the Hotel Marbella and Fiesta Americana hotel. It's $2 per hour, with printers and copiers available. It's open Monday through Friday from 9am to 8pm, Saturday from 9am to 2pm. They also have computer repair services available.

Police Both the general police and Tourism Police are available by calling © **314/332-1004.**

Post Office The *correo,* Dr. Miguel Galindo 30, opposite Farmacia de Guadalajara, downtown (© **314/332-0022**), is open Monday through Friday from 9am to 2pm.

ACTIVITIES ON & OFF THE BEACH

Activities in Manzanillo revolve around its golden sand beaches, which frequently accumulate a film of black mineral residue from nearby rivers. Most of the resort hotels are completely self-contained. Manzanillo's public beaches provide an opportunity to see more local color and scenery. They are the daytime playground for those staying at places off the beach or without pools.

BEACHES   Playa Audiencia, on the Santiago Peninsula, offers the best swimming as well as snorkeling, but **Playa San Pedrito,** shallow for a long way out, is the most popular beach for its proximity to downtown. **Playa Las Brisas** offers an optimal combination of location and good swimming. **Playa Miramar,** on the Bahía de Santiago past the Santiago Peninsula, is popular with body-surfers, windsurfers, and boogie boarders. It's accessible by local bus from town. The major part of **Playa Azul** drops off sharply but is noted for its wide stretch of golden sand.

BIRDING   Several lagoons along the coast offer good birding. As you go from Manzanillo past Las Brisas to Santiago, you'll pass **Laguna de Las Garzas (Lagoon of the Herons)**, also known as Laguna de San Pedrito, where you can see many white pelicans and huge herons fishing in the water. They nest here in December and January. Directly behind downtown is the **Laguna de Cuyutlán** (follow the signs to Cuyutlán), where you'll usually find birds in abundance; species vary between summer and winter.

DIVING   Underworld Scuba ☆☆ (℃/fax **314/333-0642;** cell 314/358-0327; www.gomanzanillo.com), owned by longtime resident and local diving expert Susan Dearing, conducts highly professional scuba expeditions and classes. Susan's warm enthusiasm and intimate knowledge of the area make this one of the top dive outfitters in Mexico. Many locations are so close to shore there's no need for a boat. Close-in dives include the jetty with coral growing on the rocks at 14m (45 ft.), and a nearby sunken frigate downed in 1959 at 8m (28 ft.). Divers can see abundant sea life, including coral reefs, seahorses, giant puffer fish, and moray eels. A dive requiring a boat costs $60 per person for one tank (with a three-person minimum), or $70 for two tanks ($10 discount if you have your own gear). You can also rent weights and a tank for beach dives for $10. A three-stop snorkel trip is $35. Guides are certified divemasters, and the shop runs intensive certification classes (PADI, YMCA, and CMAS). The owner offers a 10% discount on your certification when you mention Frommer's. MasterCard and Visa are accepted.

ESCORTED TOURS   Because Manzanillo is so spread out, you might consider a city tour. Reputable options include **Hectours** (℃ **314/333-1707**) and **Bahías Gemelas Travel Agency** (℃ **314/ 333-1000;** fax 314/333-0649). Schedules are flexible; a half-day tour is around $25. Other tours include the daylong Colima Colonial Tour ($67), which stops at a sugar-cane plantation, the Archaeological Museum, and principal colonial buildings, and passes the active volcano. Offerings change regularly, so ask about new tours.

FISHING   Manzanillo is famous for its fishing—particularly sailfish, which is abundant year-round, as is marlin. Winter is best for dolphin fish and dorado (mahi-mahi); in summer, wahoo and rooster

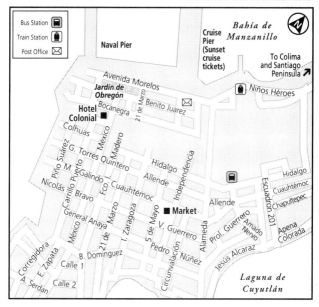

fish are in greater supply. The international sailfish competition is held around the November 20 Revolution Day holiday, and the national sailfish competition is in February. You can arrange fishing through travel agencies or directly at the fishermen's cooperative (© **314/332-1031**), located downtown where the fishing boats moor. Call from 7am to 7pm. A fishing boat is approximately $40 to $65 per hour, with most trips lasting about 5 hours.

GOLF The 18-hole **La Mantarraya Golf Course** (© **314/331-0101**) is open to nonguests as well as guests of Las Hadas. At one time, La Mantarraya was among the top 100 courses in the world, but newer entries have passed it. Still, the compact, challenging 18-hole course designed by Roy and Pete Dye is a beauty, with banana trees, blooming bougainvillea, and coconut palms at every turn. A lush and verdant place (12 of the 18 holes are played over water), it remains a favorite among Mexico's 125 courses. When the course was under construction, workers dug up pre-Hispanic ceramic figurines, idols, and beads where the 14th hole is—believed to have been an important ancient burial site. Greens fees are $122 for 18 holes, $73 for 9 holes; cart rental costs $50.

The fabulous 27-hole golf course associated with the **Grand Bay Hotel** in Barra de Navidad, an easy distance from Manzanillo, is also open to the public. The Robert Von Hagge design is long and lovely, with each hole amid rolling, tropical landscapes. It is wide open, with big fairways and big greens, and features plenty of water (2 lagoon holes, 13 lakeside holes, and 8 holes along the Pacific). The greens fees are $166 for 18 holes, $192 for 27 holes for hotel guests, $216 and $240, respectively, for nonguests, including a motorized cart. Barra is about a 1- to 1½-hour drive north of Manzanillo on Highway 200. (See "Activities On & Off the Beach" under "Barra de Navidad & Melaque," in chapter 4.)

A MUSEUM   The **Museum of Archaeology and History** (© 314/332-2256) is a small but impressive structure that houses exhibits depicting the region's history, plus rotating displays of contemporary Mexican art. It's on Avenida Niños Héroes at Avenida Teniente Azueta, on the road leading between the downtown and Las Brisas areas. Every Friday evening, the museum hosts free cultural events, which might be a trio playing romantic ballads or a chamber music ensemble. Performances begin at 8pm. Hours are Tuesday through Saturday from 10am to 2pm and 5 to 8pm, Sunday from 10am to 1pm. The museum is undergoing a complete renovation, scheduled to be completed in November 2006.

SHOPPING   Various shops carry Mexican crafts and clothing, mainly from nearby Guadalajara. Almost all are downtown on the streets near the central plaza. Shopping downtown is an experience—for example, you won't want to miss the shop bordering the plaza that sells a combination of shells, religious items (including shell-framed Virgin of Guadalupe nightlights), and orthopedic supplies. The Plaza Manzanillo is an American-style mall on the road to Santiago, and there's a traditional *tianguis* (outdoor) market in front of the entrance to Club Maeva, with touristy items from around Mexico. Most resort hotels also have boutiques or shopping arcades.

SUNSET CRUISES   To participate in this popular tour, buy tickets from a travel agent or your hotel tour desk. Most cost around $25. Trips last 1½ to 2 hours and vary in terms of drinks, music, and entertainment. Departing from Las Hadas is the **El Explorer** (© 314/352-4882) and **Antares** (© 314/376-0144).

WHERE TO STAY

Manzanillo's strip of coastline consists of three areas: **downtown,** with its shops, markets, and commercial activity; **Las Brisas,** the hotel-lined beach area immediately north of the city; and **Santiago,** the town and peninsula, now virtually a suburb, to the north at the end of Playa Azul. Transportation by bus or taxi makes all three areas fairly convenient to each other. Reservations are recommended during the Easter, Christmas, and New Year's holidays.

DOWNTOWN

Hotel Colonial ☆ An old favorite, this three-story colonial-style hotel is in the central downtown district. Popular for its consistent quality, ambience, and service, it has beautiful blue-and-yellow tile, and colonial-style carved doors and windows in the lobby and restaurant. Rooms are decorated with minimal furniture, red-tile floors, and basic comforts. The hotel is 1 block inland from the main plaza at the corner of Juárez and Galindo.

Av. México 100 and González Bocanegra, 28200 Manzanillo, Col. ☎ **314/332-1080,** 314/332-0668, 314/332-1230, or 314/332-1134. 42 units. $34 double. MC, V. **Amenities:** Restaurant; bar; tour desk. *In room:* A/C, TV.

LAS BRISAS

Some parts of the Las Brisas area look run-down; however, it still lays claim to one of the best beaches in the area and is known for its constant gentle sea breezes—a pleasure in the summer.

Hotel La Posada ☆ This small inn has a bright-pink stucco facade with a large arch that leads to a broad tiled patio on the beach. The rooms have exposed brick walls and simple furnishings with Mexican decorative accents. It remains popular with longtime travelers to Manzanillo. The atmosphere is casual and informal—help yourself to beer and soft drinks, and at the end of your stay, owners Juan and Lisa Martinez will count the bottle caps you tossed in a bowl with your room number on it. The restaurant is open daily during high season from 8 to 11am and 1:30 to 8pm; nonguests are welcome. A meal is about $7. During low season, the restaurant is open from 8am to 3pm. Stop by for a drink at sunset; the bar's open until 9pm year-round. The hotel is at the end of Las Brisas Peninsula, closest to downtown, and is on the local Las Brisas bus route.

Av. Lázaro Cárdenas 201, Las Brisas (Apdo. Postal 135), 28200 Manzanillo, Col. ☎ fax **314/333-1899.** www.hotel-la-posada.info or www.mexonline.com/laposada. htm. 23 units. High season $78 double; low season $58 double. Rates include full breakfast. MC, V. **Amenities:** Restaurant; bar; Internet cafe; laundry service; money exchange; safe-deposit boxes.

SANTIAGO

Five kilometers (3 miles) north of Las Brisas is the wide Santiago Peninsula. The settlement of Salahua is on the highway where you enter the peninsula to reach the hotels Las Hadas, Plaza Las Glorias, and Sierra Manzanillo, as well as the Mantarraya Golf Course. Buses from town marked LAS HADAS pass by these hotels every 20 minutes. Past the Salahua turnoff, at the end of the settlement of Santiago, an obscure road on the left is marked ZONA DE PLAYAS and leads to the hotels on the other side of the peninsula and Playa de Santiago.

Brisas Las Hadas Golf Resort & Marina 👫👫 Las Hadas—the setting for the movie *10,* with Bo Derek—is the most compelling reason to visit Manzanillo. This elegant, Moorish-style, beachside resort is built into the side of the rocky peninsula. The service is gracious, warm, and unobtrusive. Rooms need some updating, but they spread over landscaped grounds and overlook the bay; cobbled lanes lined with colorful flowers and palms connect them. The resort is large but maintains an air of seclusion. (Motorized carts are on call for transportation within the property.)

Views, room size, and amenities differentiate the six types of accommodations, which can vary greatly. If you're not satisfied with your room, ask to be moved—a few of the rooms are significantly less attractive than others. Understated and spacious, the better units have white-marble floors, sitting areas, and large, comfortably furnished balconies. Nine suites have private pools. The lobby is a popular place for curling up in one of the overstuffed seating areas or, at night, for enjoying a drink and live music. Pete and Roy Dye designed La Mantarraya, the hotel's 18-hole, par-71 golf course.

Av. de los Riscos s/n, Santiago Peninsula, 28200 Manzanillo, Col. ℂ **888/559-4329** in the U.S. and Canada, or 314/331-0101. www.brisas.com.mx. 233 units. High season $250–$300 double, $462–$557 Fantasy Suite; low season $190–$232 double, $395–$495 Fantasy Suite. AE, DC, MC, V. Free guarded parking. **Amenities:** 3 restaurants, including the elegant Legazpi (see "Where to Dine," below); 3 lounges and bars; 2 pools; small workout room; scuba diving, snorkeling, water-skiing, sailing, and trimaran cruises; concierge; tour desk; travel agency; car rental; shopping arcade; 24-hr. room service; in-room massage; babysitting; laundry service; dry cleaning; marina for 70 vessels; shade tents on the beach. *In room:* A/C, TV, dataport, minibar, hair dryer, safe-deposit box, bathrobes.

Hotel Sierra Manzanillo 👫 (Kids) This 21-floor hotel, with all-inclusive package options, overlooks La Audiencia beach. Its full program of sports, dining, entertainment, and kids' activities makes its a top choice for families. Architecturally, it mimics the white Moorish style of Las Hadas, which has become so popular in Manzanillo. Inside, it's palatial in scale and awash in pale-gray marble. Room decor picks up the pale-gray theme with armoires that conceal the TV and minibar. Most standard rooms have two double beds or a king-size bed, plus a small table, chairs, and desk. Several rooms at the end of most floors are small, with one double bed, small porthole-size windows, no balcony, and no view. Most rooms, however, have balconies and ocean or hillside views. The 10 honeymoon suites have sculpted, shell-shaped headboards, king-size beds, and chaises. Junior suites have a sitting area with couch, and large bathrooms. Scuba-diving lessons take place in the pool, and excellent scuba-diving sites are within swimming distance.

Av. La Audiencia 1, Los Riscos, 28200 Manzanillo, Col. 🕐 800/564-7556 in the U.S., or 314/333-2000. Fax 314/333-2611. 332 units. High season $342 double, $392–$412 suite; low season $175 double, $248–$308 suite. Rates are all-inclusive. AE, MC, V. **Amenities:** 3 restaurants; 4 bars; grand pool on the beach; children's pool; 4 lighted tennis courts; health club w/exercise equipment, aerobics, hot tub, men's and women's sauna and steam rooms; travel agency; salon w/massage; room service; laundry service; 24-hr. currency exchange. *In room:* A/C, TV, dataport, minibar, hair dryer.

Karmina Palace ★★★ *(Kids)*   The quality of rooms and services at this all-inclusive resort makes the newest of Manzanillo's hotels probably one of the area's best values. It's the best choice for families in Manzanillo. The buildings resemble Maya pyramids, and even though the architecture at first might seem a little overdone, somehow it works. Rooms are all very large suites, with rich wood accents, comfortable recessed seating areas with pull-out couches, and two 27-inch TVs in each room. The extralarge bathrooms have marble floors, twin black marble sinks, separate tubs, and glassed-in showers. Most rooms have terraces or balconies with views of the ocean, overlooking the tropical gardens and swimming pools. Master suites have spacious sun terraces with private splash pools, plus a full wet bar, full refrigerator, and a large living room area with 42-inch TV. Two full-size bedrooms close off from the living/dining area.

The Kid's Club offers a host of activities, while adults have numerous choices for fun—all included in the price. There's also an exceptionally well-equipped gym and European-style spa.

Av. Vista Hermosa 13 Fracc. Península de Santiago, 28200 Manzanillo, Col. 🕐 888/234-6222 in the U.S. and Canada, or 314/334-1300, 314/331-1313, or 01-800/234-6222 in Mexico. Fax 314/334-1108. www.karminapalace.com. Reservations: reservations@karminapalace.com. 324 units. $364–$384 double; $850–$1,000 2-bedroom suites for quad occupancy. Rates are all-inclusive. Special packages and Web specials available. 2 children under 8 stay free in parent's room. Ask about seasonal specials. AE, MC, V. **Amenities:** 2 restaurants; snack bar; 5 bars; 8 connected swimming pools; tennis courts; health club w/treadmills and Cybex equipment; full spa facilities, including men's and women's sauna and steam rooms; kids' activity program; 24-hr. concierge; car rental; 24-hr. room service; beach volleyball; windsurfing; money exchange; safe-deposit box in reception area. *In room:* A/C, TV, dataport, minibar, hair dryer, iron, safe-deposit box ($2).

Plaza Tucanes ✷   The sunset-colored walls of this pueblolike hotel ramble over a hillside on the Santiago Peninsula. The restaurant on top and most rooms afford a broad vista of other red-tiled rooftops and either the palm-filled golf course or the bay. It's one of Manzanillo's undiscovered resorts, known more to wealthy Mexicans than to Americans. Conceived as private condominiums, the accommodations were designed for living; each spacious unit is stylishly furnished, and very comfortable. Each has a huge living room; a small kitchen/bar; one, two, or three large bedrooms with tile or brick floors; large Mexican-tiled bathrooms; huge closets; and large furnished private patios with views. Some units have whirlpool tubs, and a few can be partitioned off and rented by the bedroom only. Rooms can be a long walk from the main entrance, through a succession of stairways and paths. If stair climbing bothers you, try to get a room by the restaurant and pool—you'll have a great view, and a hillside rail elevator goes straight from top to bottom.

Av. de Tesoro s/n, Santiago Peninsula, 28200 Manzanillo, Col. ✆ **314/334-1098.** Fax 314/334-0090. www.plazatucanes.com. 103 units. $75–$95 double. Packages available. AE, MC, V. **Amenities:** Two restaurants, including Argentine steakhouse; pool; kids' club; minigolf, "recreational park," game area; room service; babysitting (w/advance notice); beach club on Las Brisas beach, w/pool and small restaurant; transportation to and from beach club (once daily in each direction). *In room:* A/C, TV, safe-deposit box.

WHERE TO DINE
DOWNTOWN
Roca del Mar MEXICAN/INTERNATIONAL   Join the locals at this informal cafe facing the plaza. The large menu includes club sandwiches, hamburgers, *carne asada a la tampiqueña* (thin grilled steak served with rice, poblano pepper, an enchilada, and refried beans), fajitas, fish, shrimp, and vegetable salads. A specialty is its *paella* (served on Sun and Tues), and the economical *pibil* tacos are outstanding. This cafe is very clean and offers sidewalk dining.

21 de Marzo 204 (across from the plaza). ✆ **314/332-0302.** Main courses $3–$12. No credit cards. Daily 7:30am–noon.

LAS BRISAS
The Hotel La Posada (see "Where to Stay," above) offers breakfast to nonguests at its beachside restaurant; it's also a great place to mingle with other tourists and enjoy the sunset and cocktails.

La Toscana ★★★ *Finds* SEAFOOD/INTERNATIONAL   You're in for a treat at La Toscana (by the same owner of the now-closed Willy's), one of Manzanillo's most popular restaurants, on the beach in Las Brisas. It's homey, casual, and small (reservations are highly recommended). The modest atmosphere belies the cuisine, with starters that include escargot and salmon carpaccio. Among the grilled specialties are shrimp imperial wrapped in bacon, red snapper tarragon, dorado basil, sea bass with mango and ginger, and tender fresh lobsters (four to a serving). Live music frequently sets the scene.

Bulevar Miguel de la Madris 3177, 100m (300 ft.) from Hotel Fiesta Mexicana. ℃ **314/333-2515**. Reservations required. Main courses $8–$17. MC, V. Daily 6pm–2am.

SANTIAGO ROAD

The restaurants below are on the Costera Madrid between downtown and the Santiago Peninsula, including the Salahua area.

Benedetti's Pizza PIZZA   Benedetti's has several branches in town, so you'll probably find one near your hotel. The variety is extensive, but Benedetti's specializes in seafood pizzas, such as smoked oyster and anchovy. (If you order sesame-crust pizza, add some *chimichurri* sauce to enhance the flavor.) You can also select from pastas, sandwiches, fajitas, salads, Mexican soups, and desserts.

Bulevar Miguel de la Madrid, near the Las Brisas Glorietta on the ocean side (west). ℃ **314/333-1592** or 314/334-0141. Pizza $9–$12; main courses $2–$5.55. AE, MC, V. Daily 1–11:30pm.

Bigotes II *Finds* SEAFOOD   Locals flock to this large, breezy restaurant by the water for large portions of grilled seafood and a festive atmosphere. Strolling singers serenade patrons as they dine.

Puesta del Sol 3. ℃ **314/333-1236**. Main courses $9.50–$23. MC, V. Daily noon–10pm. From downtown, follow the Costera Madrid past the Las Brisas turnoff; the restaurant is behind the Penas Coloradas Social Club, across from the beach.

SANTIAGO PENINSULA

Legazpi ★★ INTERNATIONAL   This is a top choice in Manzanillo for sheer elegance, gracious service, and outstanding food. The candlelit tables are set with silver and flowers. Enormous bell-shaped windows on two sides show off the sparkling bay below. The sophisticated menu includes prosciutto with melon marinated in port wine, crayfish bisque, broiled salmon, roast duck, lobster, veal, and flaming desserts from crepes to Irish coffee.

In the Brisas Las Hadas hotel, Santiago Peninsula. ℃ **314/331-0101**. Main courses $8.50–$16. AE, MC, V. High season daily 7–11:30pm. Closed low season.

MANZANILLO AFTER DARK

Manzanillo is not only a resort town—it's a thriving commercial center, with a much more exuberant nightlife than you might expect. Clubs and bars tend to change from year to year, so check with your concierge for current hot spots. Some area clubs have a dress code prohibiting shorts or sandals, principally applying to men.

El Bar de Félix, between Salahua and Las Brisas by the Avis rental-car office (© **314/333-1875**), is open Tuesday through Sunday from 2pm to midnight, and has an $8 minimum consumption charge. With music ranging from salsa and ranchero to rock and house, it's the most consistently lively place in town. **Vog Disco** (© **314/333-1875**), Bulevar Costera Miguel de la Madrid Km 9.2, features alternative music in a cavernous setting; it's Manzanillo's current late-night hot spot, open until 5am, but only on Friday and Saturday. The cover charge for women is $10, for men $15. Also very popular—with a built-in crowd—is the nightclub at the **Club Maeva Hotel & Resort** (© **01-800/523-8450**), on the inland side of the main highway, north of the Santiago Peninsula. It's open Tuesday, Thursday, and Saturday from 11pm to 2am. Couples are given preferential entrance. Nonguests are welcome but must pay an entrance fee, after which all drinks are included. *Note:* When Club Maeva is full, entrance to nonguests is difficult—or impossible. Ask your hotel front desk if they can secure a pass for you. The fee varies depending on the night of the week and the time of year.

A SIDE TRIP TO COLIMA & ITS VOLCANO

The city of Colima makes an interesting and accessible day trip from Manzanillo. It's about an hour's drive along the well-maintained, four-lane Highway 54 to this charming colonial city, the capital of Colima state. Well-preserved colonial buildings, such as the city's 1527 **cathedral** and the **Palacio de Gobierno,** with its murals depicting Mexican history, are key attractions in the city's center.

Colima has several interesting museums, including the **Museo de las Culturas del Occidente,** which displays an impressive permanent collection of pre-Columbian pottery and artifacts. It's open Tuesday through Sunday from 10am to 5pm; admission is free. The **Casa de la Cultura** hosts changing exhibitions of contemporary art and offers free art, music, and dance classes. It's open Tuesday through Sunday from 10:30am to 5:30pm; admission is free.

Two imposing volcanoes (one still active) border the town. The **Volcán de Fuego** is 24km (15 miles) north, next to the taller, extinct **Nevado de Colima.** In 1999, the Volcán de Fuego became active, sometimes blowing smoke and ash up to 5km (3 miles) high, but it has since settled down.

6

Settling into Guadalajara

by David Baird

Guadalajara is the second-largest city in Mexico (with 3.5 million inhabitants, it's a very distant second to Mexico City), but because it's the homeland of mariachi music, the jarabe tapatío (the Mexican hat dance), and tequila, many consider it the most Mexican of cities. Despite its size, Guadalajara isn't hard to navigate, and the people are friendly and helpful. And unlike in Mexico City, visitors can enjoy big-city pleasures without big-city hassles.

While in Guadalajara, you will undoubtedly come across the word *tapatío* (or *tapatía*). In the early days, people from the area were known to trade in threes, called *tapatíos*. Gradually, the locals came to be called Tapatíos, too, and the word now signifies Guadalajaran when referring to a thing, a person, or a manner of doing something.

1 Orientation

GETTING THERE

BY PLANE Guadalajara's international airport is a 25- to 45-minute ride from the city. Taxis are the only transport ($15 to downtown). Tickets, priced by zone, are sold in front of the airport.

Major Airlines See chapter 1 for a list of toll-free numbers for international airlines serving Mexico. Numbers in Guadalajara are: **AeroMar** (© 33/3615-8509), **Aeromexico** (© 01-800/021-4010), **American** (© 01-800/904-6000), **Continental** (© 01-800/900-5000), **Delta** (© 33/3630-3530), **Mexicana** (© 01-800/502-2000), and **United** (© 33/3616-9489).

Of the smaller airlines, **Aviacsa** (© 33/3123-1751) connects to Los Angeles, Las Vegas, Houston, and Chicago. **Aero California** (© 33/3616-2525) connects to Tijuana, Mexico City, Los Mochis, La Paz, and Puebla. **Azteca** (© 33/3630-4615) offers service to and from Mexico City, and from there to several cities in Mexico. **Allegro** (© 33/3647-7799) operates flights to and from Oakland and

Greater Guadalajara

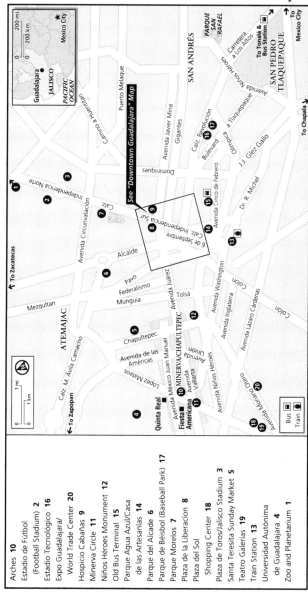

Las Vegas via Tijuana. **Alaska Airlines** (© 01-800/426-0333) flies to Los Angeles and Reno.

BY CAR   Guadalajara is at the hub of several four-lane toll roads (called *cuotas* or *autopistas*), which cut travel time considerably but are expensive. From Nogales on the **U.S. border,** follow Highway 15 south (21 hr.). From **Tepic,** a quicker route is toll road 15D (5 hr., $37). From **Puerto Vallarta,** go north on Highway 200 to Compostela; toll road 68D heads east to join the Tepic toll road. Total time is 5½ hours, and the tolls add up to $28. From **Barra de Navidad,** on the coast southeast of Puerto Vallarta, take Highway 80 northeast (4½ hr.). From **Manzanillo,** you might also take this road, but toll road 54D through Colima to Guadalajara (3½ hr., $25) is faster. From **Mexico City,** take toll road 15D (7 hr., $48).

BY BUS   Guadalajara has two bus stations. The old one, south of downtown, is for buses to Lake Chapala and other nearby areas; the new one, 10km (6 miles) southeast of downtown, is for longer trips.

   The Old Bus Station—for destinations within 100km (60 miles) of town, including the Lake Chapala area, go to the old bus terminal, on Niños Héroes off Calzada Independencia Sur. For Lake Chapala, take **Transportes Guadalajara-Chapala,** which runs frequent buses and *combis* (minivans).

   The New Bus Station—the **Central Camionera** is 15 to 30 minutes from downtown. The station has seven terminals connected by a covered walkway. Each terminal contains different bus lines, offering first- and second-class service for different destinations. You can buy bus tickets from several travel agents in Guadalajara. Ask at your hotel for the closest to you. There are several major bus lines. The best service (big seats and lots of room) is provided by **ETN.**

VISITOR INFORMATION

The **State of Jalisco Tourist Information Office,** at Calle Morelos 102 (© **33/3668-1600** or 33/3668-1601; http://visita.jalisco.gob.mx) in the Plaza Tapatía, at Paseo Degollado and Paraje del Rincón del Diablo, is open Monday through Friday 9am to 8pm, and Saturday, Sunday, and festival days 10am to 2pm. They dispense maps, a calendar of cultural events, and good information.

CITY LAYOUT

The **Centro Histórico (city center),** with all its plazas, churches, and museums, will obviously be of interest to the visitor. The **west side** is Guadalajara's modern, cosmopolitan district. In the northwest corner is **Zapopan,** home of Guadalajara's patron saint. On the opposite side of the city from Zapopan, in the southeast corner, are the crafts centers of **Tlaquepaque** and **Tonalá.**

The main artery for traffic from downtown to the west side is **Avenida Vallarta.** It starts downtown as **Juárez.** The main arteries for returning to downtown are **Mexico** and **Hidalgo,** both north of Vallarta. Vallarta heads due west, where it intersects another major artery, **Avenida Adolfo López Mateos,** at **Fuente Minerva** (or simply La Minerva, or Minerva Circle). Minerva Circle, a 15-minute drive from downtown, is the central point of reference for the west side. To go to Zapopan from downtown, take **Avenida Avila Camacho,** which you can pick up on Alcalde; it takes 20 minutes by car. To Tlaquepaque and Tonalá, take **Calzada Revolución.** Tlaquepaque is 8km (5 miles) from downtown and takes 15 to 20 minutes by car; Tonalá is 5 minutes farther. Another major viaduct, **Calzada Lázaro Cárdenas,** connects the west side to Tlaquepaque and Tonalá, bypassing downtown.

GUADALAJARA NEIGHBORHOODS IN BRIEF

Centro Histórico   The heart of the city contains many plazas, historic buildings, museums, the cathedral, and the striking murals of José Clemente Orozco, one of the great Mexican muralists. Theaters, restaurants, shops, and clubs dot the area, and an enormous market rounds out the attractions. All of this is in a space roughly 12 blocks by 12 blocks, an easy area for a good walker to explore and enjoy the several plazas and pedestrian-only areas. To the south is a large green space called Parque Agua Azul.

West Side   It's swanky here, with fine restaurants, luxury hotels, boutiques, galleries, and the American, British, and Canadian consulates. It's a large area best navigated by taxi.

Zapopan   Founded in 1542, Zapopan is a suburb of Guadalajara. In its center is the 18th-century basilica, the home of Guadalajara's patron saint, the Virgin of Zapopan. The most interesting part of Zapopan is clustered around the temple and can be explored by foot. It has a growing arts and nightlife scene.

Tlaquepaque   This was a village of artisans (especially potters) that grew into a market center. In the last 30 years, it has attracted designers from all over Mexico. Every major form of art and crafts is for sale here: furniture, pottery, glass, jewelry, woodcarvings, leather goods, sculptures, and paintings. The shops are sophisticated, yet Tlaquepaque's center retains a small-town feel that makes door-to-door browsing enjoyable and relaxing.

Tonalá This has remained a town of artisans. Plenty of stores sell mostly local products from the town's 400-plus workshops. You'll see wrought iron, ceramics, blown glass, and papier-mâché. A busy street market operates each Thursday and Sunday.

2 Getting Around

BY TAXI Taxis are the easiest way to get around town. Almost all have meters, and, though some drivers are reluctant to use them, you can insist that they do. There are three rates: for day, night, and suburbia. On my last visit typical fares were the following: downtown to the west side, $6 to $8; downtown or west side to Tlaquepaque, $6 to $9; to new bus station, $7; to airport, $14 to $18.

BY CAR Keep in mind the several main arteries (see "City Layout," above). Several important freeway-style thoroughfares crisscross the city. **González Gallo** leads south from the town center and connects with the road to Lake Chapala. **Avenida Vallarta** continues past La Minerva and eventually feeds onto **Highway 15,** bound for Tequila and Puerto Vallarta.

BY BUS There are various city bus lines that offer different grades of service. The best buses are the **Turquesa buses,** which can be identified by the large capital letters TUR. They are air-conditioned and comfortable and carry only as many passengers as there are seats; they are worth the price (about 60¢ for most destinations). For the visitor, the handiest route is the **706 tur,** which runs from the Centro Histórico southeast to Tlaquepaque, the Central Camionera (the new bus station), and Tonalá. For more information on Tlaquepaque and Tonalá, see "Shopping," in chapter 7. You can catch this bus on Avenida 16 de Septiembre. The same bus runs in the reverse direction back to the downtown area.

The electric bus is handy for travel between downtown and the Minerva area. It bears the sign PAR VIAL and runs east along Hidalgo and west along the next street to the north, Calle Independencia (not Calzada Independencia). Hidalgo passes along the north side of the cathedral. The Par Vial goes as far east as Mercado Libertad and as far west as Minerva Circle. The city also has a light rail system, **Tren Ligero,** but it doesn't serve areas that are of interest to visitors.

FAST FACTS: Guadalajara

American Express The local office is at Av. Vallarta 2440, Plaza los Arcos, Local A-1 (✆ **33/3818-2323**); it's open Monday through Friday from 9am to 6pm, Saturday from 9am to noon.

Area Code The telephone area code is **33.**

Books, Newspapers & Magazines **Gonvil,** a popular bookstore chain, has a branch across from Plaza de los Hombres Ilustres on Avenida Hidalgo, and another a few blocks south at Av. 16 de Septiembre 118 (Alcalde becomes 16 de Septiembre south of the cathedral). It carries few English selections. **Sanborn's,** at the corner of Juárez and 16 de Septiembre, does a good job of keeping English-language periodicals in stock, but most are specialty magazines. Many newsstands sell the two English local papers, the *Guadalajara Reporter* and the *Guadalajara Weekly.* For the widest selection of English-language books, try **Sandi Bookstore,** Av. Tepeyac 718 (✆ **33/3121-0863**), in the Chapalita neighborhood on the west side.

Business Hours Store hours are Monday through Saturday from 10am to 2pm and 4 to 8pm.

Climate & Dress Guadalajara is mild year-round, with the occasional freak cold spell. Generally, from November through March, you'll need a sweater in the evening. The warmest months, April and May, are hot and dry. From June through September, the city gets afternoon and evening showers that keep the temperature a bit cooler. Dress in Guadalajara is conservative; attention-getting sportswear (short shorts, halters, and the like) is out of place.

Consulates The **American consular offices** are at Progreso 175 (✆ **33/3268-2200** or 33/3268-2100). Other consulates include the **Canadian consulate,** Hotel Fiesta Americana, Local 31 (✆ **33/3615-6215**); the **British consulate,** Calle Jesús Rojas 20, Col. Los Pinos (✆ **33/3343-2296**); and the **Australian consulate,** López Cotilla 2018, Col. Arcos Vallarta (✆ **33/3615-7418**). They're all open Monday through Friday from 8am to 1pm.

Currency Exchange The best rates are found 3 blocks south of the cathedral on López Cotilla, between Corona and Degollado. There are more than 20 *casas de cambio* on these 2 blocks. Almost all post their rates, which are better than the banks', without the long lines.

Elevation Guadalajara sits at 1,700m (5,576 ft.).

Emergencies The emergency phone number is ℂ 080.

Hospitals For medical emergencies, visit the **Hospital México-Americano,** Cólomos 2110 (ℂ **33/3642-7152**).

Internet Access Ask at your hotel for the closest Internet access. Most of the big hotels have business centers that you can use. In the Centro Histórico, there are many. All you have to do is ask around.

Language Classes Foreigners can study Spanish at the **Foreign Student Study Center,** University of Guadalajara, Calle Tomás V. Gómez 125, 44100 Guadalajara, Jal. ((ℂ **33/3616-4399**). **IMAC** is a private Spanish school at Donato Guerra 180 in the Centro Histórico (ℂ **33/3613-1080**).

Luggage Storage & Lockers You can store luggage in the main bus station, the Central Camionera, and at the Guadalajara airport.

Police Tourists should first try to contact the Jalisco tourist information office in Plaza Tapatía (ℂ **33/3658-1600**). If you can't reach the office, call the municipal police at ℂ **33/3617-6060**.

Post Office The *correo* is at the corner of Carranza and Calle Independencia, about 4 blocks northeast of the cathedral. Standing in the plaza behind the cathedral, facing the Degollado Theater, walk to the left and turn left on Carranza; walk past the Hotel Mendoza, cross Calle Independencia, and look for the post office on the left. It's open Monday through Thursday from 9am to 5pm, Saturday from 10am to 2pm.

Safety Guadalajara doesn't have the violent crime that Mexico City does. Crimes against tourists and foreign students are infrequent and most often take the form of pickpocketing and purse snatching. Criminals usually work in teams and target travelers in busy places, such as outdoor restaurants: One will create a distraction while the other slips off with whatever the tourist has set down. Purse-snatchers usually target unaccompanied women at night and rarely in places with crowds. The same is true of necklace snatching (the assailant grabs a necklace, especially if it has a gold chain, and pulls hard, hoping it will break). Be especially alert if someone spills something on you—this is a common trick.

3 Where to Stay

Prices are standard rack rates including the 17% tax. In slow periods, look for discounts; the big hotels often give business discounts.

Almost all of the luxury hotels in Guadalajara are on the west side, which has most of the shopping malls, boutiques, tony restaurants, and clubs. The Centro Histórico offers lots to do, making it a good base. Finally, Tlaquepaque is a comfortable suburb, perfect for shoppers; the only drawback is that almost everything shuts down by 7 or 8pm. Chain hotels not included below are the Hilton, Marriott, Camino Real, Howard Johnson, Crowne Plaza, and Best Western.

VERY EXPENSIVE

Hotel Presidente InterContinental 🏵🏵🏵 In a 14-story glass building with an atrium lobby, across from the Plaza del Sol shopping center, this hotel boasts Guadalajara's most comprehensive list of services and amenities. There is little staff turnover, and the concierge has proven more capable and knowledgeable than any other in the city. The quiet, comfortable rooms have modern furniture, including a desk and small table with two chairs. Club rooms, on limited-access hallways, have discreet check-in; rates include continental breakfast, newspaper, and evening cocktails. The extra privacy and services are good for Mexican soap opera stars or repeat guests who want their preferences known in advance. If you're neither of these, opt for one of the other rooms. The lobby bar is popular; during the season, bullfighters relax here after the *corrida*.

Av. López Mateos Sur and Moctezuma, 45050 Guadalajara, Jal. ⓒ **800/327-0200** in the U.S. and Canada, or 33/3678-1234. Fax 33/3678-1222. www.interconti.com. 409 units. $192–$249 double; $204–$261 deluxe; $227–$285 club; $305 and up for suite. Rates include breakfast buffet. AE, DC, MC, V. Valet parking $4. **Amenities:** 2 restaurants; lobby bar; outdoor heated pool; golf at nearby clubs; health club w/saunas, steam rooms, and whirlpools; concierge; tour desk; car rental; large business center; executive business services; salon; 24-hr. room service; massage; babysitting; laundry service; dry cleaning; nonsmoking rooms; executive-level rooms. *In room:* A/C, TV w/pay movies, minibar, hair dryer, iron, safe, high-speed wireless Internet.

Quinta Real 🏵🏵🏵 This chain specializes in building properties that are suggestive of Mexico's heritage, in contrast to the comfortable but generic luxury hotel. No glass skyscraper here—two four-story buildings made of stone, wood, plaster, and tile occupy lush grounds. Rooms vary quite a bit: Eight have brick cupolas, some have balconies, and four are equipped with a whirlpool tub in the bathroom. All are large, with a split-level layout and antique decorative touches. And all come with large, fully equipped bathrooms with tub/shower combinations and excellent water pressure. You can choose between two doubles or one king-size bed. The hotel is 2 blocks from Minerva Circle in western Guadalajara. Ask for a room that doesn't face López Mateos.

Av. México 2727 (at López Mateos), 44680 Guadalajara, Jal. ℭ **800/445-4565** in the U.S. and Canada, or 33/3669-0600. Fax 33/3669-0601. www.quintareal.com. 75 suites. $357 master suite; $387 grand-class suite. AE, DC, MC, V. Free secure parking. **Amenities:** Restaurant; bar; outdoor heated pool; golf at local club; access to nearby health club; concierge; tour desk; car rental; business center; executive business services; room service until midnight; babysitting; laundry service; dry cleaning; nonsmoking rooms. *In room:* A/C, TV, dataport, minibar, hair dryer, iron, safe.

Villa Ganz 🐾🐾🐾   This small, stylish hotel on the near west side of the city is one of the most comfortable in Guadalajara. Rooms are big, comfortable, and decorated with flair. Each holds a basket of fruit and a small bottle of wine on check-in. Bathrooms are large and well lit—some have tubs, others just showers. Bed choices include a king-size, a queen-size, or two twins. Beds come with down comforters (hypoallergenic option available). Rooms facing the garden are the quietest, but those facing the street are set back from the traffic and have double-glazed windows. The common rooms and rear garden are agreeable places to relax. Service is personal and helpful. Guests can contract with a guide or taxi driver at the hotel. In-room dining can be arranged with one of three nearby restaurants or arrangements can be made to bring in a chef. Villa Ganz is a member of the Boutique Hotels of Mexico. Villa Ganz has opened a bed-and-breakfast in central Guadalajara and it also offers apartments for extended stays; see the website for more information.

López Cotilla 1739, 44140 Guadalajara, Jal. ℭ **877/278-8018** in the U.S., 866/818-8342 in Canada, or 33/3120-1416. www.villaganz.com. 10 suites. $235–$2,278 suite. Rates include continental breakfast. AE, MC, V. Free secure parking. Children under 12 not accepted. **Amenities:** Golf and tennis at local club; concierge; tour desk; airport transfer; 24-hr. room service; laundry service; dry cleaning. *In room:* A/C, TV, hair dryer, iron (on request), safe, high-speed Internet.

EXPENSIVE

Fiesta Americana 🐾🐾   A sharp, 22-story hotel, similar to the Presidente Inter-Continental but with fewer amenities, the Fiesta Americana caters mainly to business travelers. The location is excellent—in front of Minerva Circle, in western Guadalajara—and service is great. Request newly remodeled floors 4 through 10. Rooms are large and carpeted, with two doubles or one king-size bed and a soundproof door. The large, well-equipped bathrooms hold tub/shower combinations. The furniture is modern and understated.

Aurelio Aceves 225, Glorieta Minerva, 44100 Guadalajara, Jal. ⓒ **800/FIESTA-1** in the U.S. and Canada, or 33/3825-3434. Fax 33/3630-3725. www.fiestaamericana.com. 391 units. $145–$185 double; $190 Fiesta Club double; $281–$624 suite. AE, DC, MC, V. Free secure parking. **Amenities:** Restaurant; lobby bar; heated pool; golf privileges at local club; 2 lighted tennis courts; exercise room; children's activities (Fiesta kids' program on Sun); concierge; tour desk; business center; executive business services; salon; 24-hr. room service; massage; babysitting; laundry service; dry cleaning; nonsmoking rooms; executive-level rooms; 1 room for those w/limited mobility. *In room:* A/C, TV w/pay movies, dataport, minibar, coffeemaker, hair dryer.

Holiday Inn Hotel and Suites Centro Histórico 🖈🖈 This six-story hotel is the most comfortable one downtown. Its location, a few blocks from the main square, is also good. Standard rooms are carpeted and cheerfully decorated in Mexican architectural colors. The furniture is modern Mexican with a few wrought-iron pieces. Room size and lighting are good; bathrooms are midsize and well equipped, with ample counter space. For quiet, ask for a room off the street. The suites are larger, but otherwise not worth the extra cost. Room rates include transportation to (but not from) the airport.

Av. Juárez 211, 44100 Guadalajara, Jal. ⓒ **800/HOLIDAY** in the U.S. and Canada, 01-800/009-9900 in Mexico, or 33/3613-1763. www.holiday-inn.com. 90 units. $180 double; $200 suite. Ask about promotional rates. AE, MC, V. Free secure parking. **Amenities:** Restaurant; bar; fitness room; business center; room service (until 10:30pm); laundry service; dry cleaning; nonsmoking rooms. *In room:* A/C, TV, dataport, minibar, coffeemaker, hair dryer, iron.

Hotel de Mendoza 🖈 On a quiet street next to the Degollado Theater and Plaza Tapatía, 2 blocks from the cathedral, the Mendoza has the best location of any downtown hotel. The decor is a stab at old Spanish, with wood paneling and old-world accents. Standard rooms are midsize and comfortable. Bed choices are one queen-size, two full, or two queen-size. Bathrooms are midsize, with ample counter space. Suites have an additional sitting area and larger bathrooms. Rooms face the street, an interior courtyard, or the pool. ***Note:*** The bath towels are the narrowest I've ever seen— obviously the brainchild of a demented cost-cutting expert. If the hotel hasn't changed these, ask for a couple extra after you check in.

Carranza 16, 44100 Guadalajara, Jal. ⓒ **800/221-6509** in the U.S., or 33/3613-4646. Fax 33/3613-7310. www.demendoza.com.mx. 104 units. $120 double; $142 suite. Discounts available. AE, MC, V. Secure parking $4. **Amenities:** Restaurant; bar; small pool; fitness room; Jacuzzi; tour desk; room service (until 10:30pm); laundry service; dry cleaning; nonsmoking rooms. *In room:* A/C, TV, dataport.

MODERATE

El Aposento Hotel *Value* This small hotel in a colonial house in the Centro Histórico has handsomely furnished rooms in muted tones. In terms of price, comfort, and location, it is roughly equal to other downtown bargains in this category, but rooms here are larger, with more character (but maybe less light). To avoid street noise, ask for a room away from the street (especially Madero). Rooms come with a king-size or two double beds. Most bathrooms are large; half come with a tub/shower combination. Full breakfast is served.

Francisco Madero 545, 44100 Guadalajara, Jal. ©/fax **33/3614-1612.** www.el aposento.com. 28 units. $65 double. Rates include full breakfast. AE, MC, V. Free sheltered parking. **Amenities:** Massage; nonsmoking rooms. *In room:* A/C, TV.

Hotel Cervantes *Value* This six-story downtown hotel offers modern amenities at a great price. The rooms are attractive and midsize, with wall-to-wall carpeting and tile bathrooms with ample sink areas and tub/shower combos. The lower price is for one double bed; the higher price, for a king-size or two double beds. It's not particularly noisy, but if you require absolute quiet, request an interior room. The Cervantes is 6 blocks south and 3 blocks west of the cathedral.

Prisciliano Sánchez 442, Col. Centro Histórico, 44100 Guadalajara, Jal. ©/fax **33/3613-6686.** 100 units. $65–$75 double. AE, MC, V. Free secure parking. **Amenities:** Restaurant; lobby bar; small outdoor heated pool; tour desk; room service (until 10pm); babysitting; laundry service; dry cleaning. *In room:* A/C, TV.

La Villa del Ensueño *★★* This B&B in central Tlaquepaque is a lovely alternative to big-city hotels. A modern interpretation of traditional Mexican architecture, it is a delight to the eye—small courtyards and beautiful gardens bordered by old stucco walls, which have been painted in muted shades of orange oxide or covered in carefully trimmed ivy, with an occasional wrought-iron balcony or stone staircase. The rooms are individually decorated and have more character than most hotel lodgings. All contain ceiling fans and wireless Internet connections. Doubles have either two twin or two double beds. Guests receive a complimentary cocktail on arrival. The hotel is about 8 blocks from the main plaza.

Florida 305, 45500 Tlaquepaque, Jal. © **800/220-8689** in the U.S., or 33/3635-8792. Fax 818/597-0637 in the U.S. www.villadelensueno.com. 18 units. $88 double; $100 deluxe double; $117 2-bedroom unit; $140 suite. Rates include full breakfast, light laundry service. AE, MC, V. Free valet parking. **Amenities:** Bar; indoor and small outdoor pool; laundry service. *In room:* A/C, TV, dataport, hair dryer.

Quinta Don José ★★ *Value*   This small hotel, 2 blocks from Tlaquepaque's main square, is a good value with a great location and friendly, English-speaking owners. Rooms range from midsize to extralarge. All are comfortable, attractive, and quiet. Most of the standard and deluxe doubles have a king-size or two double beds and an attractive, midsize bathroom. A couple have small private outdoor spaces. Some of the suites in back come with a full kitchen and lots of space—more than twice the size of the usual suite, with one king-size and one double bed. The breakfasts are good, and would you believe high-speed wireless Internet connection? Some lodgings just have a good feel to them, and this is one.

Reforma 139, 45500 Tlaquepaque, Jal. ⓒ **866/629-3753** in the U.S. and Canada, or 33/3635-7522. Fax 33/3659-9315. www.quintadonjose.com. 15 units. $88–$99 double; $117–$152 suite. Rates include full breakfast, wireless Internet access, airport and bus station pickup for long stays. AE, MC, V. Free secure parking. **Amenities:** Restaurant; bar; heated outdoor pool; tour info; in-room massage; babysitting; laundry service; nonsmoking rooms. *In room:* A/C, TV, hair dryer, iron, high-speed wireless Internet.

INEXPENSIVE

Hotel San Francisco Plaza *Value*   This colonial-style downtown hotel is both pleasant and a bargain. Its rooms are big and comfortable, with attractive furnishings. All have rugs or carpeting, and most have tall ceilings (except in the remodeled area behind the reception desk). The hotel is built in colonial style around four courtyards, which contain fountains and potted plants. Rooms along the Sánchez Street side are much quieter now that the management has installed double windows. Some units along the back wall of the rear patio have small bathrooms. The San Francisco Plaza is 6 blocks south and 2 blocks east of the cathedral.

Degollado 267, 44100 Guadalajara, Jal. ⓒ **33/3613-8954** or 33/3613-8971. Fax 33/3613-3257. www.sanfranciscohotel.com.mx. 76 units. $47 double. AE, MC, V. Free parking. **Amenities:** Restaurant; limited room service; babysitting; laundry service; dry cleaning; ironing service. *In room:* A/C, TV.

Plaza Los Reyes *Value*   Rooms in this 10-story downtown hotel are midsize and come with either two doubles or a king-size bed. Those on the mezzanine level are larger and often cost the same. Ask for a room facing away from the busy Calzada Independencia. Midsize bathrooms are clean, with showers. Air-conditioning units are minisplits, which are quiet and effective. It's good for the money.

Calzada Independencia Sur 168, 44100 Guadalajara, Jal. ⓒ **33/3613-9770** or 33/3613-9775. 189 units. $55 double. AE, MC, V. Free valet parking. **Amenities:** Restaurant; bar; outdoor heated pool; tour info; room service (until midnight); laundry service; nonsmoking rooms. *In room:* A/C, TV.

4 Where to Dine

Guadalajara has many excellent restaurants for fine dining and for typical local fare. Most of the fine-dining spots are on the west side. Those in the Centro Histórico are uniformly bad, excepting **La Fonda de San Miguel.** Tlaquepaque has some good choices, but they all close around 8pm. Popular eateries with good local fare abound, especially in the Centro Histórico. Local dishes include *birria* (goat, lamb, or pork covered in maguey leaves and roasted), in a tomato-based broth or with the broth on the side. To get it properly prepared, go to one of the many *birrierías.* There are about a half-dozen in Las Nueve Esquinas neighborhood, downtown; in Tlaquepaque, try **Birriería El Sope.** Another local favorite is *torta ahogada,* a sandwich with a pork filling bathed in a tomato sauce. Jalisco-style *pozole* is chicken-and-hominy soup to which you add lime juice, onion, Mexican oregano, and chiles.

For a quick meal, there are several **Sanborn's** in the city. This is a popular national chain of restaurants and coffee shops; the traditional dish is *enchiladas suizas* (enchiladas in cream sauce).

Keep your guidebook handy when taking a taxi; many drivers are unfamiliar even with popular places and require an address. Make reservations in the evening, especially for west side restaurants.

EXPENSIVE

Chez Nené 🐾🐾🐾 FRENCH   You can enjoy a delicious, leisurely French meal in this small, pleasant, open-air dining room. The owner is a French expatriate (whose Mexican wife, Nené, is the restaurant's namesake) with clear ideas about food and dining—supported by everything I saw and tasted there. Freshness and quality of ingredients, shorn of all fads and pretense, are what matter for him. Everything but stews and such is cooked to order. The daily menu, written on a chalkboard, depends on what he finds that morning at the market, and includes at least a dozen main courses. Service is excellent and informative.

Juan Polomar y Arias 426 (continuación Rafael Sauzio), west side. © 33/3673-4564. Reservations recommended on weekends. Main courses $10–$20. AE, MC, V. Tues 4–11pm; Wed–Sat 1–5:30pm and 7:30–11:30pm; Sun 1–6pm.

MODERATE

Adobe Fonda 🐾🐾🐾 NUEVA COCINA   This charming restaurant shares space with a large store on pedestrian-only Independencia. The space is open and airy. The menu is inventive and thoughtfully designed. Homemade bread and tostadas come to the table with an olive oil–based chile sauce, pico de gallo, and *requezón de epazote* (ricotta-like cheese with a Mexican herb). Among the soups are *crema de cilantro* and an interesting mushroom soup with a dark beer broth. The main courses present some difficult decisions, with intriguing combinations of Mexican, Italian, and Argentine ingredients: shrimp quesadillas accompanied by *chimichurri* with *nopal* cactus; filet in creamy ancho sauce. The daily specials can be very good. Sample the margaritas, too.

Francisco de Miranda 27, corner of Independencia, Tlaquepaque. © **33/3657-2792.** Reservations recommended on weekends. Main courses $9–$17. AE, MC, V. Daily 12:30–6:30pm.

El Sacromonte ★★★ ALTA COCINA   The food here is so exquisite that I try to dine here every time I'm in Guadalajara. El Sacromonte emphasizes artful presentation and design: Order "Queen Isabel's crown," and you'll be served a dish of shrimp woven together in the shape of a crown and covered in divine lobster-and-orange sauce. Or try quesadillas with rose petals in a deep-colored strawberry sauce. For soup, consider *el viejo progreso* for its unlikely combination of flavors (blue cheese and chipotle chile). The menu features amusing descriptions in verse. The main dining area is a shaded, open-air patio. The restaurant isn't far from the downtown area, on an eastbound street just 2 blocks north of Avenida Vallarta.

In the building next door, the owners opened **El Duende,** an updated version of the classic type of Mexican bar that serves complimentary *botanas* (the Mexican equivalent of tapas). There is also a menu, which is simpler than the restaurant's.

Pedro Moreno 1398, at Colonias, west side. © **33/3825-5447** or 33/3827-0663. Reservations suggested. Main courses $9–$17. MC, V. Mon–Sat 1:30pm–midnight.

Hostería del Angel ★★ TAPAS/SPANISH-ITALIAN DELI   Sip wine and munch on tapas in this comfortable and casual restaurant and wine bar just a few blocks from the basilica in Zapopan. The chef-owner cooked for years in Spain and Italy, where he became fascinated with the making of cheeses and deli meats such as prosciutto and Spanish *jamón Serrano.* He serves a variety of tapas, and his baguette sandwiches are very popular with the locals. The menu does a poor job of explaining the dishes, so don't hesitate to ask the waitperson for explanations. The house specialty is the *rotolata*—vegetables and cold cuts surrounded by a thin layer of crispy cheese. Live music plays from 9 to 11pm Monday through

Saturday. The restaurant is a half-block off the pedestrian-only *calzada,* which leads to the plaza in front of the basilica.

5 de Mayo 295, Zapopan, west side. ✆/fax **33/3656-9516.** Reservations recommended. Menu items $4–$9. MC, V. Tues–Sat 9am–midnight; Sun 9am–8pm.

I Latina FUSION   Warehouse chic with a porcine motif (the owner tells me that the pig is a symbol of abundance in Thailand) is the setting here. Naturally, the menu must exhibit sophistication, which it does with carpaccio here, portobellos there—you probably get the picture. But the food was well prepared. I had a stir-fry of chicken flavored with ginger, and a salad with greens, fried rice noodle, and citrus-flavored dressing. I also enjoyed people-watching. The furniture—metal and plastic—is completely in character yet comfortable. There's live music Thursday from 9 to 11pm and Sunday afternoon. Go early if you want to avoid the rush, and make reservations—this restaurant is *popularísimo.*

Av. Inglaterra, west side. ✆ **33/3647-7774.** Reservations recommended. Main courses $9–$15. MC, V. Wed–Sat 7:30pm–1am; Sun 2–6pm.

La Destilería 🐷🐷 MEXICAN   You know that with a name like "The Distillery," tequila will somehow be involved. Although this museum-restaurant abounds with artifacts and photos depicting every stage of the tequila-making process, the food is what really pulls in the TapatíosThis place is sure to please everyone. Specialties include *molcajete de la casa*—steaming fajitas, *rajas* (chile strips), cheese, onion, and avocado in a large, sizzling *molcajete* (three-legged stone mortar). The steak dish *medallones a la poblana* is memorable, as is the delicately flavored fish in parsley sauce. You can order salads here without hesitation (all greens are washed in antimicrobial solution), and the dessert menu includes such favorites as *pastel de tres leches.* And, with its vast selection of tequilas, it's the perfect place to do a little tasting. La Destilería is 5 blocks northwest of Fuente Minerva.

Av. México 2916 (corner of Nelson), Fracc. Terranova, west side. ✆ **33/3640-3440** or 33/3640-3110. Reservations recommended. Main courses $9–$15. AE, MC, V. Mon–Sat 1pm–midnight; Sun 1–6pm.

La Fonda de San Miguel 🐷🐷 *Moments* MEXICAN   My favorite way to enjoy a good meal in Mexico is to dine in an elegant colonial courtyard. I love the contrast between the bright, noisy street and the cool, shaded patio. This restaurant is in the former convent of Santa Teresa de Jesús. While you enjoy the stone arches and gurgling fountain, little crisp tacos, homemade bread, and mildly spiced butter awaken the appetite. For main courses, try *chiles en nogada* (a combination of spicy and sweet) if it's in season, or perhaps a traditional *mole poblano.* The restaurant is 4 blocks west and 1 block south of the cathedral, between Pedro Moreno and Morelos. Thursday to Saturday musicians perform from 3 to 5 and 9 to 11pm.

Donato Guerra 25, downtown. © 33/3613-0809. Reservations recommended on weekends. Breakfast $4–$8; main courses $9–$16. AE, MC, V. Sun–Mon 8am–6pm; Tues–Sat 8am–midnight.

La Trattoria Pomodoro Ristorante ⍟ ITALIAN   Good food, good service, and moderate prices make this restaurant perennially popular. The price of pastas and main courses includes a visit to the well-stocked salad bar. Try the combination pasta plate (lasagna, fettuccini Alfredo, and spaghetti), shrimp linguine, and chicken parmigiana. The Italian owner stocks lots of wines from the motherland. The dining room is attractive and casual, with comfortable furniture and separate seating for smokers and nonsmokers. Reservations are not accepted during holidays.

Niños Héroes 3051, west side. © 33/3122-1817. Reservations recommended. Pasta $7–$9; main courses $8–$10. AE, MC, V. Daily 1pm–midnight. Free parking.

Mariscos Progreso SEAFOOD   On a large, open patio shaded by trees and tile roofs, waiters navigate the tables with large platters of delicious seafood. Grilling over charcoal is the specialty here, but the kitchen's repertoire includes all the Mexican standards. Try the *parrillada* (a platter of grilled dishes) for two. Sometimes there's quite a bit of ambience, with mariachis adding to the commotion. At other times, the crowd thins and one can rest peacefully with a cold drink after shopping. It's a half-block from the Parián.

Progreso 80, Tlaquepaque. © 33/3657-4995. Reservations not accepted. Main courses $7–$14. AE, MC, V. Daily 11am–7pm.

INEXPENSIVE

Café Madrid MEXICAN   This little coffee shop is like many coffee shops used to be—a social institution where people come in, greet each other and the staff by name, and chat over breakfast or coffee and cigarettes. Change comes slowly here. For example, despite the fact that it's an informal place, the waiters wear white jackets with black bow ties, as they did 20 years ago. The coffee and Mexican breakfasts are good, as is the standard Mexican fare served in the afternoon. The front room opens to the street, with a small lunch counter and another room in the back.

Juárez 264, downtown. ☎ 33/3614-9504. Breakfast $2–$4; main courses $3–$6. No credit cards. Daily 7:30am–10:30pm. From the Plaza de Armas, walk 1 block on Corona to Juárez and turn right; the cafe is on the right.

La Chata Restaurant REGIONAL/MEXICAN   This popular downtown spot offers good standards at reasonable prices. Aromas waft into the street from the kitchen in front, where women with their heads wrapped in bandanas busily stir, chop, and fry. Past this is a large dining area. Local dishes include *pozole* (chicken, pork, and hominy in a broth to which you add onions, radishes, chile, and oregano) and *torta ahogada* (a spicy pork sandwich bathed in sauce). If you're very hungry, try the sampler platter of *antojitos* for four or the *plato combinado* (*mole,* chile relleno, rice, and beans).

Corona 126 (between Juárez and López Cotilla), downtown. ☎ 33/3613-0588. Reservations not accepted. Breakfast $3–$5; main courses $4–$7. AE, DC, MC, V. Daily 8am–11:30pm. From the Plaza de Armas, walk 1½ blocks south on Corona; La Chata is on the right.

La Fonda de la Noche 🔍 *(Finds)* MEXICAN   This is my favorite place in town for a simple supper. The limited menu is excellent, the surroundings are comfortable and inviting, the lighting is soothing, and the atmosphere evokes Mexico of the '40s, '50s, and '60s. It's not far from downtown or the west side; take a cab to the intersection of Jesús and Reforma, and, when you get there, look for a door behind a small hedge. There's no sign. It's a house with five dining rooms. I like best the bar immediately to your right as you enter. Only Spanish is spoken, but the menu is simple. To try a little of everything, order the *plato combinado,* which comes with an *enchilada de "medio mole,"* an empanada called a *media luna,* a tostada, and a *sope* (soup). The owner is Carlos Ibarra, an artist originally from the state of Durango. He has decorated the place with traditional Mexican pine furniture and cotton tablecloths and his personal collection of paintings, mostly the works of close friends.

Jesús 251, corner with Reforma, Col. El Refugio. ☎ 33/3827-0917. Reservations not accepted. Main course $5–$7. No credit cards. Tues–Sun 7pm–midnight.

Los Itacates Restaurant 🔍 *(Value)* MEXICAN   The Mexican equivalent of down-home cooking at reasonable prices. Office workers pack the place between 2 and 4pm weekdays, and there's a good crowd weekend nights, but at other times there's no problem finding a table. You can dine outdoors in a shaded sidewalk area or in one of the three dining rooms. The atmosphere is bright and colorful. Specialties include *pozole* (chicken-and-hominy soup), *lomo* *adobado* (baked pork in dark chile sauce), and chiles rellenos. *Pollo Itacates* is a quarter of a chicken, two cheese enchiladas, potatoes, and rice. Los Itacates is 5 blocks north of Avenida Vallarta. In the evenings they serve tacos and other *antojitos*.

Chapultepec Norte 110, west side. 🕐 **33/3825-1106** or 33/3825-9551. Reservations accepted on weekends and holidays. Breakfast buffet $6; tacos $1; main courses $5–$7. MC, V. Mon–Sat 8am–11pm; Sun 8am–7pm.

7

Exploring Guadalajara & Beyond

by David Baird

Guadalajara is one of the most Mexican of Mexico's cities. Spend a few days exploring its historic downtown area, with all its cultural and architectural highlights, parks, and attractions, and even the most hard-core resort tourist will realize there is much more to Mexico than sandy beaches and souvenir shops.

1 What to See & Do in Guadalajara

SPECIAL EVENTS

There's always something going on from September to December. In September, when Mexicans celebrate independence from Spain, Guadalajara goes all out, with a full month of festivities. The celebrations kick off with the **Encuentro Internacional del Mariachi** (www.mariachi-jalisco.com.mx), in which mariachi bands from around the world play before knowledgeable audiences and hold sessions with other mariachis. Bands come from as far as Japan and Russia, and the event takes on a curious postmodern hue. There are concerts in several venues. In the Degollado Theater, you can hear orchestral arrangements of classic mariachi songs with solos by famous mariachis. You might be acquainted with many of the classics without even knowing it. The culmination is a parade of thousands of mariachis and *charros* (Mexican cowboys) through downtown. It starts the first week of September.

On **September 15,** a massive crowd assembles in front of the Governor's Palace to await the traditional *grito* (shout for independence) at 11pm. The *grito* commemorates Father Miguel Hidalgo de Costilla's cry for independence in 1810. The celebration features live music on a street stage, spontaneous dancing, fireworks, and shouts of *"¡Viva México!"* and *"¡Viva Hidalgo!"* The next day is the official Independence Day, with a traditional parade; the plazas downtown resemble a country fair and market, with booths, games

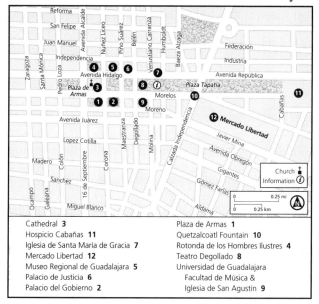

Downtown Guadalajara

Cathedral **3**
Hospicio Cabañas **11**
Iglesia de Santa María de Gracia **7**
Mercado Libertad **12**
Museo Regional de Guadalajara **5**
Palacio de Justicia **6**
Palacio del Gobierno **2**

Plaza de Armas **1**
Quetzalcoatl Fountain **10**
Rotonda de los Hombres Ilustres **4**
Teatro Degollado **8**
Universidad de Guadalajara
  Facultad de Música &
  Iglesia de San Agustín **9**

of chance, stuffed-animal prizes, cotton candy, and candied apples. Live entertainment stretches well into the night.

On **October 12**, a **procession** 🐦🐦 honoring Our Lady of Zapopan celebrates the feast day of the Virgin of Zapopan. Around dawn, her small, dark figure begins the 5-hour ride from the Cathedral of Guadalajara to the suburban Basilica of Zapopan (see "Other Attractions," below). The original icon dates from the mid-1500s; the procession began 200 years later. Today, crowds spend the night along the route and vie for position as the Virgin approaches. She travels in a gleaming new car (virginal in that it must never have had the ignition turned on), which her caretakers pull through the streets. During the previous months, the figure visits churches all over the city. You will likely see neighborhoods decorated with paper streamers and banners honoring the Virgin's visit to the local church.

The celebration has grown into a month-long event, **Fiestas de Octubre,** which kicks off with an enormous parade, usually on the first Sunday or Saturday of the month. Festivities include performing arts, *charreadas* (rodeos), bullfights, art exhibits, regional dancing, a food fair, and a Day of Nations incorporating all the consulates in

Guadalajara. By the time this is over, you enter the **holiday season of November and December,** with Revolution Day (Nov 20), the Virgin of Guadalupe's feast day (Dec 12), and several other celebrations.

DOWNTOWN GUADALAJARA

The most easily recognized building in the city is the **cathedral** ✦, around which four open plazas make the shape of a Latin cross. Later, a long swath of land was cleared to extend the open area from the cathedral east to the Instituto Cultural Cabañas, creating **Plaza Tapatía.**

Construction on the cathedral started in 1561 and continued into the 18th century. Over such a long time, it was inevitable that remodeling would take place before the building was ever completed. The result is an unusual facade that is an amalgam of several architectural styles, including baroque, neoclassical, and Gothic. An 1818 earthquake destroyed the original large towers; their replacements were built in the 1850s, inspired by designs on the bishop's dinner china. Blue and yellow are Guadalajara's colors. The nave is open, airy, and majestic. Items of interest include a painting in the sacristy ascribed to the 17th-century Spanish artist Bartolomé Estaban Murillo (1617–82).

To the cathedral's left is the **Plaza de Armas,** the oldest and loveliest of the plazas. A cast-iron Art Nouveau bandstand is its dominant feature. Made in France, it was a gift to the city from the dictator Porfirio Díaz in the 1890s. The female figures on the bandstand exhibited too little clothing for conservative Guadalajarans, who clothed them. The dictator, recognizing when it's best to let the people have their way, said nothing.

Facing the plaza is the **Palacio del Gobierno** ✦✦, a broad palace two stories high, built in 1774. The facade blends Spanish and Moorish elements and holds several details that catch the eye. Inside the central courtyard, above the staircase to the right, is a spectacular mural of Hidalgo by the modern Mexican master José Clemente Orozco. The Father of Independence appears high overhead, bearing directly down on the viewer and looking as implacable as a force of nature. On one of the adjacent walls Orozco painted *The Carnival of Ideologies,* a dark satire on the prevailing fanaticisms of his day. Another of his murals is inside the second-floor chamber of representatives, depicting Hidalgo again, this time in a more conventional posture, writing the proclamation to end slavery in Mexico. The *palacio* is open daily from 10am to 8pm.

In the plaza on the opposite side of the cathedral from the Plaza de Armas is the **Rotonda de los Hombres Ilustres.** Sixteen white columns, each supporting a bronze statue, stand as monuments to Guadalajara's and Jalisco's distinguished sons. Across the street from the plaza you will see a line of horse-drawn buggies. A spin around the Centro Histórico lasts about an hour and costs $20 for one to four people.

Facing the east side of the rotunda is the **Museo Regional de Guadalajara,** Liceo 60 (© **33/3614-9957**). Originally a convent, it was built in 1701 in the churrigueresque (Mexican baroque) style and contains some of the region's important archaeological finds, fossils, historic objects, and art. Among the highlights are a giant reconstructed mammoth's skeleton and a meteorite weighing 1,715 pounds, discovered in Zacatecas in 1792. On the first floor, there's a fascinating exhibit of pre-Hispanic pottery, and some exquisite pottery and clay figures recently unearthed near Tequila during the construction of the toll road. On the second floor is a small ethnography exhibit of the contemporary dress of the state's indigenous peoples, including the Coras, Huicholes, Mexicaneros, Nahuas, and Tepehuanes. It's open Tuesday through Sunday from 9am to 5pm. Admission is $3 for adults, $1 for children.

Behind the cathedral is the Plaza de la Liberación, with the **Teatro Degollado** (Deh-goh-*yah*-doh) on the opposite side. This neoclassical 19th-century opera house was named for Santos Degollado, a local patriot who fought with Juárez against Maximilian and the French. Apollo and the nine muses decorate the theater's pediment, and the interior is famous for both the acoustics and the rich decoration. It hosts a variety of performances during the year, including the Ballet Folclórico on Sunday at 10am. It's open Monday through Friday from 10am to 2pm and during performances.

To the right of the theater, across the street, is the sweet little **church of Santa María de Gracia,** built in 1573 as part of a convent for Dominican nuns. On the opposite side of the Teatro Degollado is the **church of San Agustín.** The former convent is now the **University of Guadalajara School of Music.**

Behind the Teatro Degollado begins the Plaza Tapatía, which leads to the Instituto Cabañas. It passes between a couple of low, modern office buildings. The Tourism Information Office is in a building on the right-hand side.

Beyond these office buildings, the plaza opens into a large expanse, now framed by department stores and offices and dominated by the abstract modern **Quetzalcoatl Fountain.** This fluid steel structure represents the mythical plumed serpent Quetzalcoatl, who figured so prominently in pre-Hispanic religion and culture, and exerts a presence even today.

At the far end of the plaza is the Hospicio Cabañas, formerly an orphanage and known today as the **Instituto Cultural Cabañas** *ﷻ*, Cabañas 8 (© **33/3617-4322**). This vast structure is impressive for both its size (more than 23 courtyards) and its grandiose architecture, especially the cupola. Created by the famous Mexican architect Manuel Tolsá, it housed homeless children from 1829 to 1980. Today, it's a thriving cultural center offering art shows and classes. The interior walls and ceiling of the main building display murals painted by Orozco in 1937. His *Man of Fire,* in the dome, is said to represent the spirit of humanity projecting itself toward the infinite. Other rooms hold additional Orozco works, as well as excellent contemporary art and temporary exhibits.

Just south of the Hospicio Cabañas (to the left as you exit) is the **Mercado Libertad** *ﷻ*, Guadalajara's gigantic covered central market, the largest in Latin America. This site has been a market plaza since the 1500s; the present buildings date from the early 1950s (see "Shopping," below).

OTHER ATTRACTIONS

At **Parque Agua Azul (Blue Water Park),** plants, trees, shrubbery, statues, and fountains create a perfect refuge from the bustling city. Many people come here to exercise early in the morning. The park is open daily from 7am to 6pm. Admission is $1 for adults, 50¢ for children.

Across Independencia from the park, cater-cornered from a small flower market, is the **Museo de Arqueología del Occidente de México,** Calzada Independencia at Avenida del Campesino. It houses a fine collection of pre-Hispanic pottery from Jalisco, Nayarit, and Colima. The museum is open Tuesday through Sunday from 10am to 2pm and 4 to 7pm. There's a small admission charge.

The state-run **Casa de las Artesanías** (© **33/3619-4664**) is at the Instituto de la Artesanía Jalisciense, just past the park entrance at Calzada Independencia and González Gallo (for details, see "Shopping," below).

Also near the park is Guadalajara's rodeo arena, **Lienzo Charro de Jalisco** (© **33/3619-0315**). Mexican cowboys, known as *charros,* are famous for their riding and lasso work, and the arena in Guadalajara is considered the big time. There are shows and competitions every Sunday at noon. The arena is at Av. Dr. R. Michel 577, between González Gallo and Las Palomas.

The Basilica of the Virgin of Zapopan ☆   A wide promenade several blocks long leads to a large, open plaza and the basilica. This is the religious center of Guadalajara. On the Virgin's feast day (see "Special Events," above) the plaza fills with thousands of Tapatíos. The 18th-century church is a lovely (and somewhat anachronistic) combination of baroque and plateresque styles. The cult of the Virgin of Zapopan practically began with the foundation of Guadalajara itself. She is much revered and the object of many pilgrimages. In front of the church are several stands selling religious figures and paraphernalia. On one side of the church is a lovely museum and store dedicated to the betterment of the Huichol Indians. It is well worth a visit.

Main Plaza, Zapopan (10km/6 miles northwest of downtown). No phone. Free admission. Daily 7am–7pm; museum daily 10am–7pm.

Museo de las Artes de la Universidad de Guadalajara
Inside the main lecture hall of this building are some more murals by Orozco. On the wall behind the stage is a bitter denunciation of corruption called *The People and Their False Leaders*. But in the cupola is a more optimistic work—*The Five-fold Man*, who works to create a better society and better self. There is also a small permanent collection of modern art, which will look all too familiar because the works seem so derivative of many of the modern masters.

Juárez 975 (enter on López Cotilla). ℂ **33/3134-2222**. Free admission. Tues–Sun 10am–8pm.

Museo de la Ciudad   This museum opened in 1992 in a former convent. It chronicles Guadalajara's past. The eight rooms, beginning on the right and proceeding in chronological order, cover the period from just before the city's founding to the present. Unusual artifacts, including rare Spanish armaments and equestrian paraphernalia, give a sense of what day-to-day life was like. Descriptive text is in Spanish only.

Independencia 684 (at M. Barcena). ℂ **33/3658-2531**. Free admission. Tues–Sun 10am–5pm.

2 Shopping

Many visitors to Guadalajara come specifically for the shopping in Tlaquepaque and Tonalá (see below). If you have little free time, try the government-run **Instituto de la Artesanía Jalisciense** ☆,

González Gallo 20 at Calzada Independencia (© **33/3619-4664**), in Parque Agua Azul, just south of downtown. This place is perfect for one-stop shopping, with two floors of pottery, silver jewelry, dance masks, glassware, leather goods, and regional clothing from around the state and the country. As you enter, on the right are museum displays showing crafts and regional costumes from the state of Jalisco. The crafts store is open Monday through Friday from 10am to 6pm, Saturday from 10am to 5pm, and Sunday from 10am to 3pm.

Guadalajara is known for its shoe industry; if you're in the market for a pair, try the **Galería del Calzado,** a shopping center made up exclusively of shoe stores. It's on the west side, about 6 blocks from Minerva Circle, at avenidas Mexico and Yaquis.

Mariachis and *charros* come to Guadalajara from all over Mexico to buy their highly worked belts and boots, wide-brimmed sombreros, and embroidered shirts. Several tailor shops and stores specialize in these outfits. One is **El Charro,** which has a store in the Plaza del Sol shopping center, across the street from the Hotel Presidente InterContinental, and one downtown on Juárez.

To view a good slice of what constitutes the material world for most Mexicans, try the mammoth **Mercado Libertad** 🏵 downtown. Besides food and produce, you'll see crafts, household goods, clothing, magic preparations, and more. Although it opens at 7am, the market isn't in full swing until around 10am. Come prepared to haggle.

SHOPPING IN TLAQUEPAQUE & TONALA

Almost everyone who comes to Guadalajara for the shopping has Tlaquepaque (Tlah-keh-*pah*-keh) and Tonalá in mind. These two suburbs are traditional handicraft centers that produce and sell a wide variety of *artesanía* (crafts).

TLAQUEPAQUE

Located about 20 minutes from downtown, **Tlaquepaque** 🏵🏵🏵 has the best shopping for handicrafts and decorative arts in all of Mexico. Over the years, it has become a fashionable place, attracting talented designers in a variety of fields. Even though it's a suburb of a large city, it has a cozy, small-town feel; it's a pleasure simply to stroll through the central streets from shop to shop. No one hassles you; no one does the hard sell. There are some excellent places to eat (see "Where to Dine," in chapter 6, or you can grab some simple fare at **El Parián,** a building in the middle of town that houses a number of small eateries.

A taxi from downtown Guadalajara costs $5, or you can take one of the deluxe **Turquesa buses** that make a fairly quick run from downtown to Tlaquepaque and Tonalá (see "Getting Around," in chapter 6).

The **Tlaquepaque Tourism Office,** Juárez 238 (© **33/3635-1220,** ext. 104 or 113), has a helpful, English-speaking staff. It's open Monday through Friday from 9am to 3pm. Most stores in Tlaquepaque close between 2 and 4pm and stay open until 7 or 8pm. Most are closed or have reduced hours on Sunday.

If you are interested in pottery and ceramics, two museums are worth a visit. The **Regional Ceramics Museum,** Independencia 237 (© **33/3635-5404**), displays several aspects of traditional Jalisco pottery as produced in Tlaquepaque and Tonalá. The examples date back several generations and are grouped according to the technique used to produce them. Note the crosshatch design known as *petatillo* on some of the pieces; it's one of the region's oldest traditional motifs and is, like so many other motifs, a real pain to produce. Look for the wonderful old kitchen and dining room, complete with pots, utensils, and dishes. The museum is open Tuesday through Saturday from 10am to 6pm, Sunday from 10am to 3pm; admission is free. The **Museo Pantaleón Panduro** ✦✦✦ (© **33/3635-1089,** ext. 17) is at P. Sánchez 191, at Florida. It is a must-see. Named after a famous local 19th-century artisan, it displays prize-winning pieces from the national ceramics contest held each year in Tlaquepaque. Many of the pieces exhibit an astounding virtuosity. Categories include miniatures, traditional designs, and original designs. It's open Tuesday through Sunday from 10am to 6pm; admission is free. If you still haven't had your fill, the Museo Nacional de Cerámica is in Tonalá (see below).

A number of workshops permit visitors to watch artisans at work. A popular workshop is **La Rosa de Cristal,** Contreras Medillín 173, a glassblowing factory. It's open Monday through Saturday from 10am to 7pm. If you're interested in a particular craft, talk to the city tourism office; the staff can help locate workshops that are open to the public.

The following list of Tlaquepaque shops will give you an idea of what to expect. This is just a small fraction of what you'll find; the best approach might be to just follow your nose. The main shopping is along **Independencia,** a pedestrian-only street that starts at El Parián. You can go door-to-door visiting the shops until the street ends, then work your way back on **Calle Juárez,** the next street over, north of Independencia.

> ### ⌒Tips **Packing It In**
>
> If you need your purchases packed safely so that you can check them as extra baggage, or if you want them shipped, talk to **Margaret del Río**. She is an American who runs a large packing and shipping company at Juárez 347, Tlaquepaque (② **33/3657-5652**). Paying the excess baggage fee usually is cheaper than shipping, but less convenient.

Agustín Parra So you bought an old hacienda and are trying to restore its chapel—where do you go to find traditional baroque sculpture, religious art, gold-leafed objects, and even entire *retablos* (altarpieces)? Parra is famous for exactly this kind of work, and the store is lovely. It's open Monday through Saturday from 10am to 7pm. Independencia 158. ② **33/3657-8530**.

Bazar Hecht One of the village's longtime favorites. Here you'll find wood objects, handmade furniture, and a few antiques. It's open Monday through Saturday from 10am to 2:30pm and 3:30 to 7pm. Juárez 162. ② **33/3657-0316**.

Casa Canela One of the most elegant stores in Tlaquepaque, this is a feast for the eyes. Browse through rooms full of furniture and decorative objects. It's open Monday through Friday from 10am to 2pm and 3 to 7pm, Saturday from 10am to 6pm, and Sunday from 11am to 3pm. Independencia 258, near Calle Cruz Verde. ② **33/3635-3717**.

Sergio Bustamante Sergio Bustamante's imaginative, original bronze, ceramic, and papier-mâché sculptures are among the most sought-after in Mexico—as well as the most copied. He also designs silver jewelry. This exquisite gallery showcases his work. It's open Monday through Saturday from 10am to 7pm, Sunday from 11am to 4pm. Independencia 236 at Cruz Verde. ② **33/3639-5519**.

Tete Arte y Diseño Architectural decorative objects mix with pottery, antiques, glassware, and paintings at this shop. It's open Monday through Saturday from 10am to 7pm. Juárez 173. ② **33/3635-7347**.

Tierra Tlaquepaque Here you'll find unusual, rustic, and finely finished pottery, as well as wood sculptures, table textiles, and decorative objects. Open Monday through Saturday from 10am to 7pm, Sunday from 11am to 5pm. Independencia 156. ② **33/3635-9770**.

TONALA: A TRADITION OF POTTERY MAKING

Tonalá ✦✦ is a pleasant town 5 minutes from Tlaquepaque. The streets were paved only recently, and there aren't any fancy shops. The village has been a center of pottery making since pre-Hispanic times; half of the more than 400 workshops here produce a wide variety of high- and low-temperature pottery. Other local artists work with forged iron, cantera stone, brass and copper, marble, miniatures, papier-mâché, textiles, blown glass, and gesso. This is a good place to look for custom work in any of these materials; you can locate a large pool of craftspeople by asking around a little.

Market days are Thursday and Sunday. Expect large crowds, and blocks and blocks of stalls displaying locally made pottery and glassware, as well as cheap manufactured goods, food, and all kinds of bric-a-brac. "Herb men" sell a rainbow selection of dried medicinal herbs from wheelbarrows; magicians entertain crowds with sleight-of-hand; and craftspeople spread their colorful wares on the plaza's sidewalks. I prefer to visit Tonalá on non-market days, when it's much easier to get around and see the glass and pottery stores. This is the place for buying sets of margarita glasses, the widely

Tonalá

seen blue-rimmed rustic glassware, as well as the pottery typically associated with Mexico and finely painted *petatillo* ware.

The **Tonalá Tourism Office** (© **33/3683-1740;** fax 33/3683-0590) is in the Artesanos building, set back from the road at Atonaltecas 140 Sur (the main street leading into Tonalá) at Matamoros. Hours are Monday through Friday from 9am to 3pm, Saturday from 9am to 1pm. The office offers free walking tours on Monday, Tuesday, Wednesday, and Friday at 9am and 2pm, Saturday at 9am and 1pm. They include visits to artisans' workshops (where you'll see ceramics, stoneware, blown glass, papier-mâché, and the like). Tours last 3 to 4 hours and require a minimum of five people. Visitors can request an English-speaking guide. Also in Tonalá, cater-cornered from the church, you'll see a small tourism information kiosk that's staffed on market days and provides maps and useful information.

Tonalá is also the home of the **Museo Nacional de Cerámica,** Constitución 104, between Hidalgo and Morelos (© **33/3683-0494**). The museum occupies a two-story mansion and displays work from Jalisco and all over the country. There's a large shop in the front on the right as you enter. The museum is open Tuesday through Friday from 10am to 5pm, Saturday and Sunday from 10am to 2pm. Admission is free; the fee for using a video or still camera is $8.50 per camera.

3 Guadalajara After Dark

MARIACHIS

You can't go far in Guadalajara without coming across some mariachis, but seeing really talented performers takes some effort. Try **Casa Bariachi,** Av. Vallarta 2221 (© **33/3615-0029**). In Tlaquepaque, go to **El Parián,** the building on the town square where mariachis serenade diners under the archways.

THE CLUB & MUSIC SCENE

Guadalajara, as you might expect, has a lot of variety in entertainment. For the most extensive listing of clubs and performances, get your hands on a copy of *Ocio,* the weekly insert of *Público.* You'll find listings in the back, categorized by type of music.

Bar Copenhagen 77   On weekends, this snug little den with upholstered walls and wood trim is the perfect setting for catching a little modern jazz. The house band of three to five musicians plays bebop and Latin jazz on Friday and Saturday nights. You can have just drinks, or you can order from the small, well-thought-out menu; the specialty is paella. Monday through Thursday it's classical guitar. The club faces the Parque de la Revolución (along Juárez, 9 blocks west of the Plaza de Armas), on your left as you walk down López Cotilla. The restaurant is open Monday through Saturday 2pm to 1am; music begins at 9pm. Marcos Castellanos 140-Z. © 33/3826-7306.

El Cubilete   El Cubilete ("the dice cup") is a small club tucked away in an old downtown neighborhood called Las Nueve Esquinas (The Nine Corners). This up-and-coming area has a couple of other clubs that are worth checking out. The house band, Son de Cuba, plays a number of salsa and *cumbia* standards from Wednesday to Saturday from 10:30pm to 1am. The club is open Monday through Saturday 2pm to 1am. Gral. Río Seco 9. © 33/3658-0406 or 33/3613-2096. $5 cover on weekends.

Tequila: The Name Says It All

Tequila is an entertaining (and intoxicating) town, well worth a day trip from Guadalajara. Several taxi drivers charge about $55 to take you to the town, get you into a tour of a distillery, take you to a restaurant, and haul you back to Guadalajara. A few of them speak English. One driver is named José Gabriel Gómez (© 33/3649-0791; jgabriel-taxi@hotmail.com); he has a new car and drives carefully. Call him in the evening. Tour companies also arrange bus trips to Tequila; see a travel agency in Guadalajara.

Tequila has many distilleries, including the famous brands **Sauza** and **José Cuervo.** All the distilleries—the big, modern ones and the small, more traditional ones—offer tours. If you're on your own, a good place to hook up with a tour is at the little booth outside the city hall on the main square. Two young women who speak English run tours to any of the local factories. The tour costs $5 and lasts about 2 hours. All tours show how tequila is made, what traditions the process follows, and what differences exist between tequilas; they end, of course, with a tasting. Avenida Vallarta runs straight to the highway to Tequila, which is about an hour outside of Guadalajara.

Another approach is to take the **Tequila Express** 🏚🏚 to the town of Amatitán, home of the Herradura distillery. It leaves from the train station on Friday and Saturday, and sometimes on Sunday during vacation and holiday season. You need to be there by 10am. The Guadalajara Chamber of Commerce (Cámara de Comercio), at Vallarta and Niño Obrero (© 33/3880-9099), organizes this trip. Buy tickets ahead of time at the main office; at the small office in the Centro Histórico at Morelos 395, at Calle Colón (no phone); or through Ticketmaster (© 33/3818-3800). Office hours are Monday through Friday from 9am to 2pm and 4 to 6pm. Tickets cost $65 for adults, $35 for children 6 to 12. The tour includes an open bar with tequila tasting that begins on the train, a visit to the Hacienda San José del Refugio, a tour of a distillery, dinner, and, of course, mariachis. It returns to Guadalajara at about 8pm. Travel time is 1¾ hours each way. For more information, see www.tequilaexpress.com.mx.

Appendix:
Useful Terms & Phrases

1 Telephones & Mail
USING THE TELEPHONES

All phone numbers listed in this book have a total of 10 digits—a two- or three-digit area code plus the telephone number. Local numbers in Mexico City, Guadalajara, and Monterrey are eight digits; everywhere else, local numbers have seven digits.

To call long distance within Mexico, dial the national long-distance code **01** before dialing the area code and then the number. Mexico's *claves* (area codes) are listed in the front of telephone directories. Area codes are listed before all phone numbers in this book. For long-distance dialing, you will often see the term "LADA," which is the automatic long-distance service offered by Telmex, Mexico's former telephone monopoly and its largest phone company. To make a person-to-person or collect call inside Mexico, dial **020.** You can also call 020 to request the correct area codes for the number and place you are calling.

To make a long-distance call to the United States or Canada, dial **001,** then the area code and seven-digit number. For international long-distance numbers in Europe, Africa, and Asia, dial **00,** then the country code, the city code, and the number. To make a person-to-person or collect call to outside Mexico, to obtain other international dialing codes, or for further assistance, dial **090.**

For additional details on making calls within and to Mexico, see chapter 1 and the inside front cover of this book.

POSTAL GLOSSARY

Airmail **Correo aéreo**

Customs **Aduana**

General delivery **Lista de correos**

Insurance (insured mail) **Seguro (correo asegurado)**

Mailbox **Buzón**

Money order **Giro postal**

Parcel **Paquete**

Post office	**Oficina de correos**
Post office box (abbreviation)	**Apdo. Postal**
Postal service	**Correos**
Registered mail	**Registrado**
Rubber stamp	**Sello**
Special delivery, express	**Entrega inmediata**
Stamp	**Estampilla** or **timbre**

2 Basic Vocabulary

Most Mexicans are very patient with foreigners who try to speak
their language; it helps a lot to know a few basic phrases. I've
included simple phrases for expressing basic needs, followed by
some common menu items.

ENGLISH-SPANISH PHRASES

English	Spanish	Pronunciation
Good day	**Buen día**	bwehn *dee*-ah
Good morning	**Buenos días**	*bweh*-nohss *dee*-ahss
How are you?	**¿Cómo está?**	*koh*-moh ehss-*tah?*
Very well	**Muy bien**	mwee byehn
Thank you	**Gracias**	*grah*-syahss
You're welcome	**De nada**	deh *nah*-dah
Good-bye	**Adiós**	ah-*dyohss*
Please	**Por favor**	pohr fah-*vohr*
Yes	**Sí**	see
No	**No**	noh
Excuse me	**Perdóneme**	pehr-*doh*-neh-meh
Give me	**Déme**	*deh*-meh
Where is . . . ?	**¿Dónde está . . . ?**	*dohn*-deh ehss-*tah?*
the station	**la estación**	lah ehss-tah-*syohn*
a hotel	**un hotel**	oon oh-*tehl*
a gas station	**una gasolinera**	*oo*-nah gah-soh-lee-*neh*-rah

English	Spanish	Pronunciation
a restaurant	**un restaurante**	oon res-tow-*rahn*-teh
the toilet	**el baño**	el *bah*-nyoh
a good doctor	**un buen médico**	oon bwehn *meh*-dee-coh
the road to . . .	**el camino a/hacia . . .**	el cah-*mee*-noh ah/*ah*-syah
To the right	**A la derecha**	ah lah deh-*reh*-chah
To the left	**A la izquierda**	ah lah ees-*kyehr*-dah
Straight ahead	**Derecho**	deh-*reh*-choh
I would like	**Quisiera**	key-*syeh*-rah
I want	**Quiero**	*kyeh*-roh
to eat	**comer**	koh-*mehr*
a room	**una habitación**	*oo*-nah ah-bee-tah-*syohn*
Do you have . . . ?	**¿Tiene usted . . . ?**	tyeh-neh oo-*sted*?
a book	**un libro**	oon *lee*-broh
a dictionary	**un diccionario**	oon deek-syow-*nah*-ryo
How much is it?	**¿Cuánto cuesta?**	*kwahn*-toh *kwehss*-tah?
When?	**¿Cuándo?**	*kwahn*-doh?
What?	**¿Qué?**	keh?
There is (Is there . . . ?)	**(¿)Hay (. . . ?)**	eye?
What is there?	**¿Qué hay?**	keh eye?
Yesterday	**Ayer**	ah-*yer*
Today	**Hoy**	oy
Tomorrow	**Mañana**	mah-*nyah*-nah
Good	**Bueno**	*bweh*-noh
Bad	**Malo**	*mah*-loh
Better (best)	**(Lo) Mejor**	(loh) meh-*hohr*
More	**Más**	mahs
Less	**Menos**	*meh*-nohss

English	Spanish	Pronunciation
No smoking	**Se prohibe fumar**	seh proh-*ee*-beh foo-*mahr*
Postcard	**Tarjeta postal**	tar-*heh*-ta pohs-*tahl*
Insect repellent	**Repelente contra insectos**	reh-peh-*lehn*-te *cohn*-trah een-*sehk*-tos

MORE USEFUL PHRASES

English	Spanish	Pronunciation
Do you speak English?	**¿Habla usted inglés?**	*ah*-blah oo-*sted* een-*glehs*?
Is there anyone here who speaks English?	**¿Hay alguien aquí que hable inglés?**	eye *ahl*-gyehn ah-*kee* keh *ah*-bleh een-*glehs*?
I speak a little Spanish.	**Hablo un poco de español.**	*ah*-bloh oon *poh*-koh deh ehss-pah-*nyohl*
I don't understand Spanish very well.	**No (lo) entiendo muy bien el español.**	noh (loh) ehn-*tyehn*-doh mwee byehn el ehss-pah-*nyohl*
The meal is good.	**Me gusta la comida.**	meh *goo*-stah lah koh-*mee*-dah
What time is it?	**¿Qué hora es?**	keh *oh*-rah ehss?
May I see your menu?	**¿Puedo ver el menú (la carta)?**	*pueh*-do vehr el meh-*noo* (lah *car*-tah)?
The check, please.	**La cuenta, por favor.**	lah *quehn*-tah pohr fa-*vorh*
What do I owe you?	**¿Cuánto le debo?**	*kwahn*-toh leh *deh*-boh?
What did you say?	**¿Mande?** (formal) **¿Cómo?** (informal)	*mahn*-deh? *koh*-moh?

| I want (to see) . . . | **Quiero (ver)** . . . | *kyeh*-roh (vehr) |
| a room | **un cuarto** or **una habitación** | oon *kwar*-toh, *oo*-nah ah-bee-tah-*syohn* |

English	**Spanish**	**Pronunciation**
for two persons	**para dos personas**	*pah*-rah dohss pehr-*soh*-nahs
with (without) bathroom	**con (sin) baño**	kohn (seen) *bah*-nyoh
We are staying here only . . .	**Nos quedamos aquí solamente** . . .	nohs keh-*dah*-mohss ah-*kee* soh-lah-*mehn*-teh
one night.	**una noche.**	*oo*-nah *noh*-cheh
one week.	**una semana.**	*oo*-nah seh-*mah*-nah
We are leaving . . .	**Partimos (Salimos)** . . .	pahr-*tee*-mohss (sah-*lee*-mohss)
tomorrow.	**mañana.**	mah-*nya*-nah
Do you accept . . . ?	**¿Acepta usted . . . ?**	ah-*sehp*-tah oo-*sted*
traveler's checks?	**cheques de viajero?**	*cheh*-kehss deh byah-*heh*-roh?
Is there a laundromat . . . ? near here?	**¿Hay una lavandería . . . ? cerca de aquí?**	eye *oo*-nah lah-*vahn*-deh-*ree*-ah *sehr*-kah deh ah-*kee*
Please send these clothes to the laundry.	**Hágame el favor de mandar esta ropa a la lavandería.**	*ah*-gah-meh el fah-*vohr* deh mahn-*dahr ehss*-tah *roh*-pah a lah lah-*vahn*-deh-*ree*-ah

NUMBERS

1	**uno** (*ooh*-noh)	18	**dieciocho** (dyess-ee-*oh*-choh)
2	**dos** (dohss)	19	**diecinueve** (dyess-ee-*nweh*-beh)
3	**tres** (trehss)	20	**veinte** (*bayn*-teh)
4	**cuatro** (*kwah*-troh)	30	**treinta** (*trayn*-tah)
5	**cinco** (*seen*-koh)	40	**cuarenta** (kwah-*ren*-tah)
6	**seis** (sayss)	50	**cincuenta** (seen-*kwen*-tah)
7	**siete** (*syeh*-teh)	60	**sesenta** (seh-*sehn*-tah)
8	**ocho** (*oh*-choh)	70	**setenta** (seh-*tehn*-tah)
9	**nueve** (*nweh*-beh)	80	**ochenta** (oh-*chehn*-tah)
10	**diez** (dyess)	90	**noventa** (noh-*behn*-tah)
11	**once** (*ohn*-seh)	100	**cien** (syehn)
12	**doce** (*doh*-seh)	200	**doscientos** (do-*syehn*-tohs)
13	**trece** (*treh*-seh)	500	**quinientos** (kee-*nyehn*-tohs)
14	**catorce** (kah-*tohr*-seh)	1,000	**mil** (meel)
15	**quince** (*keen*-seh)		
16	**dieciseis** (dyess-ee-*sayss*)		
17	**diecisiete** (dyess-ee-*syeh*-teh)		

TRANSPORTATION TERMS

English	Spanish	Pronunciation
Airport	**Aeropuerto**	ah-eh-roh-*pwehr*-toh
Flight	**Vuelo**	*bweh*-loh
Rental car	**Arrendadora de autos**	ah-rehn-da-doh-rah deh ow-tohs
Bus	**Autobús**	ow-toh-*boos*
Bus or truck	**Camión**	ka-*myohn*
Lane	**Carril**	kah-*reel*
Nonstop (bus)	**Directo**	dee-*rehk*-toh
Baggage (claim area)	**Equipajes**	eh-kee-*pah*-hehss
Intercity	**Foraneo**	foh-rah-*neh*-oh
Luggage storage area	**Guarda equipaje**	gwar-dah eh-kee-*pah*-heh
Arrival gates	**Llegadas**	yeh-*gah*-dahss
Originates at this station	**Local**	loh-*kahl*

English	Spanish	Pronunciation
Originates elsewhere	**De paso**	deh *pah*-soh
Stops if seats available	**Para si hay lugares**	*pah*-rah see eye loo-*gah*-rehs
First class	**Primera**	pree-*meh*-rah
Second class	**Segunda**	seh-*goon*-dah
Nonstop (flight)	**Sin escala**	seen ess-*kah*-lah
Baggage claim area	**Recibo de equipajes**	reh-see-boh deh eh-kee-*pah*-hehss
Waiting room	**Sala de espera**	*sah*-lah deh ehss-*peh*-rah
Toilets	**Sanitarios**	sah-nee-*tah*-ryohss
Ticket window	**Taquilla**	tah-*kee*-yah

3 Menu Glossary

Achiote   Small red seed of the *annatto* tree.

Achiote preparado   A Yucatecan prepared paste made of ground *achiote*, wheat and corn flour, cumin, cinnamon, salt, onion, garlic, and oregano.

Agua fresca   Fruit-flavored water, usually watermelon, cantaloupe, chia seed with lemon, hibiscus flour, rice, or ground melon-seed mixture.

Antojito   Typical Mexican supper foods, usually made with *masa* or tortillas and having a filling or topping such as sausage, cheese, beans, and onions; includes such things as *tacos, tostadas, sopes,* and *garnachas.*

Atole   A thick, lightly sweet, hot drink made with finely ground corn and usually flavored with vanilla, pecan, strawberry, pineapple, or chocolate.

Botana   An appetizer.

Buñuelos   Round, thin, deep-fried crispy fritters dipped in sugar.

Carnitas   Pork deep-cooked (not fried) in lard, and then simmered and served with corn tortillas for tacos.

Ceviche   Fresh raw seafood marinated in fresh lime juice and garnished with chopped tomatoes, onions, chiles, and sometimes cilantro.

Chayote   A vegetable pear or mirliton, a type of spiny squash boiled and served as an accompaniment to meat dishes.

Chiles en nogada   Poblano peppers stuffed with a mixture of ground pork and beef, spices, fruits, raisins, and almonds. Can be served either warm—fried in a light batter—or cold, sans the batter. Either way it is then covered in walnut-and-cream sauce.

Chiles rellenos   Usually poblano peppers stuffed with cheese or spicy ground meat with raisins, rolled in a batter, and fried.

Churro   Tube-shaped, breadlike fritter, dipped in sugar and sometimes filled with *cajeta* (milk-based caramel) or chocolate.

Cochinita pibil   Pork wrapped in banana leaves, pit-baked in a *pibil* sauce of *achiote,* sour orange, and spices; common in the Yucatán.

Enchilada   A tortilla dipped in sauce, usually filled with chicken or white cheese, and sometimes topped with *mole* (*enchiladas rojas* or *de mole*), or with tomato sauce and sour cream (*enchiladas suizas*—Swiss enchiladas), or covered in a green sauce *(enchiladas verdes),* or topped with onions, sour cream, and guacamole *(enchiladas potosinas).*

Escabeche   A lightly pickled sauce used in Yucatecan chicken stew.

Frijoles refritos   Pinto beans mashed and cooked with lard.

Garnachas   A thickish small circle of fried *masa* with pinched sides, topped with pork or chicken, onions, and avocado, or sometimes chopped potatoes and tomatoes, typical as a *botana* in Veracruz and Yucatán.

Gorditas   Thick, fried corn tortillas, slit and stuffed with choice of cheese, beans, beef, chicken, with or without lettuce, tomato, and onion garnish.

Horchata   Refreshing drink made of ground rice or melon seeds, ground almonds, cinnamon, and lightly sweetened.

Huevos mexicanos   Scrambled eggs with chopped onions, hot green peppers, and tomatoes.

Huitlacoche   Sometimes spelled "cuitlacoche." A mushroom-flavored black fungus that appears on corn in the rainy season; considered a delicacy.

Manchamantel   Translated, means "tablecloth stainer." A stew of chicken or pork with chiles, tomatoes, pineapple, bananas, and jicama.

Masa   Ground corn soaked in lime; the basis for tamales, corn tortillas, and soups.

Mixiote   Rabbit, lamb, or chicken cooked in a mild chile sauce (usually chile *ancho* or *pasilla*), and then wrapped like a tamal and steamed. It is generally served with tortillas for tacos, with traditional garnishes of pickled onions, hot sauce, chopped cilantro, and lime wedges.

Pan de muerto   Sweet bread made around the Days of the Dead (Nov 1–2), in the form of mummies or dolls, or round with bone designs.

Pan dulce   Lightly sweetened bread in many configurations, usually served at breakfast or bought in any bakery.

Papadzules   Tortillas stuffed with hard-boiled eggs and seeds (pumpkin or sunflower) in a tomato sauce.

Pibil   Pit-baked pork or chicken in a sauce of tomato, onion, mild red pepper, cilantro, and vinegar.

Pipián   A sauce made with ground pumpkin seeds, nuts, and mild peppers.

Poc chuc   Slices of pork with onion marinated in a tangy sour orange sauce and charcoal-broiled; a Yucatecan specialty.

Pozole   A soup made with hominy in either chicken or pork broth.

Pulque   A drink made of fermented juice of the maguey plant; best in the state of Hidalgo and around Mexico City.

Quesadilla   Corn or flour tortillas stuffed with melted white cheese and lightly fried.

Queso relleno   "Stuffed cheese," a mild yellow cheese stuffed with minced meat and spices; a Yucatecan specialty.

Rompope   Delicious Mexican eggnog, invented in Puebla, made with eggs, vanilla, sugar, and rum.

Salsa verde   An uncooked sauce using the green tomatillo and puréed with spicy or mild hot peppers, onions, garlic, and cilantro; on tables countrywide.

Sopa de flor de calabaza   A soup made of chopped squash or pumpkin blossoms.

Sopa de lima   A tangy soup made with chicken broth and accented with fresh lime; popular in Yucatán.

Sopa de tortilla   A traditional chicken broth–based soup, seasoned with chiles, tomatoes, onion, and garlic, served with crispy fried strips of corn tortillas.

Sopa tlalpeña (or *caldo tlalpeño*)   A hearty soup made with chunks of chicken, chopped carrots, zucchini, corn, onions, garlic, and cilantro.

Sopa tlaxcalteca   A hearty tomato-based soup filled with cooked nopal cactus, cheese, cream, and avocado, with crispy tortilla strips floating on top.

Sope   Pronounced "*soh*-peh." An *antojito* similar to a *garnacha,* except spread with refried beans and topped with crumbled cheese and onions.

Tacos al pastor   Thin slices of flavored pork roasted on a revolving cylinder dripping with onion slices and juice of fresh pineapple slices. Served in small corn tortillas, topped with chopped onion and cilantro.

Tamal   Incorrectly called a tamale (*tamal* singular, *tamales* plural). A meat or sweet filling rolled with fresh *masa,* wrapped in a corn husk or banana leaf, and steamed.

Tikin xic   Also seen on menus as "tik-n-xic" and "tikik chick." Charbroiled fish brushed with *achiote* sauce.

Torta   A sandwich, usually on *bolillo* bread, typically with sliced avocado, onions, tomatoes, with a choice of meat and often cheese.

Xtabentun   Pronounced "shtah-behn-*toon.*" A Yucatecan liquor made of fermented honey and flavored with anise. It comes *seco* (dry) or *crema* (sweet).

Zacahuil   Pork leg tamal, packed in thick *masa,* wrapped in banana leaves, and pit-baked, sometimes pot-made with tomato and *masa;* a specialty of mid- to upper Veracruz.

Index

See also Accommodations and Restaurant indexes below.

HIT THE ROAD WITH FROMMER'S DRIVING TOURS!

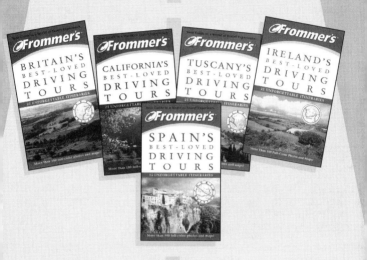

Frommer's Britain's Best-Loved Driving Tours
Frommer's California's Best-Loved Driving Tours
Frommer's Florida's Best-Loved Driving Tours
Frommer's France's Best-Loved Driving Tours
Frommer's Germany's Best-Loved Driving Tours
Frommer's Ireland's Best-Loved Driving Tours
Frommer's Italy's Best-Loved Driving Tours
Frommer's New England's Best-Loved Driving Tours
Frommer's Northern Italy's Best-Loved Driving Tours
Frommer's Scotland's Best-Loved Driving Tours
Frommer's Spain's Best-Loved Driving Tours
Frommer's Tuscany & Umbria's Best-Loved Driving Tours

Available at bookstores everywhere.

Frommer's® Budget Guides

Live Large
and Spend Little

The guide that shows you how to have lots of fun without spending too much cash.

- Australia from $50 a Day
- California from $70 a Day
- England from $75 a Day
- Europe from $85 a Day
- Florida from $70 a Day
- Hawaii from $80 a Day
- Ireland from $80 a Day
- Italy from $70 a Day

- London from $90 a Day
- New York City from $90 a Day
- Paris from $90 a Day
- San Francisco from $70 a Day
- Washington, D.C. from $80 a Day

Frommer's®

FROMMER'S® COMPLETE TRAVEL GUIDES

Alaska
Alaska Cruises & Ports of Call
American Southwest
Amsterdam
Argentina & Chile
Arizona
Atlanta
Australia
Austria
Bahamas
Barcelona
Beijing
Belgium, Holland & Luxembourg
Bermuda
Boston
Brazil
British Columbia & the Canadian
 Rockies
Brussels & Bruges
Budapest & the Best of Hungary
Calgary
California
Canada
Cancún, Cozumel & the Yucatán
Cape Cod, Nantucket & Martha's
 Vineyard
Caribbean
Caribbean Ports of Call
Carolinas & Georgia
Chicago
China
Colorado
Costa Rica
Cruises & Ports of Call
Cuba
Denmark
Denver, Boulder & Colorado Springs
Edinburgh & Glasgow
England
Europe
Europe by Rail
European Cruises & Ports of Call
Florence, Tuscany & Umbria

Florida
France
Germany
Great Britain
Greece
Greek Islands
Halifax
Hawaii
Hong Kong
Honolulu, Waikiki & Oahu
India
Ireland
Italy
Jamaica
Japan
Kauai
Las Vegas
London
Los Angeles
Madrid
Maine Coast
Maryland & Delaware
Maui
Mexico
Montana & Wyoming
Montréal & Québec City
Munich & the Bavarian Alps
Nashville & Memphis
New England
New Mexico
Newfoundland & Labrador
New Orleans
New York City
New York State
New Zealand
Northern Italy
Norway
Nova Scotia, New Brunswick &
 Prince Edward Island
Oregon
Ottawa
Paris
Peru

Philadelphia & the Amish Country
Portugal
Prague & the Best of the Czech
 Republic
Provence & the Riviera
Puerto Rico
Rome
San Antonio & Austin
San Diego
San Francisco
Santa Fe, Taos & Albuquerque
Scandinavia
Scotland
Seattle
Seville, Granada & the Best of
 Andalusia
Shanghai
Sicily
Singapore & Malaysia
South Africa
South America
South Florida
South Pacific
Southeast Asia
Spain
Sweden
Switzerland
Texas
Thailand
Tokyo
Toronto
Turkey
USA
Utah
Vancouver & Victoria
Vermont, New Hampshire & Maine
Vienna & the Danube Valley
Virgin Islands
Virginia
Walt Disney World® & Orlando
Washington, D.C.
Washington State

FROMMER'S® DOLLAR-A-DAY GUIDES

Australia from $50 a Day
California from $70 a Day
England from $75 a Day
Europe from $85 a Day
Florida from $70 a Day
Hawaii from $80 a Day

Ireland from $80 a Day
Italy from $70 a Day
London from $90 a Day
New York City from $90 a Day
Paris from $90 a Day
San Francisco from $70 a Day

Washington, D.C. from $80 a Day
Portable London from $90 a Day
Portable New York City from $90
 a Day
Portable Paris from $90 a Day

FROMMER'S® PORTABLE GUIDES

Acapulco, Ixtapa & Zihuatanejo
Amsterdam
Aruba
Australia's Great Barrier Reef
Bahamas
Berlin
Big Island of Hawaii
Boston
California Wine Country
Cancún
Cayman Islands
Charleston
Chicago
Disneyland®
Dominican Republic

Dublin
Florence
Frankfurt
Hong Kong
Las Vegas
Las Vegas for Non-Gamblers
London
Los Angeles
Los Cabos & Baja
Maui
Miami
Nantucket & Martha's Vineyard
New Orleans
New York City
Paris

Phoenix & Scottsdale
Portland
Puerto Rico
Puerto Vallarta, Manzanillo &
 Guadalajara
Rio de Janeiro
San Diego
San Francisco
Savannah
Vancouver Island
Venice
Virgin Islands
Washington, D.C.
Whistler

FROMMER'S® NATIONAL PARK GUIDES

Algonquin Provincial Park
Banff & Jasper
Family Vacations in the National
  Parks

Grand Canyon
National Parks of the American West
Rocky Mountain

Yellowstone & Grand Teton
Yosemite & Sequoia/Kings Canyon
Zion & Bryce Canyon

FROMMER'S® MEMORABLE WALKS

Chicago
London

New York
Paris

San Francisco

FROMMER'S® WITH KIDS GUIDES

Chicago
Hawaii
Las Vegas
New York City

Ottawa
San Francisco
Toronto

Vancouver
Walt Disney World® & Orlando
Washington, D.C.

SUZY GERSHMAN'S BORN TO SHOP GUIDES

Born to Shop: France
Born to Shop: Hong Kong, Shanghai
  & Beijing

Born to Shop: Italy
Born to Shop: London

Born to Shop: New York
Born to Shop: Paris

FROMMER'S® IRREVERENT GUIDES

Amsterdam
Boston
Chicago
Las Vegas
London

Los Angeles
Manhattan
New Orleans
Paris
Rome

San Francisco
Seattle & Portland
Vancouver
Walt Disney World®
Washington, D.C.

FROMMER'S® BEST-LOVED DRIVING TOURS

Austria
Britain
California
France

Germany
Ireland
Italy
New England

Northern Italy
Scotland
Spain
Tuscany & Umbria

THE UNOFFICIAL GUIDES®

Beyond Disney
California with Kids
Central Italy
Chicago
Cruises
Disneyland®
England
Florida
Florida with Kids
Inside Disney

Hawaii
Las Vegas
London
Maui
Mexico's Best Beach Resorts
Mini Las Vegas
Mini Mickey
New Orleans
New York City
Paris

San Francisco
Skiing & Snowboarding in the West
South Florida including Miami &
  the Keys
Walt Disney World®
Walt Disney World® for
  Grown-ups
Walt Disney World® with Kids
Washington, D.C.

SPECIAL-INTEREST TITLES

Athens Past & Present
Cities Ranked & Rated
Frommer's Best Day Trips from London
Frommer's Best RV & Tent Campgrounds
  in the U.S.A.
Frommer's Caribbean Hideaways
Frommer's China: The 50 Most Memorable Trips
Frommer's Exploring America by RV
Frommer's Gay & Lesbian Europe

Frommer's NYC Free & Dirt Cheap
Frommer's Road Atlas Europe
Frommer's Road Atlas France
Frommer's Road Atlas Ireland
Frommer's Wonderful Weekends from
  New York City
Retirement Places Rated
Rome Past & Present